Personal Computing

**Communicating
With the
IBM PC Series**

1988   0 471 91667 6

**IBM PC
Upgraders Manual**

1988   0 471 63177 9

**DOS Productivity
Tips & Tricks**

1988   0 471 608955

**IBM PS/2
User's
Reference Manual**

1990   0 471 62150 1

Reference

**The Complete
Modem
Reference**

1991   0 471 52911 7

**Data and Computer
Communications:
Terms, Definitions
and Abbreviations**

1989   0 471 92066 5

NOW AVAILABLE

Save time and avoid keyboarding errors . . . . All major programs listed in this book are available on disk for your IBM PC or compatibles.

Order the program disk today from your computer store, bookseller, or by using the appropriate tear-off order card below (see over for details).

Please send me .... copies of **Held: Data Compression 3rd Edition** Program Disk at $45.00 for the 2 disk set (plus my local sales tax).
ISBN (0 471 93009 1)

☐ Payment enclosed (Wiley pays postage and handling on prepaid orders)

☐ Bill me

☐ Charge my   Am Ex   Visa   MC   (Circle one)
   (Postage and handling will be added on bill and charge orders)

CARD NUMBER ☐☐☐☐☐☐☐☐☐☐☐☐☐☐☐☐☐   Exp. date ....

NAME ....

ADDRESS ....

....

CITY/STATE/ZIP ....

SIGNATURE ....
(Order invalid without signature)

Please send me .... copies of **Held: Data Compression 3rd Edition** Program Disk at £21 for the 2 disk set (including VAT)
ISBN (0 471 93009 1)
Orders for one disk set only — please add £1.50 to cover postage.
Two or more disk sets — postage free.

☐ Remittance enclosed £ .... (payable to John Wiley & Sons Ltd)

☐ Please charge this order to my credit card (all orders subject to credit approval).
   Delete as necessary: AMERICAN EXPRESS, DINERS CLUB, BARCLAYCARD/VISA,
   ACCESS/MASTERCARD

   CARD NUMBER ☐☐☐☐☐☐☐☐☐☐☐☐☐☐☐☐☐

   Expiry date ....

☐ Please send me an invoice for prepayment.

NAME ....

ADDRESS ....

....

OFFICIAL ORDER NUMBER .... **SIGNATURE** ....
Please keep me informed of new books in my subject area which is

....

Order your disk from Wiley:

In the United States: John Wiley & Sons Inc, using the order card below to NJ.

In the United Kingdom,   John Wiley & Sons Ltd, using the order card
Europe and the rest of   below to Bognor Regis.
the world:

Affix
stamp
here

Customer Service Department
John Wiley & Sons Limited
Distribution Centre
Shripney Road
Bognor Regis
Sussex PO22 9SA
England

DATA COMPRESSION

Techniques and Applications
Hardware and Software Considerations

Third Edition

Gilbert Held

*4-Degree Consulting,
Macon, Georgia, USA*

and

Thomas R. Marshall

(Software Author)

JOHN WILEY & SONS LTD

Chichester · New York · Brisbane · Toronto · Singapore

Other Wiley Editorial Offices

John Wiley & Sons, Inc., 605 Third Avenue,
New York, NY 10158–0012, USA

Jacaranda Wiley Ltd, G.P.O. Box 859, Brisbane,
Queensland 4001, Australia

John Wiley & Sons (Canada) Ltd, 22 Worcester Road,
Rexdale, Ontario M9W 1L1, Canada

John Wiley & Sons (SEA) Pte Ltd, 37 Jalan Pemimpin 05–04,
Block B, Union Industrial Building, Singapore 2057

Library of Congress Cataloging-in-Publication Data:
Held, Gilbert, 1943–
    Data compression : techniques and applications : hardware and software considerations
    / Gilbert Held and Thomas R. Marshall. — 3rd ed.
        p.   cm.
    Includes bibliographical references and index.
    ISBN 0 471 92941 7
    1. Data compression (Computer science)   I. Marshall, Thomas
(Thomas, R.)
QA76.9.D33H44   1991
005.74′6—dc20   90-27814
                                                                    CIP

A catalogue record for this book is available from the British Library.

Typeset by Photo·graphics, Honiton, Devon
Printed in Great Britain by Courier International, East Kilbride

DEDICATION

To Beverly, Jonathan and Jessica for their patience and understanding. To Dr Alexander Ioffe and his family whom I met in Moscow, may we meet again. To Harry R. Karp for his guidance and direction and to my father Milton, who taught me to determine how when others asked why.

CONTENTS

PREFACE

The original goal of the first edition of this book was to provide
readers with an intimate awareness of practical and easy-to-implement
data-compression techniques. In writing the second edition of *Data
Compression* the original goal of the book was retained. However,
the scope and depth of coverage was expanded to include additional
data-compression techniques as well as examples of the coding
required in the BASIC programming language to develop software
to compress and decompress data using different compression
techniques. Building upon the second edition, this third edition
represents a considerable expansion of prior editions of this book.
Information concerning the structure and operation of several popular
compression algorithms that reached the market since the publication
of the second edition of this book has been added. New compression
techniques examined in this book include the Microcom Networking
Protocol (MNP) Class 5 data compression, MNP Class 7 Enhanced
Data Compression, and the CCITT V.42bis compression method
based upon the Lempel–Ziv technique. In addition, numerous
methods to enhance the efficiency of both character-oriented and
statistical compression techniques based upon the author's experience
over the past three years are now shared with readers. Concerning
character-oriented compression, a new chapter has been added which
discusses three methods readers can use to obtain the special
compression-indicating character which is the key to implementing
this type of compression.

The development of this book resulted from the response received
to a series of seminars I conducted concerning the characteristics,
operation and application of 25 data communications devices. During
these seminars, a small portion of time was devoted to examining a
few data-compression methods and how such methods could enhance

one's transmission efficiency. At the conclusion of each seminar, a common thread of questioning from participants concerned sources of information about additional data-compression algorithms, implementation techniques and hardware and software considerations. Having previously conducted a literature search prior to developing several microprocessor-based compression software modules, I realized that a literature void existed concerning practical data-compression methods that could be applied to typical data transmission problems. Based upon the success of the first and second editions of this book, it appears that *Data Compression* has significantly contributed to filling that void. I hope that this third edition will satisfy the queries of many readers who contacted me directly during the last few years for additional information concerning the compression of data.

The first chapter of this book covers the rationale and utilization of data-compression techniques and serves as a general introduction to a key interrelated subject area of the book—data compression and transmission efficiency. Since the key to the successful implementation of character-oriented compression techniques is the selection of an appropriate compression-indicating character, Chapter 2 is focused upon this topic. Due to the relationship between compression-indicating characters and data codes, Chapter 2 first reviews four popular data codes and then examines three methods readers can use to obtain compression-indicating characters. In Chapter 3, eight distinct data-compression algorithms are discussed while Chapter 4 examines statistical encoding techniques. Chapter 5 focuses on the data analysis effort required before one can select an optimum or near-optimum data-compression method. Software linkage of data-compression routines and other compression considerations are contained in Chapter 6. Topics included in this chapter concern memory requirements, software module placement buffering techniques and timing considerations.

In Chapter 7, several categories of compression performing devices are examined, providing the reader with an alternative to developing compression performing software. Topics included in this chapter include the economics of utilization and the operation of compression performing hardware and software.

Two appendices are included in this book. Both a BASIC and a FORTRAN program listing of a program whose execution permits the frequency analysis of various types of data files is included in Appendix A. This program can be used by readers to analyze their data files and determine the most beneficial data-compression method to implement. In addition, the program permits one to determine the susceptibility of data files to different compression techniques prior to actually implementing those techniques.

In Appendix B, the coding examples for compressing and decompressing data presented throughout the book have been combined into one comprehensive example with the appropriate program name of SHRINK. Readers are encouraged to review the program listing and to use the program as it appears or to modify it to satisfy their particular requirements as long as such usage is on a non-commercial basis.

With the abolition of the bulk rate discount tariff known as TELPAK coupled with private link tariff increases, many large data communications users have unfortunately become the victims of a 75 per cent communications inflation rate. Data compression represents one method of bringing that cost under control. As described in this book, most compression methods are easy to implement and their payback in the form of reduced costs may build rapidly. The effect of data compression upon one's transmission time and transmission cost can be summed up in two words—SHRINK IT.

Gilbert Held
Macon, Georgia

ACKNOWLEDGEMENTS

The author wishes to thank *Telecommunications* for permission received to reprint the tables and figures form the article 'Data Compression in High-Speed Digital Facsimile' which appeared in their June 1977 issue. The author is indebted to Mr Thomas R. Marshall who rightfully must be considered to be the software author of this book for his cooperation and assistance in developing the encoding and decoding programming examples as well as the BASIC and FORTRAN versions of the DATANALYSIS computer program listed in Appendix B, and to Mrs Carol Ferrell for her effort in converting the author's notes into a proper manuscript. I would also like to take the opportunity to thank Christine Washburn of Microcom for providing information on the different levels of MNP data compression, Kimberly Bromley of InfoTel for providing information on that firm's INFOPAK Data Compression software products, Irene M. Henderson of System Enhancement Associates for providing information on that firm's ARC archive utility that compresses data as well as permitting the program to be added to the convenience disk, and a similar 'thank you' to Mr Phil Katz of PKWARE for supplying information on his firm's file compression program as well as granting permission for its distribution on the convenience disk which is available from John Wiley & Sons.

1

RATIONALE AND UTILIZATION

In the chronology of computer development, large-scale information transfer by remote computing and the development of massive information storage and retrieval systems have witnessed a tremendous growth. Concurrent with this growth, several problem areas have developed which can result in major, but unnecessary, economic expenditures.

One problem is the so-called 'run-away database'. Here the size of the database used by an organization for its information storage and retrieval programs becomes larger and larger, requiring additional disk drives for online systems and reels of magnetic tapes for those systems that can be processed in a batch environment.

Accompanying the growth in the size of databases has been a large increase in the number of users and duration of usage by personnel at remote locations. These factors result in tremendous amounts of data being transferred between computers and remote terminals. To provide transmission facilities for the required data transfers, communications lines and auxiliary devices, such as modems and multiplexers, have been continuously upgraded by many organizations to permit higher data transfer capability.

Although the obvious solutions to these problems of data storage and information transfer are to install additional storage devices and expand existing communications facilities, to do so requires an additional increase in an organization's equipment and operating costs. One method that can be employed to alleviate a portion of data storage and information transfer problems is through the representation of data by more efficient codes. If one examines an organization's database or monitors a transmission line, there is an excellent chance that the individual characters that both make up the database and the transmission sequence could be encoded more effectively. Two techniques that can result in a more effective encoded data representation are logical and physical data compression.

1.1 LOGICAL COMPRESSION

When a database is designed, one of the first steps of the analyst is to obtain as much data reduction as possible. This data reduction results from the elimination of redundant fields of information while representing the data elements in the remaining fields with as few logical indicators as is feasible.

Although logical compression is data dependent and the method employed can vary based upon the analyst's foresight, the following two examples will illustrate the ease of implementation and benefits of this compression technique.

One simple example of logical data compression is the occupational field on a personnel database. Suppose 30 alphanumeric positions are allocated to this field. If the field is fixed, occupations such as the 10-character occupational description 'DISHWASHER' have 20 blanks inserted into the remainder of the field. Then, 30 million characters of storage would be required for the occupational field of 1 million workers. Suppose at most there were 32 768 distinct occupations. Instead of indicating the occupational title, one could encode the equivalent 5-digit data code, eliminating 25 character positions per field. The size of the field could be reduced further by allocating the binary value of 1 or more characters to the occupational code. As an example, an 8-bit character could represent $2^8 - 1$ or 255 distinct values or occupational codes. Linking two 8-bit characters through appropriate software would provide $2^{16} - 1$ or 65 535 distinct codes. This would reduce the field size from 30 to 2 characters, saving 28 million characters of storage. If our counting begins at zero instead of a conventional starting place of 1, an 8-bit character could represent 256 codes while a 16-bit character could be employed to represent 65 536 distinct values.

A second example of logical compression is a date field. This type of field frequently occurs in databases. Normally, the numeric equivalents of the subfields representing day, month and year are used in place of longhand notation. Thus, 01 04 81 would represent 1 April 1981. While this logical compression results in 6 numeric characters of storage, additional data reduction can result from storing the date as a binary value. Since the day will never exceed

31, 5 bits would suffice to represent the data field. Similarly, 4 bits could be used to represent the month value while 7 bits could represent 127 years, permitting a relative year ranging from 1900 to 2027.

Logical compression using numerical and binary representation is illustrated in Figure 1.1 for the preceding date field example. It is interesting to note that employing binary representation reduces the date field to 16 binary digits or two 8-bit concatenated characters of storage. As discussed, many logical compression methods can be considered by an analyst during the database design process. Each method may result in a distinct degree of data storage reduction. Correspondingly, when logically compressed databases or portions of such databases are transmitted between locations, transmission time is reduced since fewer data characters are transmitted.

Longhand	DAY	MONTH	YEAR
Example	1	APRIL	1981
Logical compression using numerical representation			
Example	01	04	81
Logical compression using binary representation			
Example	00001	0100	1010001

Figure 1.1   Logical compression methods. Logical compression can result from alphanumeric, numeric or binary representation of data in a shorthand notation

While logical compression can be an effective tool in minimizing the size of a database, it only reduces transmission time when logically compressed data is transmitted. Thus, the transmission of inquiry and response data, which are typically encoded as separate and distinct entities in the appropriate bit representation of the code for each character, is not normally affected. Similarly, the occurrence of repeating patterns and groups of characters, which are normally contained in reports transmitted from computer systems to terminal devices, would not be affected. For such situations, a reduction in data transmission time depends upon the physical compression of the data as it is encountered.

1.2 PHYSICAL COMPRESSION

Physical compression can be viewed as the process of reducing the quantity of data prior to its entering a transmission medium and the expansion of such data into its original format upon receipt at a distant location. Although both physical and logical compression can result in reduced transmission time, distinct application differences exist between the two techniques. Logical compression is normally used to represent databases more efficiently and does not consider the frequency of occurrence of characters or groups of characters.

Physical compression takes advantage of the fact that when data are encoded as separate and distinct entities, the probabilities of occurrence of characters and groups of characters differ. Since frequently occurring characters are encoded into as many bits as those characters that only rarely occur, data reduction becomes possible by encoding frequently occurring characters into short bit codes while representing infrequently occurring characters by longer bit codes. Like logical compression, many physical compression techniques exist. Some techniques replace repeating strings of characters by a special compression-indicator character and a quantity-count character. Other techniques replace frequently occurring characters with a short binary code while infrequently encountered characters are replaced by longer binary codes. In Chapter 3, eight distinct physical compression methods are covered in detail. For the remainder of this book we will focus our attention upon physical data compression.

1.3 COMPRESSION BENEFITS

When data compression is used to reduce storage requirements, overall program execution time may be reduced. This is because the reduction in storage will result in a reduction of disk-access attempts, while the encoding and decoding required by the compression technique employed will result in additional program instructions being executed. Since the execution time of a group of program instructions is normally significantly less than the time required to access and transfer data to a peripheral device, overall program execution time may be reduced.

With respect to the transmission of data, compression provides the network planner with several benefits in addition to the potential cost savings associated with sending less data over the switched telephone network where the cost of the call is usually based upon its duration. First, compression can reduce the probability of transmission errors occurring since fewer characters are transmitted when data is compressed while the probability of an error occurring remains constant. Second, since compression increases efficiency, it may reduce or even eliminate extra workshifts. Finally, by converting text that is represented by a conventional code such as standard ASCII into a different code, compression algorithms may provide a level of security against illicit monitoring.

For data communications, the transfer of compressed data over a medium results in an increase in the effective rate of information transfer, even though the actual data transfer rate expressed in bits per second remains the same. Data compression can be implemented on most existing hardware by software or through the use of a special hardware device that incorporates one or more compression techniques.

In Figure 1.2, a basic data-compression block diagram is illustrated. Shown as a black box, compression and decompression may occur within the user's processor to include personal computers, intelligent terminals or in a device foreign to the processor, such as a specialized communications component. Foremost among these components were data concentrators and statistical multiplexers during the 1970s and early 1980s. From approximately the mid-1980s, a revolution in the utilization of data-compression-performing products has occurred in the areas of switched network modems, personal computer and mainframe disk storage. Literally hundreds of switched network modem manufacturers have incorporated a variety of data-compression algorithms into their products, while numerous software developers have marketed programs which increase the storage capacity of disks by compressing data prior to storage.

Figure 1.2 Basic data-compression block diagram. An original data stream operated upon according to one or more compression algorithms results in the generation of a compressed data stream

To examine in some detail a portion of the benefits that may result from the employment of one or more compression techniques requires a review of some fundamental compression terminology.

1.4 TERMINOLOGY

As illustrated in Figure 1.2, an original data stream is operated upon according to a particular algorithm to produce a compressed data stream. This compression of the original data stream is sometimes referred to as an encoding process with the result that the compressed data stream is also called an encoded data stream. Reversing the process, the compressed data stream is decompressed to reproduce the original data stream. Since this decompression process results in the decoding of the compressed data stream, the result is sometimes referred to as the decoded data stream. We will use the terms original data stream and decoded data stream synonymously, as well as the terms compressed data stream and encoded data stream.

The degree of data reduction obtained as a result of the compression process is known as the compression ratio. This ratio measures the quantity of compressed data in comparison with the quantity of original data, such that (Ruth and Krentzler, 1972):

$$\text{Compression ratio} = \frac{\text{Length of original data string}}{\text{Length of compressed data string}}.$$

From the above equation, it is obvious that the higher the compression ratio the more effective the compression technique employed. Another term used when talking about compression is the figure of merit, where:

$$\text{Figure of merit} = \frac{\text{Length of compressed data string}}{\text{Length of original data string}}.$$

The figure of merit is the reciprocal of the compression ratio and must always be less than unity for the compression process to be effective. The fraction of data reduction is one minus the figure of merit. Thus, a compression technique that results in one character of compressed data for every three characters in the original data stream would have a compression ratio of 3, a figure of merit of 0.33 and a fraction of data reduction of 0.66.

Pure random data, by definition, should not have any redundancy. While the compression ratio for this type of data should be unity, in many instances the improper design of a compression algorithm or its improper application may result in a degree of data expansion, resulting in a compression ratio falling below unity.

When data is compressed, the compression ratio will vary in proportion to the susceptibility of the data to the algorithm or algorithms used. Thus, you should focus your attention upon an average compression ratio and not a ratio achieved at a particular time. In general, good algorithms can be expected to achieve an average compression ratio of 1.5, while excellent algorithms based upon sophisticated processing techniques will achieve an average compression ratio exceeding 2.0.

1.5 COMMUNICATIONS APPLICATIONS

To obtain an overview of some of the communications benefits available through the incorporation of data compression, we can consider a typical data communications application. As illustrated in the top portion of Figure 1.3, a remote batch terminal is connected

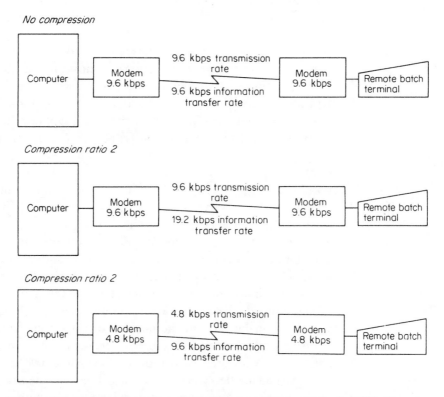

Figure 1.3 Data compression affects the information transfer ratio (ITR); through the use of data compression, the methodology and structure of one's data communications facility may be changed

to a central computer with transmission occurring at a 9.6 kbps data rate. Let us assume that the data to be transmitted has not been compressed. If through the programming of one or more compression algorithms or the installation of a hardware compression device a compression ratio of 2 is obtained, several alternatives may be available with respect to one's data communications methodology. First, our data transmission time is reduced since the effective information transfer rate has increased to approximately 19.2 kbps as shown in the middle portion of Figure 1.3. Ignoring communications software overhead, the data transmission time is halved. Thus, one may now consider using the remote batch terminal for other remote processing applications or perhaps an expensive after-hours shift or portion of such a shift can be alleviated. In the lower portion of Figure 1.3 another user option is illustrated. Here the transmission rate may be reduced to 4800 bps. With a compression ratio of 2, this is equivalent to an information transfer rate of 9600 bps. By lowering the data transmission rate, more expensive 9600 bps modems may be replaced by 4800 bps modems and line conditioning which is normally required when transmitting data at 9600 bps may be removed, resulting in an additional cost reduction.

A second type of communications application that can benefit from the utilization of data compression is illustrated in Figure 1.4. A typical multidrop network is illustrated in the top portion of Figure 1.4, connecting terminals at diverse geographical locations via a common leased line to a computer site. Typically, the transmission activity of the terminals is the governing factor that limits the multidrop line to a maximum number of drops. In the bottom portion of Figure 1.4, it is assumed that compression performing modems were substituted for the conventional modems used in the original multidrop configuration. Since data compression on a multidrop line reduces the flow of data on the line, its utilization will normally enable additional drops to be added to the line prior to the occurrence of throughput delays that affect the response time of the terminals attached to each drop. In this particular example, it is assumed that the use of compression performing modems permitted an increase in the number of line-drops from 4 to 6.

For switched network modems, data compression provides the ability to obtain an information transfer capability at a fraction of the cost of higher-speed modems. This is due to the complex modulation schemes used by modems operating at 9600 bps in comparison with less complex schemes used by 2400 bps modems. By incorporating a compression algorithm into a 2400 bps modem,

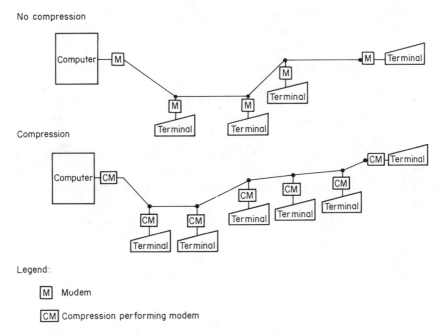

No compression

Compression

Legend:

M Modem

CM Compression performing modem

Figure 1.4 Data compression on a multidrop line reduces the flow of data on the line, permitting additional terminals to be serviced

it becomes possible to achieve a data throughput between 4800 and 9600 bps for the cost of a read only memory (ROM) chip that might have a wholesale cost of $5. In comparison, the analog circuitry required by a modem to operate at 9600 bps may have a wholesale cost of $100 or more over the circuitry required for a 2400 bps modem. Since most manufacturers must sell their products at three to five times their cost, the use of compression in lower-speed modems can translate into significant retail savings in comparison with the cost of modems operating at higher data rates. In addition, the incorporation of data compression into high-speed switched network modems provides users with an information transfer capability beyond the capacity afforded by current modem technology.

1.6 DATA STORAGE APPLICATIONS

To illustrate the applicability of data compression to data storage applications, let us examine how data is stored in a diskette. During the formatting process, a computer divides the recording space into tracks, which are concentric circles. Diskettes used with the original

IBM PC and PC XT personal computers have 40 tracks, numbered from 0 at the outer edge to 39 at the inner edge. Each track is subdivided into sectors, with the number of sectors per track a function of the storage capacity of the diskette.

Figure 1.5 illustrates the track and sector relationship for $5\frac{1}{4}$-inch diskettes used with the IBM PC and PC XT personal computers. Diskettes used with those computers have 40 tracks and eight or nine sectors per track, with the number of sectors per track based upon the FORMAT command parameter specified. Each sector can store up to 512 characters and represents the minimum amount of data that can be stored or retrieved with one disk read/write operation. If you write one character to a file you will use one sector of 512 characters, while saving a file consisting of 513 characters would require the use of two sectors.

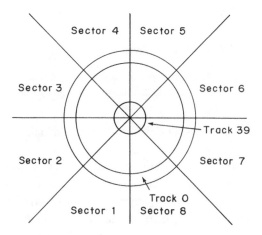

Figure 1.5 Track and sector relationship (note: diskettes can be formatted to hold either eight or nine sectors per track)

The total storage capacity of a $5\frac{1}{4}$-inch double-sided diskette formatted to hold eight sectors per track is:

2 sides × 40 tracks/side × 8 sectors/track × 512 characters/sector = 327 680 characters.

Suppose you wish to download a file that contains 350 000 characters. Without a compression program you could not store this file on one diskette. In addition, if the file is not capable of being subdivided, such as a binary file, you might have to consider upgrading your computer's storage capacity by adding a hard disk or a higher-capacity diskette drive. As an alternative, you may be able to download a compressed version of the file. Today, many bulletin boards use public domain programs to archive files into a compressed format both to reduce downloading time as well as storage requirements. If we assume that a 2:1 compression ratio is achieved, the 350 000 character file would be compressed into 175 000 characters. Not only would the file fit on one diskette, but, in addition, it could be stored using 342 sectors. This would leave 298 sectors available for other purposes, such as storing a decompression program. Once downloaded you may be able to expand the program in memory or, if you have a hard disk, expand the program onto that storage facility. If you want to distribute the program to other personal computer users you could consider distributing the compressed version of the program. This would allow you to distribute the program on one diskette. In comparison, the distribution of the normal version of the file would require two diskettes if the file could be logically separated.

For detailed information concerning the operation and utilization of two programs developed to compress IBM PC and compatible personal computer files, the reader is referred to Chapter 7. In addition, readers may wish to consider the purchase of the convenience disk which accompanies this book and which contains those programs in their original form.

1.7 DATA COMPRESSION AND INFORMATION TRANSFER

When data is transmitted between terminals, a terminal and a computer or two computers, several delay factors may be encountered which cumulatively affect the information transfer rate. Data transmitted over a transmission medium must be converted into an acceptable format for that medium. When digital data is transmitted over analog telephone lines, modems must be employed to convert the digital pulses of the business machine into a modulated signal acceptable for transmission on the analog telephone circuit. The time between the first bit entering the modem and the first modulated signal produced by the device is known as the modem's internal delay time. Since two such devices are required for a point-to-point circuit, the total internal delay time encountered during a transmission sequence equals twice the modem's internal delay time. Such times can range from a few to 10 or more milliseconds (ms). The second delay encountered on a circuit is a function of the distance between points and is known as the circuit or propagation delay time. This is the time required for the signal to be propagated or transferred down the line to the distant end. Propagation delay time can be approximated by equating 1 millisecond for every 150 circuit miles and adding 12 milliseconds to the total.

Once data is received at the distant end it must be acted upon, resulting in a processing delay which is a function of the computer or terminal employed as well as the quantity of transmitted data which must be acted upon. Processing delay time can range from a few milliseconds where a simple error check is performed to determine if the transmitted data was received correctly to many seconds where a search of a database must occur in response to a transmitted query. Each time the direction of transmission changes in a typical half duplex protocol, control signals change at the associated modem to computer and modem to terminal interfaces. The time required to switch control signals to change the direction of transmission is known as line turnaround time and can result in delays up to 250 or more milliseconds, depending upon the transmission protocol employed. We can denote the effect of data compression by examining the transmission protocol commonly known as BISYNC communications and a few of its derivations.

BISYNC communications

One of the most commonly employed transmission protocols is the Binary Synchronous Communications (BISYNC) communications control structure. This line control structure was introduced in 1966 by International Business Machine Corporation and is used for transmission by many medium-speed and high-speed devices to include terminal and computer systems. BISYNC provides a set of rules which govern the synchronous transmission of binary-coded data. While this protocol can be used with a variety of transmission codes, it is limited to the half duplex transmission mode and requires the acknowledgement of the receipt of every block of transmitted data. In an evolutionary process, a number of synchronous protocols have been developed to supplement or serve as a replacement to BISYNC, the most prominent being the high-level data link control (HDLC) protocol defined by the International Standard Organization (ISO).

The key difference between BISYNC and HDLC protocols is that BISYNC is a half duplex, character-oriented transmission control structure while HDLC is a bit-oriented, full duplex transmission control structure. We can investigate the efficiency of these basic transmission control structures and the effect of data compression upon their information transfer efficiency. To do so, an examination of some typical error control procedures is first required.

Error control

The most commonly employed error-control procedure is known as automatic request for repeat (ARQ). In this type of control procedure, upon detection of an error, a request is made by the receiving station to the sending station to retransmit the message. Two types of ARQ procedures have been developed: 'stop and wait ARQ' and 'go back n ARQ', which is sometimes called continuous ARQ.

'Stop and wait ARQ' is a simple type of error-control procedure. Here the transmitting station stops at the end of each block and waits for a reply from the receiving terminal pertaining to the block's accuracy (ACK) or error (NAK) prior to transmitting the next block. This type of error-control procedure is illustrated in Figure 1.6. Here the time between transmitted blocks is referred to as dead time which acts to reduce the effective data rate on the circuit. When

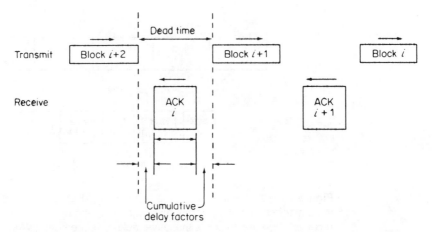

Figure 1.6 Stop and wait ARQ. In this type of error control procedure, the receiver transmits an acknowledgement after each block. This can result in a significant amount of cumulative delay time between data blocks

the transmission mode is half duplex, the circuit must be turned around twice for each block transmitted, once to receive the reply (ACK or NAK) and once again to resume transmitting. These line turnarounds, as well as such factors as the propagation delay time, station message processing time and the modem internal delay time, all contribute to what is shown as the cumulative delay factors.

When the 'go back n ARQ' type of error control procedure is employed, the dead time can be substantially reduced to the point where it may be insignificant. One way to implement this type of error control procedure is by the utilization of a simultaneous reverse channel for acknowledgement signalling as illustrated in Figure 1.7. In this type of operating mode, the receiving station sends back the ACK or NAK response on the reverse channel for each transmitted block. If the primary channel operates at a much higher data rate than the reverse channel, many blocks may have been received prior to the transmitting station receiving the NAK in response to a block at the receiving station being found in error. The number of blocks one may go back to request a transmission, n, is a function of the block size and buffer area available in the business machines and terminals at the transmitting and receiving stations, the ratio of the data transfer rates of the primary and reverse channels and the processing time required to compute the block check character and transmit an acknowledgement. For the latter, this time is shown as small gaps between the ACK and NAK blocks in Figure 1.7.

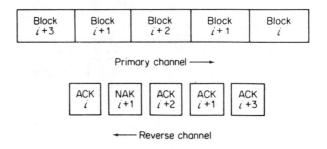

Figure 1.7 Go back n ARQ. In a 'go back n ARQ' error-control procedure, the transmitter continuously sends messages until the receiver detects an error. The receiver then transmits a negative acknowledgement (NAK) on the reverse channel and the transmitter retransmits the block received in error. Some versions of this technique require blocks sent before the error indication was encountered to be retransmitted in addition to the block received in error

Half duplex throughout model

When a message block is transmitted in the BISYNC control structure, a number of control characters are contained in that block in addition to the message text. If the variable C is assigned to represent the number of control characters per block and the variable D is used to represent the number of data characters, then the total block length is $C + D$. If the data transfer rate expressed in bps is denoted as T_R and the number of bits per character is denoted as B_C, then the transmission time for one character is equal to B_C/T_R which can be denoted as T_C. Since $D + C$ characters are contained in a message block, the time required to transmit the block will become $T_C * (D + C)$. Once the block is received, it must be acknowledged. To do so, the receiving station is required to first compute a block check character (BCC) and compare it with the transmitted BCC character appended to the end of the transmitted block. Although the BCC character is computed as the data is received, a comparison is performed after the entire block is received and only then can an acknowledgement be transmitted. The time to check the transmitted and computed BCC characters and form and transmit the acknowledgement is known as the processing and acknowledgement time (T_{PA}).

When transmission is half duplex, the line turnaround time (T_L) required to reverse the transmission direction of the line must be added. Normally, this time includes the request-to-send/clear-to-send (RTS/CTS) modem delay time as well as each of the modems' internal delay time. For the acknowledgement to reach its destination, it must propagate down the circuit and this propagation delay time, denoted as T_p, must also be considered. If the acknowledgement message contains A characters then, when transmitted on the primary channel, $A * B_C/T_R$ seconds are required to send the acknowledgement.

Once the original transmitting station receives the acknowledgement it must determine if it is required to retransmit the previously sent message block. This time is similar to the processing and acknowledgement time previously discussed. To transmit either a new message block or repeat the previously sent message block, the line must be turned around again and the message block will require time to propagate down the line to the receiving station. Thus, the total time to transmit a message block and receive an acknowledgement, denoted as T_B, becomes:

$$T_B = T_C * (D + C) + 2 * (T_{PA} + T_L + T_p) + (A * B_C/T_R). \quad (1.1)$$

Since efficiency is the data transfer rate divided by the theoretical data transfer rate, the transmission control structure efficiency (E_{TCS}) becomes:

$$E_{TCS} = \frac{B_C * D * (1 - P)}{T_R * T_B}. \qquad (1.2)$$

In equation (1.2) the numerator represents the number of actual data bits that are received correctly. Here B_C is the number of bits per character and D is the number of data characters in the block. Thus, $B_C * D$ represents the number of bits contained in the data characters which form a block. Since there is a probability, P, that one or more bits in the block will be in error, multiplying $B_C * D * (1 - P)$ results in the average number of bits per block not in error.

Focusing our attention upon the denominator, T_R represents the data transfer rate while T_B represents the total time to transmit a message block and receive an acknowledgement. This results in the denominator containing the theoretical number of bits that could be transferred and received. Dividing the number of bits received correctly (numerator) by the theoretical number of bits that could be transferred (denominator) provides us with the efficiency of the transmission control structure.

Although the preceding is a measurement of the transmission control structure efficiency, it does not consider the data code efficiency which is the ratio of information bits to total bits per character. When the data code efficiency is included, we obtain a measurement of the information transfer efficiency. We can call this ratio the information transfer ratio (ITR) which will provide us with a measurement of the protocol's information transfer efficiency. This results in:

$$ITR = \frac{B_{IC} * E_{TCS}}{B_C} \qquad (1.3)$$

where:

ITR = Information transfer ratio
B_{IC} = Information bits per character
B_C = Total bits per character
D = Data characters per message block
A = Characters in the acknowledgement message

C = Control characters per message block
T_R = Data transfer rate (bps)
T_C = Transmission time per character (B_C/T_R)
T_{PA} = Processing and acknowledgment time
T_L = Line turnaround time
T_p = Propagation delay time
P = Probability of one or more errors in block.

From the preceding, the information transfer ratio provides us with a measurement of the efficiency of the transmission control structure without considering the effect of compression. When compression is considered we obtain a new term which we will denote as the effective information transfer ratio (EITR).

When data is compressed, the original data stream will be reduced in size prior to transmission, the actual reduction being dependent upon the compression algorithms employed as well as the composition of the data acted upon. In general, we can assume that the compression ratio considers the number of characters in the compressed data stream to include special control characters required to indicate one or more compression algorithms. This reasonable assumption simplifies the effect of considering data compression when examining a particular protocol. As an example, consider a 160-character data block compressed into 78 data characters plus 2 compression indicator characters. Here the compression ratio would be 160/(78 + 2) or 2. The effect upon the previously developed equation to compute the information transfer ratio would be to change D in the numerator to the non-compressed string length of 160 characters while D in the denominator would be the actual 78 compressed data characters plus the two additional special characters required to indicate data compression, resulting in a total of 80 characters. If the total number of control characters framing the data block is relatively small, the effective information transfer ratio can be approximated by multiplying the information transfer ratio by the compression ratio.

Computation examples

We will assume that our data transmission rate is 4800 bps and we will transmit information using a BISYNC transmission control structure employing a 'stop and wait ARQ' error control procedure. Furthermore, let us assume the following parameters:

A = 4 characters per acknowledgement
B_{IC} = 8 bits per character
B_{C} = 8 bits per character
D = 80 data characters per block
C = 10 control characters per block
T_{R} = 4800 bps
T_{C} = 8/4800 = 0.001 66 seconds (s) per character
T_{PA} = 20 ms = 0.02 s
T_{L} = 100 ms = 0.10 s
T_{p} = 30 ms = 0.03 s
P = 0.01.

Then:

$$\mathrm{ITR} = \frac{8*80*(1 - 0.01)}{4800*[0.001\,66*(80 + 10) + 2*(0.02 + 0.03 + 0.1) + 4*8/4800]}$$

$$= 0.2894.$$

Since the transfer rate of information in bits (TRIB) is equal to the product of the data transfer rate and the information transfer ratio, we obtain:

$$\mathrm{TRIB} = \mathrm{ITR}*T_{\mathrm{R}} = 0.2894*4800 = 1389 \text{ bps.}$$

For the preceding example, approximately 29 per cent of the data transfer rate is effectively used.

Let us now examine the effect of doubling the text size to 160 characters while the remaining parameters except P continue as before. Since the block size has doubled, P approximately doubles, resulting in the ITR becoming:

$$\mathrm{ITR} = \frac{8*160*(1 - 0.02)}{4800*[0.001\,66*(1600 + 10) + 2*(0.02 + 0.03 + 0.1) + 4*8/4800]}$$

$$= 0.4438.$$

With an ITR of 0.4438 the TRIB now becomes:

$$\mathrm{TRIB} = \mathrm{ITR}*T_{\mathrm{R}} = 0.4438*4800 = 2130 \text{ bps.}$$

Here, doubling the block size raises the percentage of the data transfer rate effectively used to 44.38 per cent.

Compression effect

Suppose one or more data-compression algorithms are employed which result in a compression ratio of 2. What effect would this have upon the effective information transfer ratio?

The effective information transfer ratio (EITR) can be obtained by modifying equation (1.2) as follows:

$$EITR = \frac{B_{IC}*D_1*(1 - P)}{T_R*[T_C*(D_2 + C)+2*(T_{PA} + T_L + T_P)+(A*B_C/T_R)]}$$

(1.4)

where:

D_1 = original data block size in characters prior to compression
D_2 = compressed data block size in characters to include special compression indication characters

If on the average 160 data characters are transmitted in a compressed format of 80 characters we obtain:

$$EITR = \frac{8*160*(1 - 0.01)}{4800*[0.001\,66*(80 + 10) + 2*(0.02 + 0.03 + 0.1) + (4*8/4800)]}$$

$$= 0.5788.$$

As previously discussed, the effective information transfer ratio can be approximated as follows:

$$EITR \simeq ITR*CR.$$

(1.5)

Substituting, we obtain:

$$EITR \simeq 0.2861*2 \simeq 0.5722.$$

From the preceding you will note that the difference between the computed EITR (0.5788) and the approximated EITR (0.5722) is essentially insignificant. Thus, if you know the ITR you can simply multiply it by the compression ratio to obtain a reasonable approximation of the effective information transfer ratio.

Since the transfer rate of information in bits (TRIB) is the product of the effective information transfer ratio and the operating data rate, we obtain:

$$TRIB = 0.5788*4800 = 2778 \text{ bps.}$$

In Table 1.1, the reader will find a comparison of the variations in the ITR, EITR and TRIB when non-compressed and compressed data are transmitted for two different block sizes.

Table 1.1 Compression effect comparison

	Non-compressed data		Compressed data	
Block size (characters)	80	160	80	160
ITR (dimensionless)	0.2894	0.4438	N/A	N/A
EITR (dimensionless)	N/A	N/A	0.5788	0.8678
TRIB (bps)	1389	2130	2778	4165

From Table 1.1, it is apparent that two methods can be employed to increase one's transmission efficiency. First, you may alter the protocol or transmission control sequence by varying the size of the data blocks transmitted. Alternatively, you can compress data prior to transmitting a block of information. Both methods can result in more information passing over a transmission line per unit time.

To facilitate the computation of the ITR based upon varying block sizes, a BASIC language program was developed. This program, which is listed in Table 1.2, computes the ITR for block sizes varying from 40 to 4000 characters in increments of 40 characters. In examining the program listing in Table 1.2, note that the probability of a block being in error is 0.005. This is one-half of 0.01 since we are now varying block sizes by 40 characters instead of 80 characters. Also note that as each block increases by 40 characters the probability that the block contains one or more bits in error has increased by 0.005 since the probability of a block having one or more bits in error is proportion to its size.

In Table 1.3, the reader will find a tabulation of the execution of the program which calculated the ITR as the block size varied from 40 to 4000 characters in increments of 40. In examining this table one should note that the maximum ITR of 0.7358 is obtained when

Table 1.2 BASIC program listing to compute ITR as a function of block size

```
A = 4
BIC = 8
BC = 8
D = 80
C = 10
TR = 4800
TC = 8 / 4800
TPA = 0.02
TL = 0.1
TP = 0.03
P = 0.005
FOR BLOCK = 40 TO 4000 STEP 40
NUMERATOR = BIC * BLOCK * (1 − P)
DENOM = (TR * (0.00166 * (BLOCK + 10) + 2 * (TPA + TL + TP) + A *
BIC / TR))
ITR = NUMERATOR / DENOM
PRINT USING " #.#### ####"; ITR; BLOCK
P = P + 0.005
NEXT BLOCK
```

Table 1.3 Information transfer ratio and block size. Probability of block error = 0.01 per 80 characters

ITR	Block size	ITR	Block size
0.1702	40	0.6828	2040
0.2894	80	0.6794	2080
0.3771	120	0.6759	2120
0.4438	160	0.6723	2160
0.4960	200	0.6687	2200
0.5376	240	0.6651	2240
0.5714	280	0.6614	2280
0.5992	320	0.6576	2320
0.6222	360	0.6539	2360
0.6415	400	0.6501	2400
0.6577	440	0.6462	2440
0.6714	480	0.6423	2480
0.6830	520	0.6384	2520
0.6928	560	0.6345	2560
0.7011	600	0.6305	2600
0.7082	640	0.6265	2640
0.7142	680	0.6224	2680
0.7191	720	0.6184	2720

Table 1.3 (*continued*)

ITR	Block size	ITR	Block size
0.7233	760	0.6143	2760
0.7267	800	0.6102	2800
0.7295	840	0.6060	2840
0.7317	880	0.6019	2880
0.7333	920	0.5977	2920
0.7345	960	0.5935	2960
		0.5893	3000
0.7353	1000	0.5850	3040
0.7357	1040	0.5808	3080
0.7358	1080	0.5765	3120
0.7356	1120	0.5722	3160
0.7350	1160	0.5679	3200
0.7343	1200	0.5635	3240
0.7332	1240	0.5592	3280
0.7320	1280	0.5548	3320
0.7306	1320	0.5504	3360
0.7290	1360	0.5460	3400
0.7272	1400	0.5416	3440
0.7252	1440	0.5372	3480
0.7231	1480	0.5328	3520
0.7209	1520	0.5283	3560
0.7185	1560	0.5239	3600
0.7161	1600	0.5194	3640
0.7135	1640	0.5149	3680
0.7108	1680	0.5104	3720
0.7080	1720		
0.7051	1760	0.5059	3760
0.7021	1800	0.5014	3800
0.6991	1840	0.4969	3840
0.6960	1880	0.4924	3880
0.6928	1920	0.4878	3920
0.6895	1960	0.4833	3960
0.6862	2000	0.4787	4000

the block size is 1080 characters. This indicates that as the block size increases with a constant error rate, a certain point is reached where the time to retransmit a long block every so often negates the enlargement of the block size. For the parameters considered, the optimum block size is 1080 characters. Only for the ideal situation, where $P = 0$ would a continuous increase in block size produce additional efficiencies.

In Figure 1.8 the ITR is plotted as a function of block size for the error-free condition and 0.01 probability of error conditions. The 0.01 probability of error condition per 80-character block was held constant by incrementing the error rate in proportion to the increase in the block size. Since an error-free line is not something a transmission engineer can reasonably expect, a maximum block size will exist beyond which our line efficiency will decrease. At this point, only data compression will result in additional transmission efficiencies. In addition, from a physical standpoint, the buffer area of some devices may prohibit block sizes exceeding a certain number of characters. Once again, data compression can become an effective mechanism for increasing transmission efficiency while keeping data buffer requirements within an acceptable level.

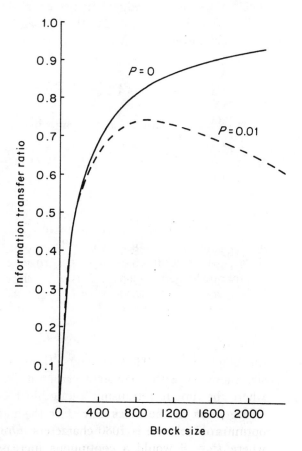

Figure 1.8 ITR and error rate

Return channel model

Consider a 'stop and wait ARQ' error control procedure where a return channel is available for the transmission of acknowledgements. The use of this return channel eliminates the necessity of line turnarounds; however, transmission is still half duplex since an acknowledgement is only transmitted after each received message block is processed.

When the message block is sent to the receiving station, both propagation delay and processing delay are encountered. When the acknowledgement is returned, one additional propagation delay and processing delay result. In addition to these delays, one must also consider the time required to transmit the acknowledgement message. If A denotes the length in characters of the acknowledgement message and T_S is the reverse channel data rate in bps, then the transmission time for the acknowledgement becomes $(A*B_C)/T_S$.

The total delay time due to the propagation and processing as well as the acknowledgement transmission time becomes:

$$2*(T_{PA} + T_p) + \frac{A*B_C}{T_S}$$

Thus, the information transfer ratio becomes:

$$\text{ITR} = \frac{B_{IC}*D_1(1 - P)}{T_R*[T_C*(D_2 + C) + 2*(T_{PA} + T_p) + A*B_C/T_S]} \quad (1.6)$$

Let us examine the effect of this modified transmission procedure on the previous example where data was packed 80 characters per block. Let us assume that a 75 bps reverse channel is available and our acknowledgement message is comprised of four 8-bit characters. Then:

$$\text{ITR} = \frac{8*80*(1 - 0.01)}{4800*[0.001\ 66*(80 + 10) + 2*(0.02 + 0.03) + 4*8/75]}$$

$$= 0.1953.$$

Note that the ITR actually decreased. This was caused by the slowness of the reverse channel where it took 0.4266 (4*8/75) seconds to transmit an acknowledgement. In comparison, the two-line turnarounds that were eliminated only required 0.2 s when the acknowledgement was sent at 4800 bps on the primary channel. This modified procedure is basically effectively when the line turnaround time exceeds the transmission time of the acknowledgement on the return channel. This situation normally occurs when the primary data transfer rate is 2400 bps or less. If the data is compressed prior to transmission and a compression ratio of 2 results in 160 data characters transmitted as a block of 80 compressed characters, the EITR can be computed as follows:

$$\text{EITR} = \frac{8*160*(1 - 0.01)}{4800*[0.001\ 66*(80 + 10) + 2*(0.02 + 0.03) + 4*8/75]} = 0.39.$$

In comparing the effect of compression, note that the transfer rate of information in bits (TRIB) rises from 0.1953*4800 or 937 to 0.39*4800 or 1872 bps. Thus, a compression ratio of 2 can be expected to approximately double throughout.

Full duplex model

A much greater throughout efficiency with the 'stop and wait ARQ' error control procedure can be obtained when a full duplex mode of transmission is employed. Although this requires the use of a four-wire leased line or modems that split a two-wire circuit into independent frequency bands, the modems and line do not have to be reversed. This permits an acknowledgement to be transmitted at the same data rate as the message block but in the reverse direction without the line turnaround. Thus, the information transfer ratio becomes:

$$\text{ITR} = \frac{B_{\text{IC}}*D_1*(1 - P)}{T_{\text{R}}*[T_{\text{C}}*(D_2 + C) + 2*(T_{\text{PA}} + T_{\text{p}})]}. \tag{1.7}$$

Again, returning to the original 80-character block example, we obtain:

$$\text{ITR} = \frac{8*80*(1 - 0.01)}{4800*[0.001\ 66*(80 + 10) + 2*(0.02 + 0.03)]} = 0.5293.$$

When data compression results in a compression ratio of 2, we obtain:

$$EITR = \frac{8*160*(1 - 0.01)}{4800*[0.001\ 66*(80 + 10) + 2*(0.02 + 0.03)]} = 1.06.$$

With an EITR greater than unity this means that the bits of information per unit time (in compressed format) exceed the data transmission rate of the equipment connected to the line. This illustrates the value of data compression, permitting one to obtain very high effective data transfer rates without requiring additional communications facilities.

A second variation of the full duplex model results if a 'go back n ARQ' error control procedure is employed. In this situation, only the block received in error is retransmitted. Here, the information transfer ratio becomes:

$$ITR = \frac{B_{IC}*D_1*(1 - P)}{T_R*[T_C*(D_2 + C)]}. \tag{1.8}$$

Again, substituting values from the original example we obtain:

$$ITR = \frac{8*80*(1 - 0.01)}{4800*[0.001\ 66*(80 + 10)]} = 0.8835.$$

This is obviously the most efficient technique since the line turnaround is eliminated and the processing and acknowledgment time (T_{PA}) and propagation delay time (T_p) in each direction are nullified due to simultaneous message block transmission and acknowledgement response. If we consider the effect of a compression ratio of 2, the effective information transfer ratio can be computed as follows:

$$EITR = \frac{8*160*(1 - 0.01)}{4800*[0.001\ 66*(80 + 10)]} = 1.767.$$

As an alternative to the previous computation you could estimate the EITR by multiplying the ITR by the compression ratio. Doing so in this situation would result in exactly the same result. For the preceding example, the TRIB becomes 1.767*4800 bps or 8482 bps.

Here, compression and protocol structure permit an effective information transfer of 8482 bps on a 4800 bps data path. In effect, the selection of an appropriate protocol coupled with effective data compression algorithms can result in a very effective data transfer. This will result in data transfers normally associated with wideband facilities occurring over conventional voice data transmission facilities.

DATA CODES AND COMPRESSION-INDICATING CHARACTERS

Prior to discussing data-compression techniques, it is important to become familiar with several data codes and the binary representation of characters of such codes. This familiarity is required since character-oriented compression techniques are based upon the employment of one or more characters in a particular character set. Such characters are used to indicate the occurrence of a compression algorithm and compression and decompression could not occur without their use.

In this chapter we will first examine the composition of four popular data codes. Once this is accomplished we will use the preceding knowledge to discuss several methods that can be used to develop compression-indicating characters as well as the advantages and disadvantages associated with the use of each method.

2.1 DATA CODES

Baudot code

The 5-level Baudot code was devised to permit teletypewriters to operate faster and more accurately than relays used to transmit information via telegraph. Since the number of different characters which can be derived from a code having two different (binary) states is 2^m, where m is the number of positions in the code, the 5-level Baudot code permits 32 unique character bit combinations. Although 32 characters could be represented normally with such a code, the necessity to transmit digits, letters of the alphabet and punctuation marks made it necessary to devise a mechanism to extend the capacity of the code to include additional character representations. The extension mechanism was accomplished by the use of two 'shift' characters—'letters shift' and 'figures shift'. The transmission of a shift character informs the receiver that the characters which follow the shift character should be interpreted as characters from a symbol and numeric set or from the alphabetic set of characters. The 5-level Baudot code is illustrated in Figure 2.1 for one particular terminal pallet arrangement. A transmission of all 1s in bit positions 1 to 5 indicates a 'letters shift' and the characters following the transmission of that character are interpreted as letters. Similarly, the transmission of 1s in bit positions 1, 2, 4 and 5 would indicate a 'figures shift' and the following characters would be interpreted as numerics or symbols based upon their code structure.

BCD and EBCDIC codes

The development of computer systems required the implementation of coding systems to convert alphanumeric characters into binary notation. One of the earliest codes used to convert data to a computer-acceptable form was the binary coded decimal (BCD) system. This coding technique permits numeric information to be represented by 4 binary bits and permits an alphanumeric character set to be represented through the use of 6 bits of information. This code is illustrated in Figure 2.2. One advantage of this code is that 2 decimal digits can be stored in an 8-bit computer word and manipulated with appropriate computer instructions. Although only 36 characters are shown, a BCD code is capable of containing a set of 2^6 or 64 different characters.

In addition to transmitting letters, numerics and punctuation marks, a considerable number of control characters may be required to promote line discipline. These control characters may be used to switch on and off devices which are connected to the communications line, control the actual transmission of data, manipulate message formats and perform additional functions. Thus, an extended character set is usually required for data communications. One such

Characters

Letters	Figures	Bit selection 1	2	3	4	5
	–	1				
A	?	1				1
B	:	·			1	
C	$	1	1	1		
D	3	1			1	
E	!	1	1		1	
F	¢			1		1
G					1	1
H	8			1	1	
I	'	1	1	1		
J	(	1				
K	)		1	1	1	1
L	.		1		1	1
M	,		1	1		
N	9		1	1	1	1
O	0				1	1
P	1	1		1	1	1
Q	4			1		
R		1	1			
S	5		1	1	1	
T	7	1	1			
U	;			1	1	1
V	2	1		1		1
W	/	1	1		1	1
X	6	1	1	1		1
Z	"	1	1	1	1	1

Functions

		1	2	3	4	5
Carriage return						
Line feed			1		1	
Space						
Letters shift	<	1	1	1	1	1
Figures shift	=	1	1	1	1	1

Figure 2.1 Baudot code data representation

character set is the extended binary-coded decimal interchange code (EBCDIC) shown in Figure 2.3. This code is an extension of the binary-coded decimal system and uses 8 bits for character representation. This code permits 2^8 or 256 unique characters to be represented although, currently, a lesser number are assigned meanings. This code is primarily used for transmission by byte-oriented computers. The use of EBCDIC by computers may alleviate

Bit position						
b_6	b_5	b_4	b_3	b_2	b_1	Character
0	0	0	0	0	1	A
0	0	0	0	1	0	B
0	0	0	0	1	1	C
0	0	0	1	0	0	D
0	0	0	1	0	1	E
0	0	0	1	1	0	F
0	0	0	1	1	1	G
0	0	1	0	0	0	H
0	0	1	0	0	1	I
0	1	0	0	0	1	J
0	1	0	0	1	0	K
0	1	0	0	1	1	L
0	1	0	1	0	0	M
0	1	0	1	0	1	N
0	1	0	1	1	0	O
0	1	0	1	1	1	P
0	1	1	0	0	0	Q
0	1	1	0	0	1	R
1	0	0	0	1	0	S
1	0	0	0	1	1	T
1	0	0	1	0	0	U
1	0	0	1	0	1	V
1	0	0	1	1	0	W
1	0	0	1	1	1	X
1	0	1	0	0	0	Y
1	0	1	0	0	1	Z
1	1	0	0	0	0	0
1	1	0	0	0	1	1
1	1	0	0	1	0	2
1	1	0	0	1	1	3
1	1	0	1	0	0	4
1	1	0	1	0	1	5
1	1	0	1	1	0	6
1	1	0	1	1	1	7
1	1	1	0	0	0	8
1	1	1	0	0	1	9

Figure 2.2 Binary-coded decimal (BCD) data representation

the necessity of having the computer perform code conversion if the connected terminals transmit data in that code. If not, the computer will perform code conversion prior to operating upon the data. In Figure 2.3, the EBCDIC character set is illustrated. Note that the undefined characters in this code, or any code for that matter, can be used to signify predefined special operations or data representations. Thus, one or more data-compression techniques could be

	00				01				10				11			
	00	01	10	11	00	01	10	11	00	01	10	11	00	01	10	11
0000	NUL	DEL	DS		SP	&										0
0001	SOH	DCI	SOS			/			a	j			A	J		1
0010	STX	DC2	FS	SYN					b	k	s		B	K	S	2
0011	ETX	TM							c	l	t		C	L	T	3
0010	PF	RES	BYP	PN					d	m	u		D	M	U	4
0101	HT	NL	LF	RS					e	n	v		E	N	V	5
0110	LC	BS	ETB	UC					f	o	w		F	O	W	6
0111	DEL	IL	ESC	EOT					g	p	x		G	P	X	7
1000		CAN					h	q	y		H	Q	Y	8		
1000		CAN							h	q	y		H	Q	Y	8
1001		EM							i	r	z		I	R	Z	9
1010	SMM	CC	SM		¢	!		:								
1001	VT	CU1	CU2	CU3	.	$	,	*								
1100	FF	IFS		DC4	<	*	%	®								
1101	CR	IGS	ENQ	NAK	{	}	–	'								
1110	SP	IPS	ACK		+	;	>	=								
1111	SI	IUS	BEL	SUB			?	"								

ACK Acknowledge
BEL Bell
BS   Backspace
BYP By pass
CAN Cancel
CC   Cursor control
CR   Carriage return
CU1 Customer use 1
CU2 Customer use 2
CU3 Customer use 3
DC1 Device control 1
DC2 Device control 2
DC4 Device control 4
DEL Delete
DLE Data link escape
DS   Digit select
EDM End of medium
ENQ Enquiry

EOT End of transmission
ESC Escape
ETB End of transmission block
ETX End of text
FF   Form feed
FS   Field separator
HT   Horizontal tab
IFS Interchange file separator
IGS Interchange group separator
IL   Idle
IRS Interchange record separator
IUS Interchange unit separator
LC   Lower case
LF   Line feed
NAK Negative acknowledge
NL   New line
NUL Null
PF   Punch off

PN   Punch on
RES Restore
RS   Reader stop
SI   Shift in
SM   Set mode
SMM Start of manual message
SO   Shift out
SOH Start of heading
SOS Start of significance
SP   Space
STX Start of text
SUB Substitute
SYN Synchronous idle
TM   Tape mark
UC   Upper case
VT   Vertical tab

Special graphic characters

¢   Cent sign
.   Period, decimal point
<   Less-than sign
(Left parenthesis
+   Plus sign
| Logical OR
&   Ampersand
!   Exclamation mark
$ Dollar sign
*   Asterisk
)   Right parenthesis
;   Semicolon
¬   Logical NOT

–   Minus sign, hyphen
/   Slash
,   Comma
%   Per-cent
—   Underscore
>   Greater-than sign
?   Question mark
:   Colon
Number sign
@   At sign
'   Prime, apostrophe
=   Equal sign
"   Quotation mark

Figure 2.3 EBCDIC character set

indicated by an 8-bit sequence that represents a character, defined or undefined, from the EBCDIC character set. Normally, it is best to employ an undefined character since the delineated characters, in addition to being numeric, graphic and alphabetic characters, include control characters which govern the operation of the terminal and the communications sequence.

When data is compressed according to a certain algorithm, an 8-bit sequence is typically inserted into a data stream to signify both the fact that compression has occurred as well as the type of algorithm employed. In this book, we refer to the use of such characters as special compression-indicator characters or special characters for brevity. When the compressed data is received, the same 8-bit sequence would indicate the presence of compressed data. In addition, it would inform the receiving station of the data compression algorithm employed which would enable the receiver to decompress the compressed data stream.

The ASCII code

Due to the proliferation of the number of data transmission codes, attempts to standardize such codes resulted. Out of this quest for standardization was the development of the American standard code for information interchange (ASCII). This 7-level code is illustrated in Figure 2.4 and is based upon a 7-bit code developed by the International Standards Organization (ISO).

ASCII characters are encoded in 7 bits while an eighth bit is available for use as a parity bit. Eight-level ASCII is commonly used for transmission by interactive asynchronous teletype devices where the parity bit can represent odd or even parity.

Another popular version of ASCII is represented by the character set used by the IBM PC and compatible personal computers. Known as extended ASCII, this character set uses 8 bits instead of the 7 used by conventional ASCII. The first 128 ASCII characters whose codes are 0 to 127 are exactly the same as those characters listed in Figure 2.4. The next 128 characters are formed by the setting of the eighth bit and define block graphics and other special characters.

2.2 SELECTING COMPRESSION-INDICATING CHARACTERS

The key to character-oriented compression is the selection and utilization of one or more compression-indicating characters. The

b_7					0 0 0	0 0 1	0 1 0	0 1 1	1 0 0	1 0 1	1 1 0	1 1 1
b_4	b_3	b_2	b_1	→	0	1	2	3	4	5	6	7
0	0	0	0	0	NUL	DLE	SP	0	@	P		P
0	0	0	1	SOH	DC1	!	1	A	Q	a	q	
0	0	1	0	2	STX	DC2	"	2	B	R	b	f
0	0	1	1	3	ETX	DC3	*	3	C	S	c	s
0	1	0	0	4	EOT	DC4	$	4	D	T	d	t
0	1	0	1	5	ENQ	NAK	%	5	E	U	e	u
0	1	1	0	6	ACK	SYN	&	6	F·	V	f	v
0	1	1	1	7	BEL	ETB	'	7	G	W	g	w
1	0	0	0	8	BS	CAN	(	8	H	X	h	x
1	0	0	1	9	HT	EM	)	9	I	Y	i	y
1	0	0	10	LF/SUB		*	:	J	Z	j	z	
1	0	1	1	1	VT	ESC	+	;	K	[	k	[
1	1	0	0	12	FF	FS	,	<	L	\	l	|
1	1	0	1	13	CR	GS	-	=	M	]	m	}
1	1	1	0	14	SO	RS	.	>	N	ˆ	n	~
1	1	1	1	15	SI	US	/	?	£	—	o	DEL

Control characters

NUL	Null/idle	DLE	Data link escape (CC)
SOH	Start of heading (CC)	DC1	
STX	Start of text (CC)	DC2	Device controls
ETX	End of text (CC)	DC3	
EOT	End of transmission (CC)	DC4	Device control (stop)
ENQ	Enquiry (CC)	NAK	Negative acknowledge (CC)
ACK	Acknowledge (CC)	SYN	Synchronous idle (CC)
BEL	Audible or attention signal	ETB	End of transmission block (CC)
BS	Backspace (FE)	CAN	Cancel
HT	Horizontal tabulation (punch card skip) (FE)	EM	End of medium
		ESC	Escape
LF	Line feed	FS	File separator (IS)
VT	Vertical tabulation (FE)	GS	Group separator (IS)
FF	Form feed (FE)	RS	Record separator (IS)
CR	Carriage return (FE)	US	Unit separator (IS)
SO	Shift out	DEL	Delete
SI	Shift in		

Note: (CC) Communication control
(FE) Formal effector
(IS) Information separator

Special graphic characters

SP	Space	(	Opening parenthesis
!	Exclamation mark	)	Closing parenthesis
	Logical OR	*	Asterisk
"	Quotation marks	+	Plus
*	Number signs	,	Comma
$	Dollar sign	-	Hyphen
%	Per cent	·	Period
&	Ampersand	/	Slant
'	Semicolon	:	Colon
<	Less than	]	Closing bracket
=	Equals	—	Underline
>	Greater than	ˆ	Grave accent
?	Question mark	{	Opening brace
@	Commercial at	|	Vertical line
[	Opening bracket	}	Closing brace
\	Reverse slant	~	Tilde

Figure 2.4 The ASCII data code

compression-indicating character will serve as a flag, informing the receiving device that compression has occurred as well as the type of compression that was performed. The receiving device can then apply an appropriate decompression algorithm to restore the data to its original form.

To illustrate the use of a compression-indicating character, assume a string of repeating characters occurred, such as XXXXXX. One possible method to compress this string would be to encode a special compression-indicating character, followed by a count and the actual character that was compressed. This encoding technique is known as run length encoding and will be discussed in more detail in Chapter 3 when we examine a variety of character-oriented compression techniques. Under this encoding technique any repeating string of characters in excess of three can be encoded as illustrated in Figure 2.5.

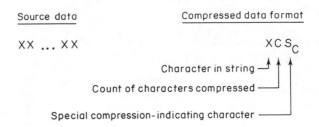

Figure 2.5 Run length encoding

The key to the selection of appropriate compression-indicating characters depends upon several factors, including the data code employed, the number of character-oriented compression schemes you will use, and, upon occasion, prior knowledge of the data to be transmitted or stored. Of these three factors, by far the most important is the data code employed which will have a major bearing upon the other factors.

Some data codes, such as EBCDIC, have unassigned characters in the character set. In such situations, the selection of special compression-indicating characters involves selecting unassigned characters from the character set you are using.

As you incorporate a mixture of character-oriented compression techniques you may run out of unassigned characters. In addition, if you use Baudot, 7-level ASCII, or other codes that do not have unassigned characters in the character set you must use a different technique to obtain compression-indicating characters. In such situations you can consider using the extended code capability of certain data codes or the insert and delete technique.

Extended code utilization

Some character sets, including ASCII and EBCDIC, have the built-in capability to redefine characters through the utilization of Shift Out (SO) and Shift In (SI) characters. The Shift Out character, in effect, denotes that all characters following that character until a Shift In (SI) character is encountered have new meanings represented by a new character set you have defined. Figure 2.6 illustrates the use of an extended code to implement run length compression. Note that the compressed data format now requires five characters. In comparison, the use of an existing character in the character set for the special compression-indicating character only required three characters. Thus, an extended code for run length compression would only be beneficial when a string of repeating characters exceeded five.

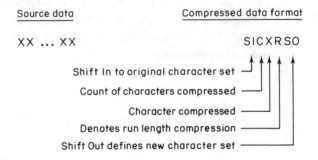

Figure 2.6 Run length encoding using an extended code

Insert and delete technique

The insert and delete technique can be considered as similar to techniques used in many data transmission schemes to effect data transparency and prevent sequences of runs of set bits from being misinterpreted as a flag in the HDLC protocol. Under the insert and delete technique you should select compression-indicating characters that are not frequently encountered in the data to be

Source data	Compressed data
JOHN Q. PUBLIC	JOHN QQ. PUBLIC
$XXXXXX 5.15	$QX65.15

Figure 2.7 Run length encoding using the insert and delete technique to form a special compression-indicating character

compressed. In the English language you might select such characters as Q and Z, since their frequency of occurrence is very low in comparison to other characters.

Once your compression-indicating characters are selected, your compression algorithm must also examine data for the natural occurrence of compression-indicating characters. If those characters naturally appear in data, the encoding process will add a second character, while the decoding process must then delete the previously inserted character, hence the term insertion and deletion. Figure 2.7 illustrates the use of the character Q as a special compression-indicating character when two strings are operated upon using the insert and delete technique to form the compression-indicating character. Note that in the first example the compressed data stream actually represents data expansion since run length compression could not be used to compress the source data and the character Q naturally occurred in the data string. In the second example, the string of six Xs was compressed with Q serving as the compression-indicating character.

3

DATA-
COMPRESSION
TECHNIQUES

The tremendous growth in remote computing during the last decade has focused the interest of communications personnel upon data compression techniques. Originally brought to data-processing user attention during the 1960s as a mechanism for increasing the capacity of mass storage devices, compression is now being applied to the data communications field. Here, compression results in the transfer of data in shorter time periods than if such data was transmitted without the employment of a compression technique.

In this chapter, eight distinct methods that can be employed to compress data are covered. Each of the methods described in this chapter is implemented based upon the use of a special compression-indicating character and can be classified as a character-oriented data-compression technique. Although each of the techniques can be implemented on an individual basis, from a practical standpoint it is very common to implement two or more character-oriented compression techniques since the data to be compressed will normally be more susceptible to a mixture of compression methods.

Character-oriented compression, while offering the potential to significantly reduce data storage or transmission requirements, should not be viewed as an end to itself. In many instances, character-oriented compression may be the first level of a multi-level compression scheme, with other levels employing a statistical-based compression method which encodes data based upon the frequency of occurrence of all characters, including special compression-indicating characters. The reader is referred to Chapter 4 for specific information concerning statistical-based methods of data compression.

In addition to examining character-oriented compression methods, various combinations of techniques are discussed with emphasis placed upon their utilization and efficiency. Some of the techniques covered in this chapter require a careful analysis of current or projected data traffic to be effective. None of the techniques presented requires more than a moderate level of difficulty in developing software to conduct the encoding and decoding algorithms. In fact, most of the techniques in this chapter should be easy for end-users to implement and their implementation may result in a high degree of data reduction for a minimal amount of effort.

By the application of one or more character-oriented compression techniques, operational efficiencies may be increased or transmission costs reduced. For the former, data compression will permit an increase in information transferred over a data link per unit time interval. Concerning the latter, reducing the amount of data to be physically transferred may make the employment of a lower-speed data link permissible, resulting in a reduction in cost in comparison with the expense of a data link operated at a higher data rate.

3.1 NULL SUPPRESSION

Null or blank suppression was one of the earliest data-compression techniques developed. Today, this simplistic technique is employed in the commonly used IBM 3780 BISYNC transmission protocol. In addition, null suppression is commonly used with a mixture of other character-oriented compression techniques to reduce data storage and data transmission.

Technique overview

As the name implies, null suppression is a data-compression technique that scans a data stream for repeated blanks or nulls. Upon encountering such a sequence, the blank or null characters are replaced by a special ordered pair of characters whose format is illustrated in Figure 3.1. First, a compression-indicator character is employed to denote that null suppression has occurred. The second character is used to indicate the quantity of null characters that were

A. *Compression format*

| NULL COUNT | COMPRESSION INDICATOR CHARACTER |

B. *Data compression example*

Original data stream   XYZ$\not{b}\not{b}\not{b}\not{b}\not{b}\not{b}$QRX

Compressed data stream   XYZS$_c$5QRX

where: S_c = special compression indicator character

C. *Data scan process*

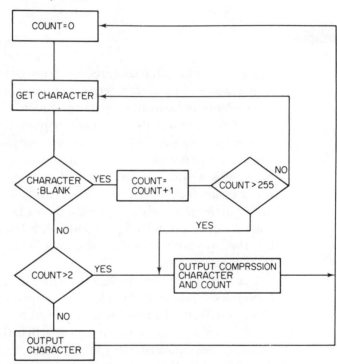

Figure 3.1   Null suppression

encountered and replaced by the two-character sequence (Aronson, 1977; Ruth and Kreutzer, 1972).

When the two-character sequence is transmitted within a data stream, the receiving device performs a search for the special character used to indicate null suppression. Upon detection of that character, the receiver knows that the next character contains the count of the number of nulls that were compressed. From this information, the original data stream can be reconstructed.

In the middle portion of Figure 3.1 is an example of the application of null suppression upon a data stream. Here, the character S_C

indicates a special compression-indicating character, denoting that null suppression has transpired.

In the lower portion of Figure 3.1, a flow chart of the null suppression scanning process is illustrated. If we assume an 8-bit format for data characters, then the character counter can store values for up to 255 sequentially encountered nulls prior to overflowing if we start our numbering at 1, or 256 if our numbering commences by assuming a zero counter represents a value of 1.

Limitations

Since a two-character compression sequence always results from the compression of up to 255 sequentially encountered nulls, no savings are possible unless three or more sequential nulls are found. Thus a sequence of two nulls should not be placed into the null suppression compressed format. This is be because no savings would result, while the compression and decompression process requires a portion of processor time. In addition, if one is employing several data-compression techniques, we will see that two sequentially encountered nulls can be effectively compressed by the Diatomic encoding process. This compression technique results in a 100 per cent data reduction for the two-null sequence situation where the null suppression technique is ineffective.

One key limitation associated with the use of null suppression concerns the selection of the special compression-indicating character. If an undefined character is available from the character set you are using, then savings begin to accrue when three or more sequential nulls are encountered. If you must use an extended character set first defined by the shift out (SO) character, you will require a four-character sequence to encode a run of nulls. Figure 3.2 illustrates the compression format and an example of null suppression using an extended code.

As noted from the example in Figure 3.2, null suppression is only viable for a sequence of five or more nulls when an extended code must be used to form the special compression-indicating character.

To consider the insert and delete technique for the use of the compression-indicating character you should have knowledge of the frequency of occurrence of the selected character for insertion and deletion in comparison to the potential saving that may accrue from null suppression. If the frequency of occurrence exceeds the potential percentage of data reduction, your algorithm would result in data

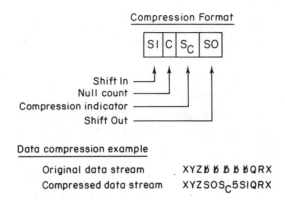

Figure 3.2 Null suppression using an extended code

expansion even though it would actually suppress all occurrences of three or more nulls.

While null suppression is viewed as an elementary data-compression technique, it is very easy to implement and its payoff can be substantial. Throughput gains of between 30 and 50 per cent have been reported for a number of computer installations that switched from the 2780 bisynchronous transmission control sequence that does not compress data to the 3780 sequence that performs null suppression.

Technique variations

Two variations of null suppression can be used to compress portions of documents containing predefined or variable indentations. In one situation, it might be beneficial to reserve a group of characters from the character set to represent several predefined numbers of spaces or nulls. Thus, one character might then represent the indentation in a letter of 5 spaces, while a second character could be used to represent 20 spaces required to tab over to the beginning of a column within a document.

Since predefined indentations represent tab stop positions, a second variation of null suppression is obtained from the employment of the tab character. If tab stops are predefined, you have only to replace a sequence of spaces or nulls by the tab character to signify that the next character begins in a particular column on the line, and all columns between the last character and the location where the next character begins are spaces or null characters. To illustrate this concept, let us assume that a portion of the document we wish to transmit is as follows:

> Now is the time to examine the relationship of defence expenditures upon the economy.
> For the years 1980 to 1984 our analysis shows:
>
> | Year | Guns | Butter |
> |------|------|--------|
> | *xxxx* | *yyyy* | *zzzz* |

Note that there are four distinct tab stop locations in this document—the indentation of a paragraph and the three column positions. Thus, a tab stop followed by the character 'N' could be used to position the beginning of the paragraph into its appropriate location. Since the indentation occurs prior to the first column position, to position the 'Y' in year would require two tab stops to be issued. Similarly, the 'G' in guns would have to be preceded by three tab stop characters and so on.

As the number of unique indentation and column location positions increases in a document or between different documents, the number of tab stop characters that may have to be issued to represent a predefined location could result in the expansion of data instead of its compression. To prevent such situations from occurring, as well as to eliminate the requirement of having prior knowledge about indentation and column locations, a variable tab stop procedure can be employed. In using variable tab stops one simply substitutes a tab stop character and the column position to tab to in place of the spacing between columns. Returning to the previous example, if 'year' began in column 15 while 'guns' and 'butter' began in columns 30 and 45 respectively, the line column heading labels could be replaced by the sequence Ts15 Year Ts30 Guns Ts45 Butter, where Ts represents the tab stop character.

One of the key applications for the replacement of strings of nulls by tab stops is IBM mainframe CICS transmissions. Several third party software developers market products which intercept outbound CICS transmissions to terminals and, among many functions, replace strings of nulls by tabbing sequences. By transmitting a lesser amount of data both the efficiency of the transmission system as well as user response times are improved.

3.2 BIT MAPPING

This compression technique is effective when the data to be operated upon consists of a high proportion of specific data types, such as numerics, or a large proportion of a specific character, such as blanks. As the name implies, a bit map is employed to indicate the presence or absence of data characters or the fact that certain data characters have been operated upon previously and must be operated upon again to return the data into its original format.

Encoding process

To examine the bit mapping technique and its applications, we will first see how it can be employed to implement a version of null suppression. In the left-hand portion of Figure 3.3, a portion of a data stream consisting of 3 data characters and 5 nulls is illustrated. Here, the 5 nulls represent $62\frac{1}{2}$ per cent of the content of the string and are spread throughout the data stream in a random sequence. Since null suppression is only effective when 3 or more sequential blanks are encountered, its use would only reduce the string from 8 to 7 characters in length.

Through the use of a bit map appended in front of the string, we can indicate the presence or absence of nulls and thereby reduce the size of the data string. In the lower portion of Figure 3.3, the employment of a bit map character is illustrated where all nulls are

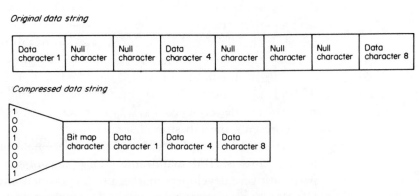

Figure 3.3 The bit mapping process. In a typical data stream, there is a high probability that one or more characters are repeated. Using one character to serve as a bit map can serve to eliminate the high frequency of occurrence of characters from a data stream

dropped from the data string and the bit which corresponds to the null position is set to zero while the bit position in the map which corresponds to a non-null or data character is set to one.

In comparing the compressed data string with the original data string, the 8 characters of data to include nulls have been reduced to 4 characters, 3 data characters and the bit map character. This results in a compression ratio of 2:1 for this particular application.

Hardware considerations

The bit map character illustrated in Figure 3.3 denotes non-null data character positions by location, from left to right. By reversing the bit map order, the data element positions can be indicated from right to left. Figure 3.4 indicates the two different methods of forming the bit map to represent the compressed data string. Using the bit map data element positioning technique illustrated in the lower portion of Figure 3.4, the bit map character resulting from the original data stream as illustrated in Figure 3.3 would become 10001001. The instruction set of the hardware device under consideration for performing the bit map suppression technique will govern the method of bit map element positioning to be employed. This can be easily explained by first examining a flow chart of the functions that have to be performed on the original data string in order to construct the bit map and the compressed data string.

The bit map suppression process is illustrated functionally in Figure 3.5. The software routine to compress data must first initialize the bit map position counter (1), the bit map (2) and a character

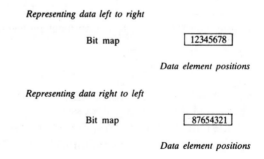

Figure 3.4 Bit map element positioning. Two methods can be employed to represent the compressed data string in the bit map—data represented left to right and right to left

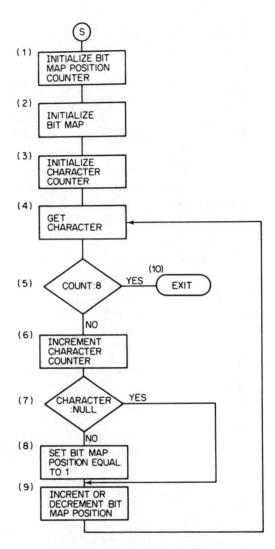

Figure 3.5 Bit map suppression function flow chart

counter (3). After a character is obtained (4), the character counter is compared with eight (5). If a match occurs, eight incoming characters have been processed and we can exit from the routine (10). If no match occurs, the character counter is incremented (6) and the character under examination is compared with a null character (7). If the character under examination is not a null, the bit map position is set equal to a binary one (8). If the character is a null, this function (8) is bypassed. Next, the bit map position is either incremented or decremented (9) so that the bit map is prepared to be set to a zero in the following bit location if the next character examined is a null. Finally, after eight characters have been processed, the count equals eight (5) and the routine exit branch is taken (10).

From a hardware standpoint, the method used to perform the functions indicated in blocks (8) and (9) of Figure 3.5 depends upon the shift and logical instructions available for programmer utilization. This interrelationship can be viewed by denoting the effect on the bit map character as succeeding data characters are examined. In Figure 3.6, the effect on the bit map and 'mask' as a progression of data characters is examined is illustrated. Here, the mask is simply a binary one that is shifted through the 8-bit map positions and logically 'OR'd' with the bit map when the data character is not a null. In examining the mask, we can note that a logical or arithmetic left shift operation is required if we wish to position our bit map so

Data character	Initial bit map	Mask	Bit map⊖ mask (or bit map if null)
Data	00000000	00000001	00000001
Null	00000001	00000010	00000001
Data	00000001	00000100	00000101
Data	00000101	00001000	00001101
Null	00001101	00010000	00001101
Null	00001101	00100000	00001101
Null	00001101	01000000	00001101
Data	00001101	10000000	10001101

Figure 3.6 The bit map masking process. The mask character is a binary one shifted through all bit positions and logically OR'd with the bit map when the data character is not a null

that the right-hand bit indicates the presence or absence of a null character in the first element of the original data string. Thus, from a hardware viewpoint, the shift instruction available will be a governing factor with respect to how the bit map elements are positioned. Although most microprocessors, minicomputers and certainly all large computers have both left and right shift functions, a few microprocessors may have limited shifting capability. Such capability should be examined prior to attempting to implement this technique.

Suppression efficiency

In the previous example, the bit map character contained 8 bits. While the example showed a 50 per cent reduction in characters from the original data string to the compressed data string, consider what happens to the compression efficiency when the percentage of nulls in the data string decreases. Table 3.1 shows the compression ratio based upon the percentage of nulls contained in the string for an 8-bit map. When there are no null characters, the resultant data string increases in size by 1 character as a result of the addition of the bit map character, producing a compression ratio of 0.888. This means that for the worst case situation where there are no null characters to be suppressed, an extra 12.5 per cent of data will result from the employment of this compression technique.

We can develop a mathematical model of suppression efficiency as follows. If p is the probability that any given character is a null, the expected number of nulls in a string of length S characters is Sp.

Table 3.1 Compression efficiency and null percentage

Null percentage	Resultant string size	Compression ratio
0.0	9	0.888
12.5	8	1.000
25.0	7	1.143
37.5	6	1.334
50.0	5	1.600
62.5	4	2.000
75.0	3	2.667
87.5	2	4.000
100.0	1	8.000

Using null compression this will be encoded as a string of length

$$S*(1 - p) + \left[\frac{S}{8}\right]$$

and the compression ratio is then

$$\left(\frac{1}{S}\left\{S(1 - p) + \left[\frac{S}{8}\right]\right\}\right)^{-1} \simeq \left((1 - p) + \frac{1}{8}\right)^{-1}$$

for large values of S.

Bit map variations

In the previous discussion of the bit map procedure, we have assumed that either a null or another character appearing in large proportion to the remainder of the data is to be suppressed. For some applications, there is no particular character that is encountered more frequently than other characters; however, in certain cases one may encounter a situation where a specific type of data, such as numerics, frequently appears. One application where such a situation could exist is the process control area where numeric readings of various equipment are transmitted to a central site for processing and control signals are returned to the devices based upon certain predefined criteria. Depending upon the transmission code employed, certain economies may be obtained by the use of the bit map technique. If the data to be transmitted is in the extended binary-coded decimal interchange code (EBCDIC), then the first four bit positions of each numeric character are all ones. Thus, the bit map character could be employed to denote the number of packed characters in the compressed string, each character containing two digits with the leading four bit positions stripped. This technique is illustrated in Figure 3.7 and is quite similar to the half-byte packing technique that is covered later in this chapter.

Technique constraints

One key limitation of the bit map technique is that it is applicable to data having fixed size units, such as characters, bytes or words.

Original data string
1
8
4
6
2
7
9
8
3
2

Compressed data string	
00001010 BIT MAP	
8	1
6	4
7	2
8	9
2	3

Figure 3.7 Half-digit suppression. In the half-digit suppression technique, the contents of the bit map specify the number of digits that follow, packed two per character

When used to suppress a particular character, such as a null, the compression ratio of this technique is directly proportional to the percentage of occurrence of that character in the original data stream. Thus, if one character in a data string occurs 30 per cent of the time while the second most frequently encountered character occurs, say, 25 per cent of the time, this technique ignores the high percentage of occurrence of the second character or any other characters. As we shall see, a technique known as run-length encoding can be employed to take advantage of the adjacent redundancy of occurrence of all characters in a data stream.

Two other limitations associated with the bit map technique include the requirement to operate upon only one type of character, such as nulls or digits, and developing a method to recognize that a character represents a bit map instead of data. Let us examine how we can overcome the second limitation when using 7-level ASCII data and how we can develop a method to overcome that limitation when using other character sets.

If we are using 7-level ASCII we can strip the parity bit and use that eighth bit position as a bit map indicator. Although this

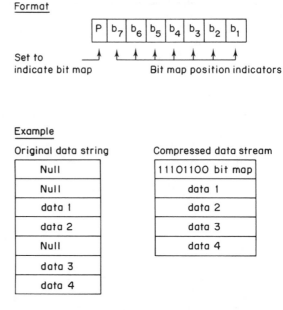

Figure 3.8 Using the parity bit as a bit map indicator

technique reduces the maximum compression ratio that can be achieved through the use of the bit map technique, it also eliminates the possibility of data expansion. To illustrate how we can avoid data expansion let us examine the operation of this revised technique.

Figure 3.8 illustrates the formation of a bit map indicator through the setting of bit position 8 which in 7-level ASCII is used as a parity bit. In the lower portion of Figure 3.8 the resulting compressed data stream is shown based upon an original data stream of seven characters. Now let us assume that the composition of the next seven characters changes so that no nulls are encountered. Under this revised technique the characters are simply placed into the compressed data stream without the necessity of adding a bit map which would result in the expansion of data. Here the data is recognized as data since the parity bit position is not set. Another advantage associated with this revised compression technique is the fact that the setting of the former parity bit position results in the automatic recognition of the character as a 7-position bit map. This allows you to eliminate coding to keep track of bit maps versus data.

If you are using each bit position within a character, such as with 8-level EBCDIC, you must then keep track of the relationship between bit map characters and data characters. To do so, you can

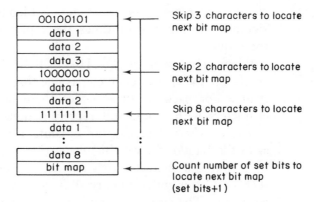

Figure 3.9 Locating bit maps. Succeeding bit maps can be located in the data stream by adding 1 to the count of the number of bit sets in the prior bit map

simply count the number of set bits in the first bit map which then tells you the number of characters to skip prior to reading the next bit map. Figure 3.9 illustrates the use of the count of the set bits in the bit map to determine the location of the next bit map in the data stream.

3.3 RUN LENGTH

Run-length encoding is a data-compression method that will physically reduce any type of repeating character sequence, once the sequence of characters reaches a predefined level of occurrence. For the special situation where the null character is the repeated character, run-length compression can be viewed as a superset of null suppression (Rubin, 1976; Ruth and Kreutzer, 1972).

Operation

In a similar way to the method used to effect null suppression, the employment of run-length encoding normally requires the use of a special character to denote that this type of compression has occurred. One exception to the use of a special compression-indicating character is the Microcom Networking Protocol (MNP) Class 5 method of data compression which is described later in this section. When a compression-indicator character is used, it is normally followed by one of the repeating characters which was in the encountered string of repetitious characters. Finally, a count character signifies the number of times the repeated character occurred in the sequence.

When codes such as ASCII or EBCDIC are employed, a good choice for the special character is one that will not occur in the data string. For each of these codes there are numerous unassigned characters with unique bit representations that can be used. For situations where the character set contains no unused character, such as in the Baudot 5-level (bit) code, this technique may still be used by selecting a character that may not be used twice in succession, such as a letter shift or figure shift, to indicate that compression has occurred. The reader should refer to Chapter 2 for additional information concerning the selection and utilization of compression-indicating characters from different character codes.

Encoding process

The run-length compression process results in a string of repeated characters being converted into a compressed data string as shown in Figure 3.10 (Aronson, 1977). With three characters required to denote compression, run-length encoding is only effective when a data string contains a sequence of four or more repeated data characters.

Three examples of the application of run-length encoding upon repeating character sequences are presented in Table 3.2. Note that S_C represents the special character used to indicate the occurrence

Data flow

→

| C_c | X | S_c |

Figure 3.10 Run-length encoding, general compression format. In run-length encoding, a special character, repeated data character and character count character are required to indicate the compression parameters

S_c = Special character indicating compression follows.

X = Any repeated data character.

C_c = Character count. This count is the number of times the compressed character is to be repeated

Table 3.2 Applying run-length encoding

Original data string	Encoded data string
\$******55.72	\$S_c*655.72
---------	S_c-9
GunsƂƂƂƂƂƂƂƂƂƂƂButter	GunsS_cƂ10Butter

of run-length encoding while the symbol Ƃ is used to indicate the presence of a blank character.

With the null suppression format requiring two characters, employing run-length compression to suppress nulls always results in one additional character generated in the compressed data stream. While this is not significant when long strings of nulls are compressed, numerous short strings of nulls could result in an excess quantity of compressed data. This suggests that one should consider the use of a mixture of several algorithms to perform data compression.

The major steps in the run-length encoding process are shown in Figure 3.11 through the use of a systems flow chart. Initially, a character counter (1) and character repetition counter (2) are set to zero. After a character in the original data string is obtained (3), the character counter is incremented (4) by one. The character count is then compared with one (5). In the first cycle, this comparison always holds true and the character is then placed in a buffer (temporary storage) area (6) for later processing if the original data string is found to contain four or more repetitive data characters. For the second and subsequent cycles, the character obtained from the original, data string (3) is compared with the character placed in storage (7). If the present character is equal to the character in storage, compression may be possible if four or more identical characters are encountered in sequence. Thus, when the character equals the stored character, the repeat counter (8) is incremented by one and another character is obtained from the original data string (3). If the present character under examination does not equal the character stored (7), the repeat counter is compared with four (9). If less than four, no compression is worthwhile since three characters must be used to encode compressed data. When the repeat counter is equal to or greater than four (9), the compression format (10) can now be set.

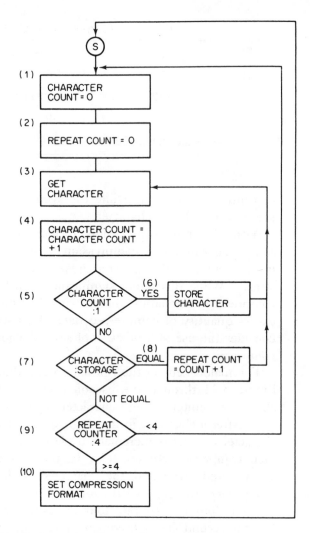

Figure 3.11 Basic run-length encoding process

Special considerations

In the basic encoding flow chart illustrated in Figure 3.11, it was
assumed that the repeat counter was capable of having an unlimited
range of values. In reality, the maximum value that the repeat
counter can contain is a function of the character code level employed.
For an 8-level (8 bits per character) character code, a maximum
between 255 and 260 repetitive characters can be represented by the
character counter. The exact value will depend upon how the

character counter is employed. In most situations, the actual character counter value is used as the number of repetitive characters. In this mode, the counter's maximum value is $2^8 - 1$ or 255. Since the compression format illustrated in Figure 3.10 occurs only when four or more repetitive characters are encountered, the presence of a character count character in itself implies that four or more repetitive characters exist. Thus, a character counter of all bits zero can be used to indicate four repetitive characters while a character counter of all bits set to 1 would then indicate 260 repetitive characters. Once the method of employing the repeat counter is determined, the flow chart in Figure 3.11 must be modified to add an additional repeat counter comparison to test for the maximum value permitted to be stored in the character counter.

Decoding

The functions necessary to decompress data compressed according to the run-length encoding process are illustrated in Figure 3.12 in flow chart format. At the beginning of the decompression procedure, a compression flag is turned off (1) and a character is obtained from the compressed data string (2). Next, if the compression flag is off (3), the character is compared with the special run-length compression-indicator character (4) to determine if run-length compression has occurred. If the character is not the special character, the next character is obtained (2). If the character is the run-length compression-indicator character, the compression flag is turned on (5) and the next character is obtained (2). On the next pass, since the compression flag is on (3), the following character obtained (6) is the repeated data character while the next character (7) contains the character count. Once these characters are obtained, the decompression format can be initiated (8).

Utilization

One of the most popular utilizations of run-length encoding is the subset known as null suppression. This compression technique is primarily encountered in the IBM 3780 BISYNC protocol. Space compression is a standard feature of this protocol when the 3780 device is operating in the line mode with non-transparent data. Here, each group of two or more consecutive space characters, up to 63,

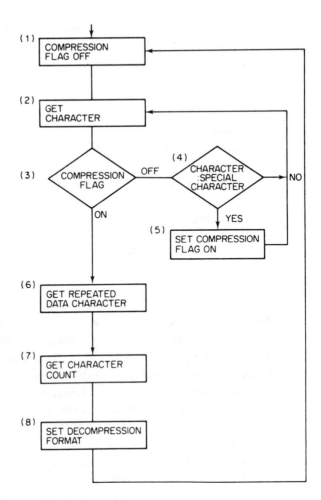

Figure 3.12 Run-length decoding process

is replaced by an IGS character if the transmission code is EBCDIC or a GS character if the code is ASCII. Either character is followed by a space-count character that defines the number of spaces removed. For the situation where 64 or more consecutive space characters occur, an additional IGS or GS character and space-count character are inserted.

On Honeywell systems, a version of run-length compression is used in their general remote terminal system (GRTS) software on front-end processors communicating with remote terminals under the remote computer (RC) protocol. In addition, the same type of compression is used on the Honeywell stand alone tape-to-tape system (SATTS) for the transmission of reels of magnetic tape between locations. In this version of run-length encoding, a record is examined for a series of three or more occurrences of the same data character. When such a situation occurs, the series is compressed and a string of repeated characters is converted into a three-character sequence as illustrated in Figure 3.13.

Figure 3.13 Honeywell version of run-length encoding. Run-length encoding as implemented on Honeywell systems differs slightly from most other computer manufacturers

X = Any repeated data character.

US = The ASCII character (0011111).

C_c = A 6-bit binary count. The BCD character represented by the binary count must be translated to ASCII for transmission to the communications subsystem. This count is the number of times the compressed character is to be repeated (maximum 63)

The most popular implementation of run-length encoding actually represents a slight variation of the previously described data-compression technique. The variation of run-length encoding that has achieved an installed base of approximately one million products is the run-length encoding technique employed by Class 5 of the Microcom Networking Protocol (MNP) which is licensed for use by over 50 manufacturers of switched network modems.

MNP Class 5 data compression uses a combination of two data compression techniques—run-length encoding and adaptive-frequency encoding. Since the adaptive-frequency encoding technique can be classified as a statistical-based compression method we will examine that technique in Chapter 4.

Under the MNP Class 5 run-length encoding method, a repetition count is inserted into the data stream to represent the number of repeated octets which follow the first three occurrences of a sequence. Since the MNP version of run-length encoding sends the first three repeated octets, those repeating characters serve as an indicator of the beginning of run-length encoding and, in effect, eliminate the necessity of utilizing a special compression-indicating character.

The top portion of Figure 3.14 illustrates the format of MNP Class 5 run-length encoding.

The lower portion of Figure 3.14 contains five examples of the operation of MNP Class 5 run-length encoding upon different strings.

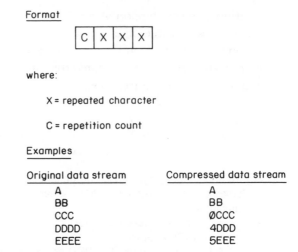

Format

C	X	X	X

where:

  X = repeated character

  C = repetition count

Examples

Original data stream	Compressed data stream
A	A
BB	BB
CCC	ØCCC
DDDD	4DDD
EEEE	5EEE

Figure 3.14 MNP Class 5 run-length encoding. Since three repeating characters indicate run-length encoding the MNP Class 5 run-length compression format does not require the use of a special compression-indicator character

Note that under this version of run-length encoding a repeated sequence of precisely three characters results in the use of a repetition count of zero being inserted into the compressed-data stream. In addition, the maximum repetition count supported by MNP is limited to 250 decimal. Thus, this portion of MNP Class 5 data compression can result in data expansion when sequences of three repeating characters are encountered in the original data stream. In addition, the MNP version of run-length encoding requires four characters, whereas the previously described method of run-length encoding uses three characters. Lastly, conventional run-length encoding can be implemented to compress up to 256 repeating characters, whereas MNP Class 5 is limited to 250. These disadvantages must be weighted against the fact that the MNP Class 5 version of run-length encoding eliminates the necessity of using a special compression-indicating character since the three repeating characters both indicate that compression has occurred and identify the character that was compressed.

Efficiency

Run-length encoding efficiency depends upon the number of repeated character occurrences in the data to be compressed, the average repeated character length and the technique employed to perform compression. In Table 3.3, the reader will find a listing of the results of the execution of a computer program written to compute the overall compression ratio based upon a varied number of repeated character occurrences in a string of 1 000 data characters. Here, the

Table 3.3 Run-length encoding efficiency based upon original data string of 1000 characters

Number of repeated character occurrences	Average repeated character length	Compression ratio
10	4	1.010
10	5	1.020
10	6	1.031
10	7	1.042
10	8	1.053
10	9	1.064
10	10	1.075
20	4	1.020
20	5	1.042
20	6	1.064
20	7	1.087
20	8	1.111
20	9	1.136
20	10	1.163
30	4	1.031
30	5	1.064
30	6	1.099
30	7	1.136
30	8	1.176
30	9	1.220
30	10	1.266
40	4	1.042
40	5	1.087
40	6	1.136
40	7	1.190
40	8	1.250
40	9	1.316
40	10	1.384
50	4	1.053
50	5	1.111
50	6	1.176
50	7	1.250
50	8	1.333
50	9	1.429
50	10	1.538

number of repeated character occurrences was varied from 10 to 50
while the average repeated character length was varied from 4 to 10.
It was assumed that three characters were used for the compressed
data format. The computed compression ratios listed in Table 3.3
ranged from a low of 1.0101 to a high of 1.5384. Table 3.3 is a
synthetic representation due to the wide divergence of actual text.
Since this table covers most common compressible occurrences, it
provides a handy tabular reference for readers to determine the effect
of run-length encoding.

A second factor affecting the efficiency of run-length encoding is
the mechanism used to implement this data-compression technique.
Table 3.4 indicates the compression ratio for three common methods
by which run-length encoding is implemented. The first column
indicates the compression ratio when a special compression character
is followed by the compressed character and a count, using a
sequence of three characters to denote the occurrence of run-length
compression. In the second column the compression ratio resulting
from the use of an extended code set (ECS) is indicated. In this
situation the SO and SI characters must be added to the beginning
(SO) and terminate (SI) the previously described three-character

Table 3.4 Efficiency of run-length encoding methods

Number of repeated characters	Compression ratio		MNP run length
	Run length	ECS run length	
3	1.0000	0.6000	0.7500
4	1.3333	0.8000	1.0000
5	1.6667	1.0000	1.2500
6	2.0000	1.2000	1.5000
7	2.3333	1.4000	1.7500
8	2.6667	1.6000	2.0000
9	3.0000	1.8000	2.2500
10	3.3333	2.0000	2.5000
11	3.6667	2.2000	2.7500
12	4.0000	2.4000	3.0000
13	4.3333	2.6000	3.2500
14	4.6667	2.8000	3.5000
15	5.0000	3.0000	3.7500
16	5.3333	3.2000	4.0000
17	5.6667	3.4000	4.2500
18	6.0000	3.6000	4.5000
19	6.3333	3.8000	4.7500
20	6.6667	4.0000	5.0000

sequence, resulting in five characters being required to encode a string of repeating characters. The third column, which is labeled MNP Run Length, indicates the compression ratio when the MNP Class 5 method of run-length encoding is used. Under this technique, strings of three or more repeating characters are encoded as four characters.

As indicated in Table 3.4, the conventional method of run-length encoding provides the greatest compression ratio. This is because it requires the fewest number of characters to implement. MNP Class 5 is the next most efficient as it requires four characters, while the use of an extended character set is the least efficient method for implementing run-length encoding.

Programming examples

To illustrate the programming required to implement run-length encoding and other compression techniques we have developed in this book several BASIC language coding examples. Each of these small program segments were written in the BASICA version of the BASIC programming language which operates on the IBM PC and compatible computers. Although a different programming language, such as assembler, Pascal or C, would be more efficient, our utilization of BASICA was based upon its wide acceptance as a programming language and the ability to use the language as a learning tool for a maximum number of readers to follow. For optimum usage of the programming examples presented in this book, we suggest that one should either employ a BASIC compiler to speed up the execution of the examples or rewrite each program segment using a more optimum programming language.

In its internal operation, the IBM PC uses an 8-bit extended ASCII character code. This extended character code results in the assignment of distinct characters to ASCII values 128 through 255. Since every character from ASCII value 0 through 255 is defined and can occur when transmitting data from an IBM PC to another computer system, one might normally employ the ASCII SO (shift out) and SI (shift in) characters in developing a compression module designed to operate on ASCII data whenever there is a probability of occurrence for each character in the character set.

The SO character is used to shift out of the current ASCII character set, resulting in the ability of the user to redefine each character in the character set. Similarly, the SI character is used to shift back into the defined ASCII character set.

By using the SO and SI characters in ASCII one obtains a set of either 128 or 256 new characters, depending upon whether one is using a system that uses the 7-bit or an extended 8-bit ASCII code. This new character set can then be used to represent compression indicating characters.

Figure 3.15 illustrates the utilization of ASCII SO and SI characters to obtain a new character set where the ASCII value 082 (conventional ASCII R) is used to denote run-length encoding. In this example, a string of six Xs was assumed to be followed by a string of seven Ys. Since the ASCII value 082 in a newly defined ASCII code will be used to indicate run-length compression, one must first shift out (SO) to the new code, issue the compression-indicating character (R) and then shift back into (SI) the normal ASCII code to transmit the character that was compressed (X) and the quantity of X characters compressed (6). Due to the requirement to shift out of the character set to issue the compression indicating character and then to shift back to the normal ASCII character set, two additional characters are required to represent a run-length encoded string. In addition to this technique requiring two extra characters, the use of a shift out code of 14 is used to turn on the double-width mode setting of most dot matrix printers while the shift in code of 15 is used to turn on the compressed character mode setting of such printers, making the graphic illustration of this technique tedious at best.

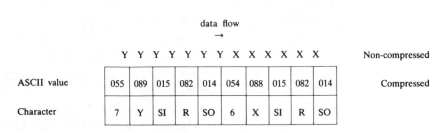

Figure 3.15 Using SO and SI characters. Using SO and SI provides a new set of characters that can be used to indicate different compression techniques, in this example, the ASCII value 082 is used to denote run-length encoding

Based upon the preceding information, it was determined that for the examples presented in this book, the use of a single character in the ASCII character set would sufficiently serve as a compression flag in addition to actually saving two characters in representing the compression of data based upon the use of run-length encoding.

Compression program

Figure 3.16 contains the listing of a BASIC program that illustrates the coding required to perform run-length compression.

To facilitate referencing BASIC programs used to illustrate the coding required to compress and decompress data, a simple naming convention has been used throughout this book. Each program filename ends with either the letter C or D, with the former used to denote a program that compresses or encodes data, while the latter references a program that decompresses or decodes data. Thus, the program labeled RUNLENC.BAS in Figure 3.16 illustrates the coding required to compress or encode data using run-length compression. The extension .BAS to the program name indicates that the file is a BASIC language program. Similarly, any data files referenced will have a filename that is a descriptor of the compression technique that will be applied against the file while its extension will be .DAT. Thus, a reference to the file RUNLEN.DAT references a data file that will be compressed by a run-length compression program.

In the RUNLENC.BAS program, the ASCII value of 125 (right brace, }) was used as the compression-indicating character, which was then followed by the ASCII character being compressed and its repetitious count in decimal notation. Thus, any string in excess of three repeating characters would be subject to compression.

Several statements in the program listing contained in Figure 3.16 warrant discussion for those readers unfamiliar with the IBM PC BASICA version of the BASIC programming language. The LINE INPUT statement in line 130 results in an entire line from a sequential file being read and assigned to the string variable X$. In line 140, the length of the string that represents one line in the data file is determined. The length of the string is then used in the FOR-NEXT loop bounded by lines 240 through 310 to process the string for repeating characters. The MID$ functions in lines 250 and 260 extract the Ith and Ith + 1 characters from the string and compare these characters to one another. When they are equal, the repeated character is saved (line 330) and the count of repeating characters is incremented (line 340). When the repeating string of characters is broken, line 260 is FALSE and a comparison of the repeating count occurs (lines 270 and 280). When the count exceeds three (line 270) data is compressed by the coding contained in lines 360 through 400. If the count equals three there is no advantage to be gained from run-length compression and the routine bounded by

```
10 REM RUNLENC.BAS PROGRAM
20 DIM O$(132)
30 WIDTH 80:CLS
40 '**********MAIN ROUTINE**********************
50 '* THIS ROUTINE READS RECORDS FROM AN ASCII *
60 '* FILE INTO A STRING CALLED X$ WHICH IS    *
70 '* THEN PASSED TO SUBROUTINES FOR COMPRESSION
80 '*******************************************
90 PRINT "ENTER ASCII FILENAME. EG, RUNLEN.DAT"
100 INPUT F$: OPEN F$ FOR INPUT AS #2
105 OPEN "RUNLENC.DAT" FOR OUTPUT AS #3
110 PRINT "PATIENCE - INPUT PROCESSING"
120 IF EOF(2) THEN GOTO 9000
130 LINE INPUT #2, X$
140 N= LEN(X$)
150 GOSUB 180
160 GOSUB 900
170 GOTO 120
180 '*****RUN LENGTH ENCODING SUBROUTINE********
190 '* THIS ROUTINE PROCESSES RECORDS FROM X$  *
200 '* AND COMPRESSES OUT REPETITIVE CHARACTERS*
210 '* USING O$ AS THE OUTPUT BUFFER.          *
220 '*******************************************
230 K=1:J=1                      'RESET INDICES
240 FOR I= 1 TO N                'STEP THRU RECORD
250 A$= MID$(X$,I,1)             'EXTRACT A CHAR
260 IF A$= MID$(X$,I+1,1) THEN 330 'SAME AS NEXT?
270 IF K>3 THEN 360              'COMPRESS
280 IF K=3 THEN 420              'DON'T COMPRESS
290 O$(J)=A$                     'STUFF IN OUTPUT BUFFER
300 J=J+1                        'BUMP BUFFER INDEX
310 NEXT I                       'GO BACK FOR MORE
320 RETURN                       'END OF STRING
330 B$=A$                        'SAVE REPEATED CHAR
340 K=K+1                        'BUMP COUNT
350 GOTO 310                     'KEEP LOOKING
355 '********************************************************
360 'INSERT COMPRESSION NOTATION IN OUTPUT BUFFER
365 '********************************************************
370 O$(J)=CHR$(125)              'SET FLAG FOR RUN-LENGTH
380 O$(J+1)=B$                   'INSERT REPEATED CHAR
390 O$(J+2)=CHR$(K)              'INSERT COUNT
400 J=J+3:K=1                    'RESET INDEX
410 GOTO 310
420 O$(J)=B$                     'STUFF 1ST REPEAT CHAR
430 O$(J+1)=B$                   'STUFF 2ND REPEAT CHAR
440 J=J+2:K=1                    'RESET INDEX
450 GOTO 310
```

Figure 3.16 RUNLENC.BAS program listing

lines 420 through 450 simply adds the input characters to the output buffer. When the Ith and Ith + 1 characters are not equal, the Ith character in the input buffer is simply placed in the output buffer (line 290). Lines 900 through 9999 are not actually part of the run-

```
900 '*****TALLY THE COMPRESSION COUNT & WRITE BUFFER******
910 '* DISPLAY BEFORE & AFTER RESULTS OF COMPRESSION    *
920 '* AND SHOW THE NET RESULTS OBTAINED BY EACH METHOD *
930 '**********************************************************
931 N1=N1+N                        'TALLY INPUT CHAR COUNT
932 T=N-J+1                        'NET DIFFERENCE IN BUFFERS
936 T1=T1+T                        'SAVE COUNT FOR SUMMARY
940 FOR I= 1 TO J-1
950 PRINT #3, O$(I);
960 NEXT I
965 PRINT #3, ""
970 RETURN
9000 CLOSE: OPEN F$ FOR INPUT AS #2
9010 PRINT "FILE ";F$;" BEFORE COMPRESSION:"
9020 LINE INPUT #2,X$
9030 IF EOF(2) THEN 9060
9040 PRINT X$
9050 GOTO 9020
9060 PRINT X$:OPEN "RUNLENC.DAT" FOR INPUT AS #3
9070 PRINT "FILE ";F$;" AFTER COMPRESSION:"
9080 LINE INPUT #3,O$
9090 IF EOF(3) THEN 9998
9100 PRINT O$
9110 GOTO 9080
9998 PRINT O$:PRINT T1;" TOTAL CHARACTERS ELIMINATED FROM ";
9999 PRINT N1;"OR ";INT((T1/N1)*100);"%":CLOSE:END
```

Figure 3.16 (continued)

length encoding process and are only included to facilitate file operations and comparison of the input and output buffers to obtain a measurement of the efficiency of this technique when applied to a data file containing a variety of repeating data strings.

Figure 3.17 illustrates a sample execution of the RUNLENC.BAS program using an ASCII file named RUNLENC.DAT as input to the program. Note that RUNLENC.BAS was purposely written to first list the contents of the file prior to its compression which is illustrated in lines 1 to 8 at the top of Figure 3.17. Next, the program lists the file after its contents were compressed based upon the application of run-length encoding to the data contained in the file.

It should be noted that string decimal values ranging below ASCII 32 were purposely omitted from inclusion in the test file since they would cause unwanted carriage returns, line feeds and other non-printable characters to be displayed, which would make an illustration of this compression technique difficult to comprehend. They would, however, be quite appropriate in normal string compression and decompression applications.

```
ENTER ASCII FILENAME. EG, RUNLEN.DAT
? RUNLEN.DAT
PATIENCE - INPUT PROCESSING
FILE RUNLEN.DAT BEFORE COMPRESSION:
1 BEGIN**********************************
2 RRRRRRRRRRRRRRRRRRRRRRRRRRRRRRRRRRR
3 EEEEEEEEEEEEEEEEEEEEEEEEEEEEEEEEEEE
4 PPPPPPPPPPPPPPPPPPPPPPPPPPPPPPPPPPP
5 EEEEEEEEEEEEEEEEEEEEEEEEEEEEEEEEEEEE
6 AAAAAAAAAAAAAAAAAAAAAAAAAAAAAAAAAAA
7 TTTTTTTTTTTTTTTTTTTTTTTTTTTTTTTTTTTT
8 *****************************************END
FILE RUNLEN.DAT AFTER COMPRESSION:
1 BEGIN}*#
2 }R!
3 }E"
4 }P#
5 }E$
6 }A%
7 }T&
8 }*%END
  261  TOTAL CHARACTERS ELIMINATED FROM  309 OR  84 %
Ok
```

Figure 3.17 Sample execution of RUNLENC.BAS

Modifications to consider

The ASCII 125 character was used as a compression-indicating character due to its representation as a right brace on most printers. Normally, if one's source data does not include characters beyond ASCII 127, then a character in the extended ASCII character set, such as ASCII 129 or another beyond ASCII 127, should be used to represent the occurrence of run-length encoding. For the preceding example, ASCII 129 was purposely excluded because its display on a monitor as the character ii will be printed on some printers as the £ (pound) character, while other printers simply ignore characters beyond ASCII 127. To correctly print characters beyond ASCII 127 using an IBM PC requires you to have a printer capable of printing the extended ASCII character set. In addition, a special disk operating system (DOS) program called GRAFTABL which is available under DOS 3.0 and higher versions of the operating system must be loaded into the computer prior to printing data. Due to this, the ASCII 125 character was used for illustrative purposes as the compression-indicating character.

If a character beyond ASCII 127 is used to indicate the occurrence of compression and that character naturally occurs in one's data a false indication of compression will result. To prevent a receiving device from misinterpreting the character as an indication that run-length compression occurred, the program can be modified to send two such characters whenever a compression-indicating character occurs naturally in a data stream. Then, at the receiving device the decompression program would first examine each character for the occurrence of a compression-indicating character; however, when encountered it would not immediately signify run-length encoding had occurred. The program would then examine the next character to ascertain if that character is also a compression-indicating character. If it is, this would serve as an indicator that one compression-indicating character occurred naturally in the data, resulting in the removal of the second compression-indicating character by the receiver. The previously described technique is more formally referenced as the insert and delete character method. This method was previously described in Chapter 2 and readers are referred to that chapter for additional information concerning the use of that technique to alleviate a false indication of the occurrence of data compression.

Decompression

In Figure 3.18, the reader will find the program listing of RUNLEND.BAS, which is the program developed to decompress data previously compressed by the RUNLENC.BAS program. To as great an extent as possible, program variables and coding modules have been kept the same between compression and decompression programs presented in this book to facilitate their utilization and explanation.

Similar to the previously examined compression program, this program processes data on a line by line basis. The LINE INPUT statement in line 130 reads a line of data from the file used for input. Next, in line 140 the length of the line is determined.

The subroutine bounded by lines 180 and 320 is then invoked. In this subroutine the string representing one line from the input file is examined on a character by character basis, using the MID$ function in line 250 to extract one character at a time from the string. In line 260, each extracted character is compared to the character value of 125 which is the right brace character to determine if a compression-indicating character occurred. If so, a branch to line 360 occurs where the repeated count and the repeated character

```
10 REM RUNLEND.BAS PROGRAM
20 DIM O$(132)
30 WIDTH 80:CLS
40 '***********MAIN ROUTINE***********************
50 '* THIS ROUTINE READS RECORDS FROM AN ASCII *
60 '* FILE INTO A STRING CALLED X$ WHICH IS     *
70 '* THEN PASSED TO DECOMPRESSION SUBROUTINE   *
80 '***********************************************
90 PRINT "ENTER ASCII FILENAME. EG, RUNLENC.DAT"
100 INPUT F$: OPEN F$ FOR INPUT AS #2
105 OPEN "RUNLEND.DAT" FOR OUTPUT AS #3
110 PRINT "PATIENCE - INPUT PROCESSING"
120 IF EOF(2) THEN GOTO 9000
130 LINE INPUT #2, X$
140 N= LEN(X$)
150 GOSUB 180
160 GOSUB 900
170 GOTO 120
180 '*****RUN LENGTH DECODING SUBROUTINE********
190 '* THIS ROUTINE PROCESSES RECORDS FROM X$  *
200 '* AND DECOMPRESSES RUN-ENCODED CHARACTERS *
210 '* USING O$ AS THE OUTPUT BUFFER.          *
220 '***********************************************
230 K=1:J=1                      'RESET INDICES
240 FOR I= 1 TO N                'STEP THRU RECORD
250 A$= MID$(X$,I,1)             'EXTRACT A CHAR
260 IF A$= CHR$(125) THEN 360    'COMPRESSION FLAG?
290 O$(J)=A$                     'STUFF IN OUTPUT BUFFER
300 J=J+1                        'BUMP BUFFER INDEX
310 NEXT I                       'GO BACK FOR MORE
320 RETURN                       'END OF STRING
355 '***********************************************************
360 'DECODE COMPRESSION NOTATION TO OUTPUT BUFFER
365 '***********************************************************
370 K$= MID$(X$,I+2,1)           'GET REPEAT COUNT
380 A$= MID$(X$,I+1,1)           'GET REPEAT CHAR
390 K= ASC(K$)                   'SET UP INDEX
400 FOR L= J TO J+K              'SET OUTPUT LOOP
410 O$(L)= A$                    'STUFF REPEAT CHAR
420 NEXT L                       'KEEP GOING
430 J= L                         'BUMP OUTPUT INDEX
440 I= I+3                       'BUMP INPUT INDEX
450 GOTO 250                     'DONE
```

Figure 3.18 RUNLEND.BAS program listing

are extracted from the string in lines 370 and 380. Next, an index is obtained based upon the numerical value of K$, using the ASC function in line 390. This is followed by the FOR-NEXT loop bounded by lines 400 to 420, which place the repeated character in the output buffer the required number of times to match the count character. Then the J and I indexes are increased and the program branches back to line 250.

```
900 '*****TALLY THE DECOMPRESSION COUNT & WRITE BUFFER****
910 '* DISPLAY BEFORE & AFTER RESULTS OF DECOMPRESSION    *
920 '* AND SHOW THE NET RESULTS OBTAINED BY EACH METHOD   *
930 '****************************************************
931 N1=N1+N                            'TALLY INPUT CHAR COUNT
932 T=N-J+1                            'NET DIFFERENCE IN BUFFERS
936 T1=T1-T                            'SAVE COUNT FOR SUMMARY
940 FOR I= 1 TO J-1
950 PRINT #3, O$(I);
960 NEXT I
965 PRINT #3, ""
970 RETURN
9000 CLOSE: OPEN F$ FOR INPUT AS #2
9010 PRINT "FILE ";F$;" BEFORE DECOMPRESSION:"
9020 LINE INPUT #2,X$
9030 IF EOF(2) THEN 9060
9040 PRINT X$
9050 GOTO 9020
9060 PRINT X$:OPEN "BYTED.DAT" FOR INPUT AS #3
9070 PRINT "FILE ";F$;" AFTER DECOMPRESSION:"
9080 LINE INPUT #3,O$
9090 IF EOF(3) THEN 9998
9100 PRINT O$
9110 GOTO 9080
9998 PRINT O$:PRINT T1;" TOTAL CHARACTERS INSERTED"
9999 CLOSE:END
```

Figure 3.18 *(continued)*

If a compression-indicating character does not occur in the data, line 290 is executed. This line causes the character extracted from the string to be placed directly into the output buffer. Next, the J index is incremented by 1 in line 300 and the boundary of the original FOR-NEXT loop checks to determine if the end of the loop was reached in line 310.

The statements from line 900 to the end of the program were included to tally the decompression count and display the before and after results of the program. Thus, this part of the program was included for illustrative purposes only.

Figure 3.19 contains a sample execution of the RUNLEND.BAS program. The reader will note that the data file RUNLENC.DAT was used as input to the program. This data file was created by the execution of the RUNLENC.BAS program and the top eight numbered lines in Figure 3.19 correspond to the lower eight numbered lines in Figure 3.17. Since the decompression program returns the compressed data to its original format, the eight numbered lines at the bottom of Figure 3.18 are exactly the same as the eight numbered lines at the top of Figure 3.17.

```
ENTER ASCII FILENAME. EG, RUNLENC.DAT
? RUNLENC.DAT
PATIENCE - INPUT PROCESSING
FILE RUNLENC.DAT BEFORE DECOMPRESSION:
1 BEGIN}*#
2 }R!
3 }E"
4 }P#
5 }E$
6 }A%
7 }T&
8 }*%END
FILE RUNLENC.DAT AFTER DECOMPRESSION:
1 BEGIN*************************************
2 RRRRRRRRRRRRRRRRRRRRRRRRRRRRRRRRR
3 EEEEEEEEEEEEEEEEEEEEEEEEEEEEEEEEEEEE
4 PPPPPPPPPPPPPPPPPPPPPPPPPPPPPPPPPPPP
5 EEEEEEEEEEEEEEEEEEEEEEEEEEEEEEEEEEEEE
6 AAAAAAAAAAAAAAAAAAAAAAAAAAAAAAAAAAAA
7 TTTTTTTTTTTTTTTTTTTTTTTTTTTTTTTTTTTT
8 **************************************END
  276  TOTAL CHARACTERS INSERTED
Ok
```

Figure 3.19 Sample execution of RUNLEND.BAS program

3.4 HALF-BYTE PACKING

This data-compression technique can be viewed as a derivative of the bit mapping process. It can be successfully used under several data structure conditions; however, unlike one version of the bit mapping technique, it will never result in a compression ratio of less than unity.

As originally developed, half-byte packing takes advantage of the structure of certain characters in a character set. This technique is effective when a portion of the bit pattern used to represent those characters becomes repetitive. As an example of this type of situation, consider the EBCDIC character set where the first four bit positions used to represent numerics are all set to binary ones as illustrated in Table 3.5.

If a non-compressed data string contains 8-level EBCDIC coded characters, then run-length encoding does not permit compression of a sequence of digits that does not repeat by character. Since the first four bits, however, do repeat, compression can be accomplished if one can pack two numerics into one character. In a similar way to several versions of run-length encoding, a special character is required to indicate that half-byte packing has occurred. Again, like

Table 3.5 EBCDIC numeric representation. When an 8-bit byte is used to contain numeric values coded in the EBCDIC character set, the first 4 bit positions are always set to all ones (1s)

Bit structure	Numeric character
1111 0000	0
1111 0001	1
1111 0010	2
1111 0011	3
1111 0100	4
1111 0101	5
1111 0110	6
1111 0111	7
1111 1000	8
1111 1001	9

versions of run-length encoding that use a special compression-indicating character, this character should be selected from one of the unassigned characters in the character set.

As an alternative, you can consider the use of the insert and delete technique or the use of an extended character set obtained by the use of the shift out (SO) character. However, since most sequences of numerics are short in comparison to runs of the same character resulting from headings and spaces between columns, the use of the alternate methods to obtain a special compression-indicating character can significantly reduce the ability of half-byte packing to compress data.

Financial applications

When data characters do not have a repetitive bit structure, half-byte packing can still be successfully employed under certain predefined conditions. One example would be to predefine the occurrence of the dollar sign, all 10 numerics, the comma, asterisk and decimal point characters in succession as suitable for compression by half-byte packing. In Table 3.6, the bit structure of ASCII data characters commonly used for financial representations is listed. If the occurrence of a string consisting of any numeric digit as well as a comma, decimal point, dollar sign and asterisk is predefined as suitable for half-byte packing, then the occurrence of such strings

Table 3.6 ASCII financial character representation. In this data representation, the parity bit was ignored. If a parity bit exists, it can be stripped along with the first three bits shown prior to the packing of the last four bits into half bytes

Bit structure	Character
011 0000	0
011 0001	1
011 0010	2
011 0011	3
011 0100	4
011 0101	5
011 0110	6
011 0111	7
011 1000	8
011 1001	9
010 0100	$
010 1100	,
010 1110	.
010 1010	*

as '$123,456.78', '123,456' or '$****123,456.78' can be compressed.

In examining the bit structure for the financial characters listed in Table 3.6, note that when the three high level bits are 'stripped', to be able to encode the reamining four bits into a half byte, that bit structure will have duplicate entries. As an example, both the dollar sign ($) and the digit four (4) would have the same bit representation of 0100. To alleviate this problem, you are required to redefine the resulting half-byte representation of each character. Table 3.7 lists one possible redefinition of a half-byte bit structure. Note that when you redefine the half bytes you can include up to six non-decimal characters as half-byte representations to be packed when encountered in a compressible string. In Table 3.7, we have added the plus (+) and minus (−) characters to the half-byte bit definitions as those characters commonly occur in strings of financial characters, such as $1,506,203− and 487.32+. Although we originally commenced our half-byte data representation using the ASCII character set, you can follow the same procedure to encode EBCDIC financial characters into a sequence of up to 16 half bytes. In doing so you can select to use the same six non-decimal characters listed in Table 3.7 or you could select any mixture of up to six non-decimal characters that you expect to encounter in strings representing financial information.

Table 3.7 Redefined half-byte bit composition

Bit structure	Character
0000	0
0001	1
0010	2
0011	3
0100	4
0101	5
0110	6
0111	7
1000	8
1001	9
1010	$
1011	,
1100	.
1101	*
1110	+
1111	−

Encoding format and technique efficiency

To compress data into half bytes, several encoding formats can be considered. Each format provides a certain level of efficiency based upon the sequence of characters encountered in the original data string. One typical format is illustrated in Figure 3.20. Using this format, up to 15 sequential numeric or predefined data characters in a string occurring sequentially can be compressed. The limit of 15 characters results from the use of a 4-bit, half-byte counter to denote the number of characters compressed.

Since, by definition, the special compression-indicating character indicates that half-byte encoding has occurred, you can assign a value of zero in the half-byte counter to indicate a count of one. Then, all four bits would indicate a run of 16 compressed characters. As an alternative, since half-byte encoding is only effective when five or more compressible characters occur in sequence, you can assign the half-byte count value of zero to indicate five half bytes are encoded. Then, a counter value of 15 (all four bits set) would indicate that 20 half bytes are encoded.

If, instead of a half-byte counter, a full byte is used to indicate the half-byte packing count, up to 2^8 (or 255) numerics can be packed or 256 if the counter starts at zero to indicate one packed character. Similarly, if a count value of zero is used to indicate a

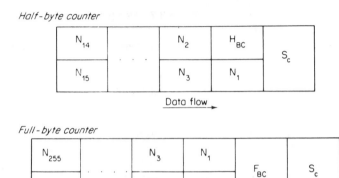

Figure 3.20 Half-byte encoding format
S   = Special character indicating half-byte encoding.
H_{BC} = Half-byte counter. Four bits are used to denote the number of numerics that have been packed.
Number $\leq$ 15, or if a count of 0 indicates five packed characters then Number $\leq$ 20.
F_BC = Full-byte counter. Number $\leq$ 255.
N_1 to N_{255} = Up to 255 numerics packed 2 per 8-bit character

string of five encoded half bytes the full-byte counter becomes capable of indicating up to 260 packed characters. Since an extra half byte is required to increase the counter capacity, only when the average number of characters in sequence is expected to exceed 15 (or 20 when a counter value of zero indicates five packed characters) should the full-byte counter be employed. Alternatively, one can use both a half-byte and a full-byte compression format and switch between the two depending upon the number of characters susceptible to half-byte packing that are encountered.

To examine the efficiency of half-byte packing, let us first explore the binary pattern of a sample data stream and the resulting compressed data stream. In Figure 3.21, the numeric sequence in the top part of the illustration consists of seven 8-bit characters or 56 bits. Through the use of the half-byte packing technique employing a half-byte (4-bit) counter, the resultant number of bits in the compressed data string is reduced to 40. In this example, the original data stream has been reduced by 28 per cent $(56 - 40)/56$ for seven sequential numerics. It should be noted that 40 bits would also be required to represent six sequentially encountered characters susceptible to half-byte packing if transmission is on a character by character basis. Thus, any even number of sequentially encountered characters suitable for packing with a half-byte counter requires the

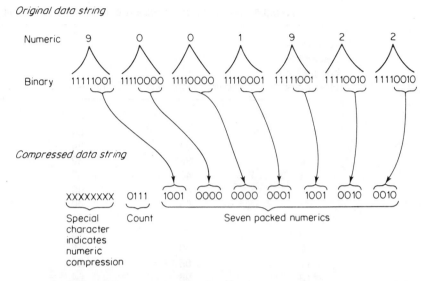

Figure 3.21 Half-byte encoding example. For 8-level character transmission, a multiple of 8 bits of compressed data is transferred. Thus, a half-byte counter with an even number of packed characters will require four trailing null bits

transmission of four additional null bits when data is transferred on a character by character basis.

In Table 3.8, the original numeric data stream and its compressed format are compared when a 4-bit counter is used. Here, the number of continuous numerics was varied from 1 to 15. Since the number of bits in the original data stream is less than or equal to the number of bits in the compressed data stream, until the number of continuous numerics exceeds four, half-byte packing should not occur until five or more sequential numerics or predefined characters are encountered in a data stream.

The preceding can be represented mathematically as follows. For a sequence of S compressible characters, $S \geq 4$, the number of bits in the uncompressed string is $8S$. The number of bits in the compressed string when a half-byte counter is used is

$$12 + 4 * \left[\frac{S}{2} \right]$$

giving a compression ratio of

$$\left(\frac{1}{8S} * \left\{ 12 + 4 * \left[\frac{S}{2} \right] \right\} \right)^{-1}.$$

Number of sequential compressible characters	Non-compressed bits	Compressed bits	Bit reduction per cent
1	8	16	N/A
2	16	24	N/A
3	24	24	N/A
4	32	32	0.00
5	40	32	20.00
6	48	40	16.66
7	56	40	28.00
8	64	48	25.00
9	72	48	33.33
10	80	56	30.00
11	88	56	36.36
12	96	64	33.33
13	104	64	38.46
14	112	72	35.71
15	120	72	40.00

When a full-byte counter is used, the number of bits in the uncompressed string remains $8S$. However, the number of bits in the compressed string now becomes:

$$16 + 4 * \left[\frac{S}{2} \right]$$

resulting in a compression ratio of:

$$\left(\frac{1}{8S} * \left\{ 16 + 4 * \left[\frac{S}{2} \right] \right\} \right)^{-1}.$$

Encoding process

A half-byte packing procedure for compressing numeric characters is illustrated in flow-chart format in Figure 3.22. After the numeric character counter is initialized in zero (1), a character is obtained from the original data string. If the character is numeric (3), the counter is incremented by one (4) and the next character in the original data string is examined (2). If the character comparison (3)

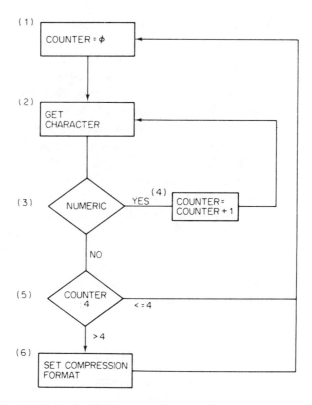

Figure 3.22 Half-byte packing process for numerics

shows that the character is not numeric, the counter is compared with four (5). If the counter is less than or equal to four, as previously discussed there is nothing to be gained by compression and the counter is reinitialized to zero (1). If the counter is greater than four (5), this means that our string of sequential numerics has ended with a sufficient number of such characters that half-byte compression is effective. At this point in time, we can set the compression format (6). Although the counter in Figure 3.22 does not have a limit, if a half-byte counter is employed, the maximum number of characters that can be packed is 15 unless you modify the assignment of values to the half-byte counter such that a value of zero indicates the compression of five half bytes, a value of one indicates the compression of six half bytes, and so on. Thus, another counter comparison would be required between symbols (5) and (6).

If we desire to compress sequentially encountered strings of predefined characters to include the dollar sign, comma, period, etc., we would test for those characters in place of testing for numerics.

Buffer considerations

When a full character or multiple characters are used as a counter, buffer memory limitations must be considered in determining the maximum number of sequential characters that can be compressed, two to a byte. In Figure 3.23 half-byte packing buffer considerations are illustrated. As the original data stream is examined, sequential characters suitable for packing two per byte are placed into a buffer as illustrated in the top portion of that figure. When the counter exceeds four and the next character is not suitable for packing, the data in the first buffer can be operated upon. One half of each character is then transferred to its proper location in the compressed data string buffer as illustrated in the lower portion of Figure 3.23. Since the special character used to indicate half-byte compression and a count character can be preplaced in the contiguous compressed data string buffer, this technique of double buffering is suitable if one wishes to employ a direct memory access (DMA) feature of the

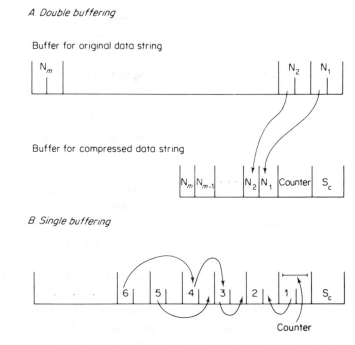

A. Double buffering

Buffer for original data string

Buffer for compressed data string

B. Single buffering

Counter

Figure 3.23 Half-byte encoding buffer considerations. Although single buffering requires additional processing, it eliminates the necessity of maintaining a separate buffer for compressed data. S_c = Special character indicating half-byte encoding

computer or microprocessor used for compression. Through the use of the DMA, data transfers can be effected independently of program control and data blocks are transferable on a word basis (bit parallel) to and from portions of main memory and peripheral devices. Thus, once the buffer in the lower portion of Figure 3.23 is completed, it can be set up for transmission through the use of a DMA transfer while the computer clears the original data string buffer and continues processing the incoming data stream. For an example of buffer size, consider the use of an 8-bit counter. In this situation, the buffer for the original data stream would have to be set up to hold up to 256 characters while the buffer for the compressed data stream would have to hold up to 130 characters, 256 compressed characters packed two per byte, a character count and the special character used to indicate half-byte packing.

Although double buffering is illustrated in the top part of Figure 3.23 for half-byte packing, single buffering can also be used. This is shown in the lower part of that illustration. In this situation, sequential characters suitable for packing are first placed into a buffer and once a non-compressible character is encountered in the original data stream and the counter exceeds four, the data elements in the buffer are manipulated as shown. In contrast to double buffering, this technique requires much more processing; however, it eliminates the necessity of having a separate buffer for compressed data. To determine total buffer requirements, the interrelationship of all data buffers must be examined as illustrated in Figure 3.24. In this example, the data to be operated upon is first read into a data-stream buffer where several different types of processing may be performed, depending upon the processing power and memory area availability of the computer being utilized. This data-stream buffer can be as small as one character or as large as a data block used for transmission. The buffer can be examined for compressible characters in several ways. First, a search can be made for any character suitable for half-byte packing; if none are encountered, the data-stream buffer can be directly transferred to the output data-stream buffer. Another method is to examine the data-stream buffer character by character. Non-compressible characters can then be sent to the output data-stream buffer while compressible characters are transferred to the original data buffer. If less than five compressible characters are in the original data buffer when a non-compressible character is encountered in the data-stream buffer, the contents of the original data buffer are transferred to the output data-stream buffer. If there are five or more characters in the original data buffer when a non-

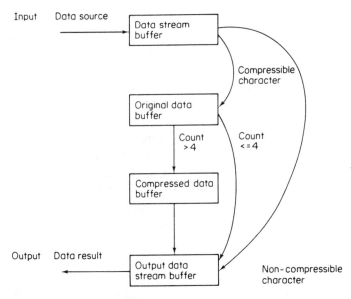

Figure 3.24 Data buffer relationships. To determine total buffer requirements, the interrelationship of all data buffers must be examined

compressible character is encountered in the data-stream buffer, the compression operation causes the contents of the original data buffer to be transferred in compressed format to the compressed data buffer. Finally, the contents of the compressed data buffer are transferred to an appropriate location in the output data-stream buffer.

Decoding

Decoding data compressed according to the half-byte packing technique is a relatively simple procedure. The decoding routine searches for the special character that is used to indicate that half-byte packing has occurred. Once that character is encountered, the next character or the following half byte will contain the count of the number of packed characters that follows. The special compression-indicator character itself can be used to inform the decoding software whether a full- or a half-byte counter is employed. Through the use of the buffering techniques previously discussed, the packed characters can be unpacked and the original data stream reconstructed.

Encoding application

Since strings of non-repeating numerics are not compressible by run-length encoding, the use of half-byte packing can be very advantageous when data files contain many numerical sequences. If predefined characters to include the dollar sign, comma, decimal point and asterisk are added to the numerics, half-byte packing becomes a very appropriate technique for compressing financial data.

Programming examples

Two different examples of half-byte encoding of data will be presented in this section. The first set of programming examples utilizes only the digits 0 to 9 for the encoding of data, following the classical approach of half-byte packing of numeric data. The second set of programming examples extends the number of characters that can be packed two per byte by including such characters as the comma, decimal point, asterisk and dollar sign as previously discussed in this section.

Encoding

The BASIC program BYTEC.BAS is listed in Figure 3.25. This program contains the coding required to perform simple half-byte encoding of strings containing five or more digits in sequence. The ASCII 126 character was used in this programming example to indicate the occurrence of half-byte encoding. This character is printed as the tilde (˜) on most printers and, therefore, provides a good visual indication of the use of a special compression-indicating character. In addition, the natural occurrence of this character in documents, correspondence, and programs written in different programming languages is minute. This also makes the tilde character suitable for the insertion and deletion method used to generate a special compression-indicating character.

Referencing the listing contained in Figure 3.25, the array 0$ is the output buffer into which each line input from an ASCII file is placed after it is first analyzed and compressed according to the half-byte encoding scheme, if so compressible. Each line from the file is read in line 130 and its length determined in line 140. Next, a branch to the subroutine starting at line 180 occurs. This subroutine steps

```
10 REM BYTEC.BAS PROGRAM
20 DIM O$(132)
30 WIDTH 80:CLS
40 '***********MAIN ROUTINE***********************
50 '* THIS ROUTINE READS RECORDS FROM AN ASCII *
60 '* FILE INTO A STRING CALLED X$ WHICH IS     *
70 '* THEN PASSED TO SUBROUTINES FOR COMPRESSION
80 '***********************************************
90 PRINT "ENTER ASCII FILENAME. EG, BYTE.DAT"
100 INPUT F$: OPEN F$ FOR INPUT AS #2
105 OPEN "BYTEC.DAT" FOR OUTPUT AS #3
110 PRINT "PATIENCE - INPUT PROCESSING"
120 IF EOF(2) THEN GOTO 9000
130 LINE INPUT #2, X$
140 N= LEN(X$)
150 GOSUB 180
160 GOSUB 900
170 GOTO 120
180 '*****HALF-BYTE ENCODING SUBROUTINE*********
190 '* THIS ROUTINE PROCESSES RECORDS FROM X$  *
200 '* AND ENCODES NUMERIC STRINGS OF DATA INTO*
210 '* HALF-BYTE OR 4 BIT REPRESENTATION USING *
215 '* DOUBLE BUFFERING WITH O$ AS OUTPUT BUFF.*
220 '***********************************************
230 K=1:J=1                       'RESET INDICES
240 FOR I=1 TO N STEP 2           'STEP THRU RECORD
250 IF (MID$(X$,I,1)<"0") OR (MID$(X$,I,1)>"9") THEN 290
260 IF (MID$(X$,I+1,1)<"0") OR (MID$(X$,I+1,1)>"9") THEN 290
270 K=K+2                         'BOTH NUMERIC-BUMP COUNT
280 NEXT I                        'GO BACK FOR MORE
285 RETURN                        'END OF STRING
290 IF K > 4 THEN GOSUB 350       'ENOUGH TO ENCODE
300 IF K > 1 THEN GOSUB 440       'DON'T ENCODE
310 O$(J) = MID$(X$,I,1)          'OUTPUT 1ST CHAR.
320 O$(J+1) = MID$(X$,I+1,1)      'OUTPUT 2ND CHAR.
330 J=J+2:K=1                     'BUMP OUTPUT-RESET COUNT
340 GOTO 280                      'AND GO FOR MORE
345 '***** SUBROUTINE TO PERFORM HALF-BYTE ENCODING *****
350 O$(J)=CHR$(126)               'FLAG FOR HALF-BYTE ENCODE
360 O$(J+1)=CHR$(K-1)             'INSERT LENGTH OF STRING
370 J=J+2                         'BUMP OUTPUT INDEX
380 FOR L=I-K+1  TO K STEP 2      'ENCODE 2 BYTES INTO 1
390 X= VAL(MID$(X$,L+1,1)):Y=VAL(MID$(X$,L,1))
400 O$(J)=CHR$(X+(Y*10))          'STUFF BYTE IN OUTPUT
410 J=J+1                         'BUMP OUTPUT INDEX
420 NEXT L                        'GO BACK FOR MORE
430 K=1:RETURN                    'RESET COUNT AND RETURN
435 '***** SUBROUTINE FOR STRING NOT WORTH ENCODING *****
440 FOR L=I-K+1 TO K              'PICKUP SHORT STRING
450 O$(J)=MID$(X$,L,1)            'STUFF IN OUTPUT BUFFER
460 J=J+1                         'BUMP OUTPUT INDEX
470 NEXT L                        'GO BACK FOR MORE
480 K=1:RETURN                    'RESET COUNT AND RETURN
```

Figure 3.25 BYTEC.BAS program listing

```
900 '*****TALLY THE COMPRESSION COUNT & WRITE BUFFER******
910 '* DISPLAY BEFORE & AFTER RESULTS OF COMPRESSION      *
920 '* AND SHOW THE NET RESULTS OBTAINED BY EACH METHOD   *
930 '****************************************************
931 N1=N1+N                          'TALLY INPUT CHAR COUNT
932 T=N-J+1                          'NET DIFFERENCE IN BUFFERS
936 T1=T1+T                          'SAVE COUNT FOR SUMMARY
940 FOR I=1 TO J-1
950 PRINT #3, O$(I);
960 NEXT I
965 PRINT #3, ""
970 RETURN
1000 PRINT
1020 RETURN
9000 CLOSE: OPEN F$ FOR INPUT AS #2
9010 PRINT "FILE ";F$;" BEFORE COMPRESSION:"
9020 LINE INPUT #2,X$
9030 IF EOF(2) THEN 9060
9040 PRINT X$
9050 GOTO 9020
9060 PRINT X$:OPEN "BYTEC.DAT" FOR INPUT AS #3
9070 PRINT "FILE ";F$;" AFTER COMPRESSION:"
9080 LINE INPUT #3,O$
9090 IF EOF(3) THEN 9998
9100 PRINT O$
9110 GOTO 9080
9998 PRINT O$:PRINT T1;" TOTAL CHARACTERS ELIMINATED FROM ";
9999 PRINT N1;"OR ";INT((T1/N1)*100);"%":CLOSE:END
```

Figure 3.25 *(continued)*

through the record obtained from the file in increments of two character positions in line 240. The record is examined in increments of two character positions since the statements in lines 250 and 260 compare character I and character $I + 1$ to the range between and including the digits 0 and 9. If either the Ith or Ith $+ 1$ character is in that range a branch to line 290 occurs.

To extend half-byte encoding to the characters $,. and * one could include them in the comparisons occurring in lines 250 and 260. This would be both tedious and slow, due to the time required to execute a group of MID functions joined together by many OR operators. A more elegant and speedier solution could be obtained by the creation of a one-dimensional array containing the characters to be encoded by half-byte compression. As an example, the following BASIC statements would initialize the array HBYTE, so each of its 14 elements would contain one of the characters that would be suitable for half-byte compression:

```
DIM HBYTE (14)
FOR I = I TO 14
READ HBYTE (I)
NEXT I
DATA "$","*",".",",","0","1","2","3",
DATA "4","5","6","7","8","9"
```

An interesting and practical assignment for the reader prior to examining the second version of this program presented in this section would be the modification of the half-byte encoding subroutine to include the compression of strings containing the characters $, . and * as well as the ten numerics.

Returning to the listing illustrated in Figure 3.25, if the Ith or Ith + 1 character is not a digit the counter is incremented by two in line 270 and the subroutine continues processing the line of input obtained from the file.

When the Ith or Ith + 1 character in the string is a numeric, a branch to line 290 in the program will occur. At this location, a comparison occurs to determine if there are enough numeric characters in sequence to encode. When K is greater than four a branch to line 350 occurs. At this program location, the subroutine actually performs the half-byte encoding of the data. In line 350 the ASCII character represented by the value 126 is placed into the Jth element of the array 0$. This character is used as the compression indicating character and, as previously discussed, will be displayed as a tilde (˜). In line 360, the length of the string is placed into the next element of the 0$ array and the output index is then incremented by 2 in line 370. Lines 380 to 420 perform the actual encoding of two bytes of non-compressed data into their half-byte representation and join two half bytes into a single byte.

Prior to examining the technique employed in line 400, let us first examine a conventional method to pack two numeric bytes into one byte in BASIC. In line 390, the VAL function is used to obtain the numeric part of the L and L + 1 characters contained in the X$ string. Thus, X represents one numeric character while Y represents the second numeric character. Suppose X was 6 and Y was 9. Their byte composition would appear as follows:

$$
\begin{array}{ll}
\boxed{\begin{array}{l} 0000\ 0110 \\ \hline 0000\ 1001 \end{array}} & \begin{array}{l} X = 6 \\ Y = 9 \end{array}
\end{array}
$$

Packing two numeric into one byte can be accomplished by multiplying one character by 16 to shift it four bit positions to the left and either add it or AND it with the second character. Assuming Y is multiplied by 16, 9 * 16 is 144 and its bit composition becomes:

$$\boxed{10010000} \qquad Y = 144$$

Then, adding X and Y results in a value of 150, whose byte composition is:

$$\boxed{10010110} \qquad X + Y \text{ packed} = 150$$

A second method to accomplish the stuffing of the two numerics into one byte was used in line 400 of the program listing contained in Figure 3.25. In this method, the numeric value of Y was first multiplied by 10 and then added to the numeric value of X. Then, the character representing the numeric value of the addition of X to Y multiplied by 10 is placed into the 0$ array as a single byte. Returning to the previous example where X was 6 and Y was 9, multiplying 9 by 10 and adding 6 results in the packing of the character that has an ASCII code of 96 into the appropriate element in the 0$ array. Thus, if this half-byte encoding routine encounters the numerical sequence of 6 followed by a 9 and there is a sufficient run of numerics to pack those two characters together they would be displayed as an apostrophe ('), since that character is represented by an ASCII 96. In this technique the ASCII codes from 00 to 99 can be employed to directly represent the 100 possible combinations of two digits.

To determine the original data one can divide the received ASCII code by 10 to obtain one numeric and use the remainder of the division process for the second numeric. Unfortunately, this technique is not applicable if the additional characters previously discussed are included in the string of characters defined as susceptible to half-byte encoding.

Again returning to the program listing contained in Figure 3.25, note that whenever the count of characters suitable for half-byte encoding is less than 5 or a non-numeric character is encountered a branch to the subroutine located at line 440 occurs. This subroutine simply takes the character from its appropriate position in the X$ string and places it in its appropriate position in the output buffer.

The last subroutine in this program was included to print a comparison of each line read from the file used for input and the half-byte encoded version of the line. In addition, the subroutine creates a file containing compressed data that will be used as an input file to test the decompression routine that will be discussed next. Starting at line 900, this subroutine also counts the characters' input and output and computes and prints the percentage of characters eliminated as a result of half-byte encoding.

Figure 3.26 illustrates the execution of the BYTEC.BAS half-byte encoding program, showing the original lines of data contained in the input file followed by its resulting compressed data. The reader should note that for clarity of illustration the input data was structured to ensure that certain numeric pairs of characters were excluded. This was done to eliminate, as an example, two encoded half-bytes representing an ASCII 31 character or below, since such characters are non-printable and would not be appropriate for illustrative purposes.

```
ENTER ASCII FILENAME. EG. BYTE.DAT
? BYTE.DAT
PATIENCE - INPUT PROCESSING
FILE BYTE.DAT BEFORE COMPRESSION:
 1  '+434567898765433345678987654333456789876⌐
 2  '-9835725789453862965739857752645749735687²⌐
 3  '$434445464748495051525354555657585960¹⌐
FILE BYTE.DAT AFTER COMPRESSION:
 1  '+˜&+-CYWA+!-CYWA+!-CY6⌐
 2  '-˜(b#H9Y-&>'9'UM4⌐9I182⌐
 3  '$˜$+,-./0123456789:;1⌐
   54  TOTAL CHARACTERS ELIMINATED FROM  132 OR  40 %
 Ok
```

Figure 3.26 Sample execution of BYTEC.BAS program

Decompression

The program BYTED.BAS listed in Figure 3.27 was written to decode or decompress data previously compressed by the BYTEC.BAS program.

Since the BYTEC.BAS program used the ASCII 126 character as a half-byte compression indicator, the BYTED.BAS program **was** written to search for the occurrence of this character. After a line of data is obtained from a file in line 130 of the program, the length of the line is determined in line 140. Then the subroutine at line 180 is invoked to scan the line character by character, looking for the occurrence of an ASCII 126. The FOR-NEXT loop bounded

```
10 REM BYTED.BAS PROGRAM
20 DIM O$(132)
30 WIDTH 80:CLS
40 '**********MAIN ROUTINE*********************
50 '* THIS ROUTINE READS RECORDS FROM AN ASCII *
60 '* FILE INTO A STRING CALLED X$ WHICH IS    *
70 '* THEN PASSED TO DECOMPRESSION SUBROUTINE  *
80 '*******************************************
90 PRINT "ENTER ASCII FILENAME. EG, BYTEC.DAT"
100 INPUT F$: OPEN F$ FOR INPUT AS #2
105 OPEN "BYTED.DAT" FOR OUTPUT AS #3
110 PRINT "PATIENCE - INPUT PROCESSING"
120 IF EOF(2) THEN GOTO 9000
130 LINE INPUT #2, X$
140 N= LEN(X$)
150 GOSUB 180
160 GOSUB 900
170 GOTO 120
180 '*****HALF BYTE  DECODING SUBROUTINE********
190 '* THIS ROUTINE PROCESSES RECORDS FROM X$  *
200 '* AND DECOMPRESSES BYTE-ENCODED CHARACTERS*
210 '* USING O$ AS THE OUTPUT BUFFER.          *
220 '*******************************************
230 K=1:J=1                       'RESET INDICES
240 FOR I= 1 TO N                 'STEP THRU RECORD
250 A$= MID$(X$,I,1)              'EXTRACT A CHAR
260 IF A$= CHR$(126) THEN 360     'COMPRESSION FLAG?
290 O$(J)=A$                      'STUFF IN OUTPUT BUFFER
300 J=J+1                         'BUMP BUFFER INDEX
310 NEXT I                        'GO BACK FOR MORE
320 RETURN                        'END OF STRING
355 '*******************************************************
360 'DECODE COMPRESSION NOTATION TO OUTPUT BUFFER
365 '*******************************************************
370 K$= MID$(X$,I+1,1)            'GET REPEAT COUNT
380 M= I+2                        'SETUP INPUT INDEX
390 K= ASC(K$)                    'SET UP LOOP INDEX
400 FOR L= J TO J+K-1 STEP 2      'SET OUTPUT LOOP
410 X= ASC(MID$(X$,M,1))          'GET ONE BYTE
420 Y= INT(X* .1)                 'SHIFT RIGHT
430 O$(L)= CHR$(Y+48)             'DECODE TENS POS
440 Z= INT(X-(Y* 10))             'SUBTRACT TENS POS
450 O$(L+1)= CHR$(Z+48)           'DECODE UNITS POS
455 M= M+1                        'BUMP INPUT INDEX
460 NEXT L                        'KEEP GOING
470 J= L+1                        'RESET OUTPUT INDEX
480 I= M                          'RESET INPUT INDEX
490 GOTO 250                      'DONE
```

Figure 3.27 BYTED.BAS program listing

by lines 240 through 320 accomplishes this, extracting a character from the string through the use of the MID$ function in line 250 and then comparing the extracted character to ASCII 126 in line 260.

If the extracted character does not equal ASCII 126, the character is simply placed into the output buffer in line 290, the index is incremented by 1 in line 300 and the processing of the data in the loop continues. If the character is equal to ASCII 126, a branch line to 360 occurs and the decoding of the compressed data commences. First the repeat count which is the next character in the string is obtained in line 370. This character is then converted into a numeric value in line 390 since it will control the loop index for decompressing the following characters in the string that were previously encoded two per byte. This decoding is controlled by the FOR-NEXT loop bounded by lines 400 through 460. First the numeric value of the byte following the repeat count is obtained the first time line 410 is executed. In line 420, the value obtained in the preceding line is multiplied by 0.1, which, in effect, functions as a right shift. By taking the integer of the multiplication of the byte's numeric value by 0.1 we obtain a numeric between 0 and 9. This numeric represents the value of Y when X and Y were previously encoded in the BYTEC.BAS program by multiplying Y by 10 and adding the value of X to the result. Since we are working with characters based upon their ASCII values, 48 is added to the value of Y in line 430 to obtain the appropriate ASCII value of the digit. This value is then an ASCII character between 0 and 9 that represents the 10s position of the previously encoded data. In line 440, the value of Y multiplied by 10 is subtracted from the value of X to obtain the numeric value representing the unit's position in the packed data. Similar to line 430, line 450 adds 48 to the value of Z to obtain the appropriate ASCII character code that represents the decoded digit.

```
ENTER ASCII FILENAME. EG, BYTEC.DAT
? BYTEC.DAT
PATIENCE - INPUT PROCESSING
FILE BYTEC.DAT BEFORE DECOMPRESSION:
 1 '+~&+-CYWA+!-CYWA+!-CY6ə
 2 '-~(b#H9Y-&>'9'UM4ə91I82ə
 3 '$~$+,-./0123456789:;1ə
FILE BYTEC.DAT AFTER DECOMPRESSION:
 1 '+4345678987654333456789876543334567 89954ə
 2 '-9835725789453862965739857752645749735650ə
 3 '$43444546474849505152535455565758594950ə
   54  TOTAL CHARACTERS INSERTED
Ok
```

Figure 3.28 Sample execution of BYTED.BAS program

Figure 3.28 illustrates the execution of the BYTED.BAS program, using the file BYTEC.DAT as input to the program. Since the half-byte compression program, BYTEC.BAS, previously created this file it should be of no surprise that lines 1 to 3 at the top of Figure 3.28 are equal to lines 1 through 3 of Figure 3.26, while lines 1 to 3 at the bottom of Figure 3.28 are equal to lines 1 to 3 at the top of Figure 3.26.

Extended half-byte encoding

A second example of half-byte encoding results from the inclusion of additional characters beyond the 10 numerics into half bytes when such characters occur sequentially. In Figure 3.29, the reader will find the program listing of the PACKC.BAS program that was developed to compress a string containing numerics and/or the dollar sign ($), comma (,), decimal point (.) and asterisk (*).

Compression program

Similar to the previously described BYTEC.BAS program, a line of input is obtained from a file in line 130, the length of the line is determined in line 140 and a branch to the half-byte encoding subroutine occurs in line 150 of the program.

The subroutine bounded by lines 180 and 550 processes the line of input and encodes sequences of numerics and the special characters previously mentioned into half bytes. The FOR-NEXT loop bounded by lines 240 and 280 searches through the character positions in the string X$ that represents a line of input data. In line 242, the C(I) array flag is reset while lines 243 and 244 extract two bytes from the string. The C(I) array flag is then set to a value between 1 and 4 if the first byte of the string (A$) is one of the special characters. If A$ is a digit between 0 and 9 the C(I) array flag is then set to 5 in line 256. Otherwise, the C(I) array flag remains set to zero and a branch to line 258 occurs where the second byte represented by B$ is processed. Next, lines 258 to 266 process the second byte, assigning the C(I + 1) flag a value between 1 and 5 depending upon whether one of four special characters or a numeric is encountered. If either C(I) or C(I + 1) equal zero and four or more bytes containing numerics or special characters have been encountered in sequence

```
10 REM PACKC.BAS PROGRAM
20 DIM O$(132),C(132)
30 WIDTH 80:CLS
40 '***********MAIN ROUTINE**********************
50 '* THIS ROUTINE READS RECORDS FROM AN ASCII *
60 '* FILE INTO A STRING CALLED X$ WHICH IS     *
70 '* THEN PASSED TO SUBROUTINES FOR COMPRESSION
80 '**********************************************
90 PRINT "ENTER ASCII FILENAME. EG, PACK.DAT"
100 INPUT F$: OPEN F$ FOR INPUT AS #2
105 OPEN "PACKC.DAT" FOR OUTPUT AS #3
110 PRINT "PATIENCE - INPUT PROCESSING"
120 IF EOF(2) THEN GOTO 9000
130 LINE INPUT #2, X$
140 N= LEN(X$)
150 GOSUB 180
160 GOSUB 900
170 GOTO 120
180 '*****HALF-BYTE ENCODING SUBROUTINE*********
190 '* THIS ROUTINE PROCESSES RECORDS FROM X$  *
200 '* AND ENCODES  MIXED  STRINGS OF DATA INTO*
210 '* HALF-BYTE OR 4 BIT REPRESENTATION USING *
215 '* DOUBLE BUFFERING WITH O$ AS OUTPUT BUFF.*
220 '**********************************************
230 K=1:J=1                       'RESET INDICES
240 FOR I=1 TO N STEP 2           'STEP THRU RECORD
242 C(I)=0:C(I+1)=0               'RESET ENCODE FLAGS
243 A$= MID$(X$,I,1)              'GET 1ST BYTE
244 B$= MID$(X$,I+1,1)            'GET 2ND BYTE
246 IF A$= "$" THEN C(I)= 1       'SET 1ST ENCODE FLAG
248 IF A$= "," THEN C(I)= 2
250 IF A$= "." THEN C(I)= 3
252 IF A$= "*" THEN C(I)= 4
254 IF A$< "0" OR A$> "9" THEN 258   'SKIP OTHERS
256 C(I)= 5
258 IF B$= "$" THEN C(I+1)= 1     'SET 2ND ENCODE FLAG
260 IF B$= "," THEN C(I+1)= 2
262 IF B$= "." THEN C(I+1)= 3
263 IF B$= "*" THEN C(I+1)= 4
264 IF B$< "0" OR B$> "9" THEN 268   'SKIP OTHERS
266 C(I+1)= 5
268 IF C(I)= 0 OR C(I+1)= 0 THEN 290   'NOT CANDIDATE
270 K=K+2                         'BOTH NUMERIC-BUMP COUNT
280 NEXT I                        'GO BACK FOR MORE
285 RETURN                        'END OF STRING
290 IF K > 4 THEN GOSUB 350       'ENOUGH TO ENCODE
300 IF K > 1 THEN GOSUB 500       'DON'T ENCODE
310 O$(J) = MID$(X$,I,1)          'OUTPUT 1ST CHAR.
320 O$(J+1) = MID$(X$,I+1,1)      'OUTPUT 2ND CHAR.
330 J=J+2:K=1                     'BUMP OUTPUT-RESET COUNT
340 GOTO 280                      'AND GO FOR MORE
350 O$(J)=CHR$(129)               'FLAG FOR BYTE PACKING
352 MASK1= &HF0                   '11110000
354 MASK2= &HF                    '00001111
360 O$(J+1)=CHR$(K-1)             'INSERT LENGTH OF STRING
```

Figure 3.29 PACKC.BAS program listing

```
370 J=J+2                              'BUMP OUTPUT INDEX
371 FOR L=I-K+1 TO K STEP 2           'SETUP ENCODE LOOP
372 ON C(L) GOTO 376,378,380,382,384  'USE FLAG TO ENCODE
376 X=&HA0:GOTO 388                    '10100000
378 X=&HB0:GOTO 388                    '10110000
380 X=&HC0:GOTO 388                    '11000000
382 X=&HD0:GOTO 388                    '11010000
384 X=VAL(MID$(X$,L,1))                'GET NUM VALUE OF BYTE 1
386 X=X*16                             'SHIFT 4 BITS LEFT
388 X=X AND MASK1                      'MASK LOWER HALF-BYTE
390 ON C(L+1) GOTO 394,396,398,400,410 'USE ENCODE FLAG
394 Y=&HA:GOTO 420                     '00001010
396 Y=&HB:GOTO 420                     '00001011
398 Y=&HC:GOTO 420                     '00001100
400 Y=&HD:GOTO 420                     '00001101
410 Y=VAL(MID$(X$,L+1,1))              'GET NUM VALUE OF BYTE 2
420 Y=Y AND MASK2                      'MASK UPPER HALF-BYTE
440 Z= X OR Y                          'OR THE TWO TOGETHER
450 O$(J)= CHR$(Z)                     'OUTPUT BYTE TO BUFFER
460 J=J+1                              'BUMP OUTPUT INDEX
470 NEXT L                             'GO BACK FOR MORE
480 K=1:RETURN                         'RESET COUNT AND RETURN
500 '***** SUBROUTINE FOR STRING NOT WORTH ENCODING *****
510 FOR L=I-K+1 TO K                   'PICKUP SHORT STRING
520 O$(J)=MID$(X$,L,1)                 'STUFF IN OUTPUT BUFFER
530 J=J+1                              'BUMP OUTPUT INDEX
540 NEXT L                             'GO BACK FOR MORE
550 K=1:RETURN                         'RESET COUNT AND RETURN
900 '*****TALLY THE COMPRESSION COUNT & WRITE BUFFER******
910 '* DISPLAY BEFORE & AFTER RESULTS OF COMPRESSION     *
920 '* AND SHOW THE NET RESULTS OBTAINED BY EACH METHOD  *
930 '*****************************************************
931 N1=N1+N                            'TALLY INPUT CHAR COUNT
932 T=N-J+1                            'NET DIFFERENCE IN BUFFERS
936 T1=T1+T                            'SAVE COUNT FOR SUMMARY
940 FOR I=1 TO J-1                     'OUTPUT FILE LOOP
950 PRINT #3, O$(I);                   'BUFFER CHAR STRING
960 NEXT I
965 PRINT #3, ""                       'NOW WRITE TO FILE
970 RETURN                             'DONE
9000 CLOSE: OPEN F$ FOR INPUT AS #2
9010 PRINT "FILE ";F$;" BEFORE COMPRESSION:"
9020 LINE INPUT #2,X$
9030 IF EOF(2) THEN GOTO 9060
9040 PRINT X$
9050 GOTO 9020
9060 PRINT X$: OPEN "PACKC.DAT" FOR INPUT AS #3
9070 PRINT "FILE ";F$;" AFTER COMPRESSION:"
9080 LINE INPUT #3,O$
9090 IF EOF(3) THEN 9998
9100 PRINT O$
9110 GOTO 9080
9998 PRINT O$:PRINT T1;" TOTAL CHARACTERS ELIMINATED FROM ";
9999 PRINT N1;"OR ";INT((T1/N1)*100);"%":CLOSE:END
```

Figure 3.29   (_continued_)

there is enough to encode and a branch to the subroutine starting at line 350 occurs. If either $C(I)$ or $C(I + 1)$ equals zero and between one and three bytes were encountered a branch to the subroutine beginning at line 500 occurs. This subroutine simply takes the encountered characters from the input string and places them into their appropriate positions in the output buffer.

When two bytes are extracted from the input string and no previous bytes were numeric or special characters $C(I)$ and $C(I + 1)$ are zero and line 268 causes a branch to line 290 to occur. Since K is zero, lines 310 to 330 are then executed, resulting in the two bytes just extracted from the input string being placed into their appropriate position in the output buffer.

Lines 350 to 480 contain the coding for generating the compression indicating character which, for this example, is ASCII 129 and then packing the characters eligible for half-byte compression into half bytes. Lines 352 and 354 enable two mask flags that will enable upper or lower half-bytes to be generated by ANDing the numerical value of a byte by the mask flag. Line 360 inserts the length of the string into the output buffer while line 372 examines the C flag and encodes the byte (lines 376 to 382) based upon the type of special character in the byte. If the byte is numeric, line 384 is executed. Here, the numeric value of the byte is extracted. In line 386, it is multiplied by 16 which is equivalent to a shift 4-bit positions to the left while line 388 ANDs the value of the newly formed character flag or shifted byte by the first mask. Similarly, lines 390 to 420 perform the same operation on the second byte by first examining the second C flag. Finally, line 440 adds the two half bytes into one byte by the use of the OR operator and the newly formed character that now represents two characters is placed into the output buffer. Like the other programs previously discussed, lines 900 to 9999 keep track of the compression count and generate a file named PACKC.DAT which represents the compressed data contained in the file PACK.DAT. Later the extended half-byte decompression program called PACKD.BAS will use the PACKC.DAT file as input to perform extended half-byte decompression.

Figure 3.30 illustrates the execution of the PACKC.BAS program using a three-line data file whose contents are listed at the top of the figure. Since the packing of some half bytes resulted in the generation of a full byte whose ASCII code was below 31 and therefore unprintable, the first two lines of compressed data may appear odd due to the effect these characters have on the printer used by the author.

```
ENTER ASCII FILENAME. EG, PACK.DAT
? PACK.DAT
PATIENCE - INPUT PROCESSING
FILE PACK.DAT BEFORE COMPRESSION:
1 '+$43,456,789.87**6543334567898765433345678987ɘɘ
2 '-$9835$72.57$89.45$386,296,573.85775264574973567ɘɘ
3 '$43444546474849505152535455565758598ɘɘ
FILE PACK.DAT AFTER COMPRESSION:
1 '+,ñ;Ekx▌eC3Eg          eC3Eg    ɘɘ

2 '-O⌐Zr┼z        -Z8k)kW<wRdWIsVɘɘ

3 '$$CDEFGHIPQRSTUVWXYɘɘ
 61   TOTAL CHARACTERS ELIMINATED FROM  146 OR  41 %
Ok
```

Figure 3.30 Sample execution of the PACKC.BAS program

Decompression program

Figure 3.31 contains the program listing of the PACKD.BAS program that was developed to decompress data compressed by the PACKC.BAS program.

Similar in construction to the PACKC.BAS program, PACKD.BAS obtains a line of data from a file in line 130, determines the length of the line in line 140 and then branches to the subroutine starting at line 180 to perform the required decoding. The FOR-NEXT loop bounded by lines 240 and 320 extracts one character at a time from the input string, searching for ASCII 129 which is the compression indicating character used to denote the occurrence of extended half-byte compression.

When the compression flag is encountered in line 260, a branch to line 330 occurs which is the beginning of the routine that decompresses the compressed data. After initializing the masks in lines 330 and 335 the length of the string is obtained in line 340 while the FOR-NEXT loop bounded by lines 350 to 498 breaks up each byte into the original two characters that were previously compressed. First line 370 takes a byte and ANDs it with the first mask and divides by 16 which is equivalent to a right shift of 4 bit positions. In line 375, the character is tested to determine if it is numeric. If so, a branch to line 430 occurs where 48 is added to the character to obtain its appropriate ASCII value. If the character is not numeric, lines 380 to 410 test to determine what special character the character represents by examining its code value and then based upon its code value the character is reset to its original value. Next,

```
10 REM PACKD.BAS PROGRAM
20 DIM O$(132)
30 WIDTH 80:CLS
40 '***********MAIN ROUTINE***********************
50 '* THIS ROUTINE READS RECORDS FROM AN ASCII *
60 '* FILE INTO A STRING CALLED X$ WHICH IS    *
70 '* THEN PASSED TO DECOMPRESSION SUBROUTINE  *
80 '***********************************************
90 PRINT "ENTER ASCII FILENAME. EG, PACKC.DAT"
100 INPUT F$: OPEN F$ FOR INPUT AS #2
105 OPEN "PACKD.DAT" FOR OUTPUT AS #3
110 PRINT "PATIENCE - INPUT PROCESSING"
120 IF EOF(2) THEN GOTO 9000
130 LINE INPUT #2, X$
140 N= LEN(X$)
150 GOSUB 180
160 GOSUB 900
170 GOTO 120
180 '*****HALF BYTE  DECODING SUBROUTINE*********
190 '* THIS ROUTINE PROCESSES RECORDS FROM X$  *
200 '* AND DECOMPRESSES BYTE-ENCODED CHARACTERS*
210 '* USING O$ AS THE OUTPUT BUFFER.          *
220 '***********************************************
230 J=1                            'RESET INDEX
240 FOR I= 1 TO N                  'STEP THRU RECORD
250 A$= MID$(X$,I,1)               'EXTRACT A CHAR
260 IF A$= CHR$(129) THEN 330      'COMPRESSION FLAG?
290 O$(J)=A$                       'STUFF IN OUTPUT BUFFER
300 J=J+1                          'BUMP BUFFER INDEX
310 NEXT I                         'GO BACK FOR MORE
320 RETURN                         'END OF STRING
322 '***********************************************************
324 'DECODE COMPRESSION NOTATION TO OUTPUT BUFFER              *
326 '***********************************************************
330 MASK1= &HF0                    '11110000
335 MASK2= &HF                     '00001111
340 K= ASC(MID$(X$,I+1,1))         'GET STRING LENGTH
345 M= I+(K/2)                     'SET END OF STRING
350 FOR L=I+2 TO M                 'SETUP LOOP TO DECODE
362 Z= ASC(MID$(X$,L,1))           'GET BYTE
370 X= (Z AND MASK1)/16            'MASK LOWER HALF-BYTE
375 IF X< 10 THEN 430              'ITS NUMERIC
380 IF X= 10 THEN O$(J)= "$"       'SPECIAL
390 IF X= 11 THEN O$(J)= ","       'SPECIAL
400 IF X= 12 THEN O$(J)= "."       'SPECIAL
410 IF X= 13 THEN O$(J)= "*"       'SPECIAL
415 GOTO 440                       'SKIP IF SPECIAL
430 O$(J)= CHR$(X+48)              'OUTPUT 1ST NUMERIC
440 Y= Z AND MASK2                 'MASK UPPER HALF-BYTE
445 IF Y< 10 THEN 490              'ITS NUMERIC
450 IF Y= 10 THEN O$(J+1)= "$"     'SPECIAL
460 IF Y= 11 THEN O$(J+1)= ","     'SPECIAL
470 IF Y= 12 THEN O$(J+1)= "."     'SPECIAL
480 IF Y= 13 THEN O$(J+1)= "*"     'SPECIAL
485 GOTO 495                       'SKIP IF SPECIAL
490 O$(J+1)= CHR$(Y+48)            'OUTPUT 2ND NUMERIC
495 J= J+2                         'BUMP OUTPUT BY TWO
498 NEXT L:I= M                    'CONTINUE, BUMP INPUT INDEX
499 GOTO 310                       'GO BACK FOR MORE
```

Figure 3.31 PACKD.BAS program listing

```
900 '*****TALLY THE DECOMPRESSION COUNT & WRITE BUFFER****
910 '* DISPLAY BEFORE & AFTER RESULTS OF DECOMPRESSION   *
920 '* AND SHOW THE NET RESULTS OBTAINED BY EACH METHOD  *
930 '****************************************************
931 N1=N1+N                          'TALLY INPUT CHAR COUNT
932 T=N-J+1                          'NET DIFFERENCE IN BUFFERS
936 T1=T1-T                          'SAVE COUNT FOR SUMMARY
940 FOR I= 1 TO J-1
950 PRINT #3, O$(I);
960 NEXT I
965 PRINT #3, ""
970 RETURN
9000 CLOSE: OPEN F$ FOR INPUT AS #2
9010 PRINT "FILE ";F$;" BEFORE DECOMPRESSION:"
9020 LINE INPUT #2,X$
9030 IF EOF(2) THEN 9060
9040 PRINT X$
9050 GOTO 9020
9060 PRINT X$:OPEN "PACKD.DAT" FOR INPUT AS #3
9070 PRINT "FILE ";F$;" AFTER DECOMPRESSION:"
9080 LINE INPUT #3,O$
9090 IF EOF(3) THEN 9998
9100 PRINT O$
9110 GOTO 9080
9998 PRINT O$:PRINT T1;" TOTAL CHARACTERS INSERTED"
9999 CLOSE:END
```

Figure 3.31   (continued)

lines 440 to 490 perform the same operation on the second half byte in the received character.

Program execution

Figure 3.32 illustrates the execution of the PACKD.BAS program using PACKC.DAT as the input data file to decompress. The reader will note that the first three lines in Figure 3.32 are identical to the

```
ENTER ASCII FILENAME. EG, PACKC.DAT
? PACKC.DAT
PATIENCE - INPUT PROCESSING
FILE PACKC.DAT BEFORE DECOMPRESSION:
1 '+,ñ;Ekx█eC3Eg          eC3Eg      ɔɔ

2 '-O-Zr╆z        -Z8k)kW<wRdWIsVɔɔ

3 '$$CDEFGHIPQRSTUVWXYɔɔ
FILE PACKC.DAT AFTER DECOMPRESSION:
1 '+$43,456,789.87**6543334567898765433345678ɔɔ
2 '-$9835$72.57$89.45$386,296,573.857752645749735ɔɔ
3 '$4344454647484950515253545556575859ɔɔ
  55  TOTAL CHARACTERS INSERTED
Ok
```

Figure 3.32   Sample execution of the PACKD.BAS program

last three lines of Figure 3.30 while the last three lines of Figure 3.32 that represents the decompressed data are identical to the top three lines of Figure 3.30. Again, this is no surprise since the decompression program simply reconstructs the compressed data into its original form. The reader should also note that the 61 characters denoted as eliminated by half-byte compression in Figure 3.30 do not take into account the additional compression characters required to indicate each occurrence of half-byte encoding. If this was done, then a total of 55 characters would have been eliminated which matches the 55 character insertion count in Figure 3.32.

Encoding variations and efficiency considerations

The coding examples previously covered in this section have illustrated the use of special compression-indicating characters by assuming that each character was available for selection. Suppose your half-byte encoding and decoding algorithms must work on 7-bit ASCII data or non-standard 8-bit ASCII as defined by the character set used by the IBM PC and compatible personal computers. Would we want to modify our selection of a compression-indicating character and, if so, how might we do so?

Let us first assume we will transmit or store 7-level ASCII data. Since computer systems operate upon 8-bit bytes, it becomes possible to use the eighth bit position as a compression indicator, similar to the alternative method described for the bit mapping encoding technique. The top of Figure 3.33 illustrates how we could define one character by the use of the parity bit (bit 8) in a 7-bit ASCII character set to represent both a compression-indicating character as well as a count of the number of compressed half bytes. In this example, the setting of bit position 8 serves as an indicator that half-byte compression has occurred, while bit positions 1 through 7 contain the binary count of the number of half bytes that were compressed. Here the 7-bit position counter can represent a sequence of up to 127 compressed half bytes.

Since we previously used this technique to indicate the occurrence of bit mapping, suppose we desire to implement both bit mapping of repeated nulls and half-byte encoding of financial data using a 7-level ASCII character set. To accomplish this task we would use the setting of bit 8 as a 'general' compression indicator. Then, we could use the value of bit 7 to denote two types of compression. Finally, bit positions 1 through 6 would either represent a 6-position

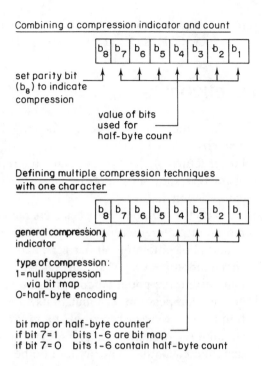

Combining a compression indicator and count

set parity bit
(b_8) to indicate
compression

value of bits
used for
half-byte count

Defining multiple compression techniques
with one character

general compression
indicator

type of compression:
1 = null suppression
    via bit map
0 = half-byte encoding

bit map or half-byte counter
if bit 7 = 1   bits 1-6 are bit map
if bit 7 = 0   bits 1-6 contain half-byte count

Figure 3.33 Using 7-level ASCII

bit map or the count of compressed half bytes based upon the value of bit 7. The lower portion of Figure 3.33 illustrates how an 8-bit character format can be used to define two types of data compression when a 7-bit data code is encapsulated in 8 bits. Of course, in using the eighth bit you eliminate the ability to use that bit for parity checking. However, since most communications software programs now include a block checking mechanism for error control purposes, the loss of a parity checking capability for most persons will be considered as a non-event.

The format illustrated in the lower portion of Figure 3.33 is only applicable for defining two types of compression. You can extend this technique further by using bit positions 6 and 7 to indicate up to four types of compression. Doing so then reduces the bit map to five bits and the maximum half-byte count to 31.

If we are using a true 8-bit character set we would not want to use the previously described technique. This is because the previous scheme could eventually generate all characters whose ASCII values exceed 127. Instead, we would probably use the insert and delete technique to obtain two characters that infrequently appear in data to use as compression-indicating characters—perhaps the characters whose ASCII values are 126 and 129!

3.5 DIATOMIC ENCODING

As the name implies, diatomic encoding is a data-compression process whereby a pair of characters is replaced by a special character. The bit structure of the special character represents the encoded pair of characters and, thus, permits a 50 per cent data reduction or a 2:1 compression ratio.

Since the number of special characters that can be employed to represent different types of compression is limited, the theoretical potential of obtaining 50 per cent data reduction by substituting one character for every pair of characters cannot be obtained. To maximize one's potential compression requires a prior understanding of the composition of your data. Once you know the expected frequency of occurrence of pairs of characters, then the most commonly encountered pairs can be selected as candidates for diatomic encoding. The actual number of pairs selected will depend upon the number of special characters available to represent those pairs of frequently occurring characters.

Operation

A block diagram representation of the diatomic encoding process will be found in the top portion of Figure 3.34. In the lower portion of that illustration is a flowchart denoting the major processes required to encode data diatomically. Note that the flowchart assumes that a continuous input data stream occurs. In actuality, the input and output buffers would be of finite length. Since the output buffer will always be less than or equal to the character size of the input buffer, you may be able to assign a pointer which will be incremented through the input buffer. Upon reaching the end of that buffer, the contents of the output buffer will be transmitted while the input buffer will be refilled with additional non-compressed data.

Pair frequency of occurrence

The major problem in the implementation of diatomic encoding is in determining what pairs should be represented by special characters.

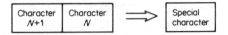

A. Diatomic encoding process

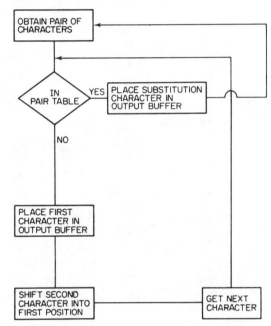

B. Diatomic encoding flow chart

Figure 3.34 The diatomic encoding process

To perform diatomic encoding and obtain a meaningful compression ratio requires the assignment of special characters to represent the most frequently occurring pairs of characters that are expected to be encountered in the original data stream. This means you must have some prior knowledge concerning the type of data to be operated upon so that one can base the assignment of special characters in a meaningful manner (Snyderman and Hunt, 1970).

To assist readers in selecting the appropriate character pairs to replace with special characters, several tables of pair combinations are presented in this section. In Table 3.9, the reader will find a table containing the first 25 most frequently encountered pairs of characters in a 12 198-character English language text (Aronson, 1977). This table, prepared by Jewell, denotes the rank, pair

Table 3.9 Jewell character-combination pairing

Rank	Combination	Occurrences	Occurrences per thousand
1	E__	328	26.89
2	__T	292	23.94
3	TH	249	20.41
4	__A	244	20.00
5	S__	217	17.79
6	RE	200	16.40
7	IN	197	16.15
8	HE	183	15.00
9	ER	171	14.02
10	__I	156	12.79
11	__O	153	12.54
12	N__	152	12.46
13	ES	148	12.13
14	__B	141	11.56
15	ON	140	11.48
16	T__	137	11.23
17	TI	137	11.23
18	AN	133	10.90
19	D__	133	10.90
20	AT	119	9.76
21	TE	114	9.35
22	__C	113	9.26
23	__S	113	9.26
24	OR	112	9.18
25	R__	109	8.94

Note: __ represents a space character

combination, number of occurrences of the pair and the occurrences per thousand data characters (Jewell, 1976).

Since many users of data transmission will transfer program files in addition to textual data, an analysis of the paired-character composition of BASIC, COBOL and FORTRAN programs is presented. The analysis of these programs was obtained by the execution of the DATANALYSIS program written by 4-Degree Consulting located in Macon, Georgia. This program performs a compression susceptibility analysis upon data files and the paired-character analysis listed in Tables 3.10 to 3.13 is but one of several compression algorithms analysed by that software package. The listing of the software statements in the DATANALYSIS program will be found in Appendix A. Its use will facilitate the selection of one or more compression algorithms based upon an analysis of the

Table 3.10 Paired-character compression analysis, BASIC data file of 9322 characters

Pair/count		Pair/count		Pair/count		Pair/count		Pair/count		Pair/count	
_P	13	NT	13	RI	13	_T	12	__	11	_I	8
O_	7	HE	7	_B	6	_S	6	T_	5	N_	5
_A	5	F_	5	_E	4	AB	4	BU	4	EX	4
_L	4	IN	4	IO	4	NI	4	_N	4	_U	4
TO	4	TS	4	_F	3	R_	3	S_	3	ND	3
E_	3	_R	3	OF	3	UR	3	OU	3	_C	3
SE	3	ET	3	_O	3	_D	2	NP	2	NS	2
EL	2	AC	2	ON	2	IR	2	OT	2	IT	2
LI	2	RO	2	LL	2	AT	2	NG	2	UT	2
IM	1	AL	1	AN	1	_K	1	BO	1	IU	1
LA	1	LD	1	BR	1	M_	1	LO	1	LU	1
MB	1	CK	1	NE	1	CO	1	CT	1	NO	1
DO	1	ED	1	_X	1	NU	1	EN	1	OL	1
EQ	1	ER	1	OS	1	ES	1	Y_	1	PP	1
PS	1	PT	1	_Y	1	GH	1	_G	1	SO	1
SS	1	ST	1	TA	1	TE	1	TH	1	TI	1
HI	1	HT	1	TU	1	UG	1	UI	1	UL	1
UN	1	IA	1	VA	1	XX	1	YE	1	YI	1
ZE	1	**	0	**	0	**	0	**	0	**	0

Total combinations found: 288

Note: __ represents a space character

susceptibility of one's anticipated or actual data traffic to several compression algorithms.

Table 3.10 shows the paired-character compression analysis results based upon an examination of a 9 322-character BASIC program. In general, most BASIC language programs contain a high proportion of input messages and prompts as well as output headings. This structure makes the paired-character consistency form a modified English text paired-character consistency. Normally, the degree of deviation from normal English textual data pairs results from the ratio of computation statements to input/output statements in the program. In Table 3.10, note that '_P' 'NT' and 'RI' are the most commonly encountered pairs. All three pairs come from PRINT statements in the program with the pair '_P' resulting from a programmer using a space to precede each PRINT statement. Similarly, the BASIC language statement of the form 'IF X:Y THEN' can be denoted by the frequently encountered pairs '_I', 'F_' and 'HE'.

Table 3.11 Paired-character compression analysis, FORTRAN data file of 20 465 characters

Pair/count		Pair/count		Pair/count		Pair/count		Pair/count		Pair/count	
_I	167	_F	116	TE	106	UT	105	OR	99	OU	99
RI	96	_W	87	MA	86	_C	86	IN	86	TP	81
IR	69	HA	66	_S	61	O_	60	ER	60	C_	57
IT	51	HE	48	EN	46	RA	44	_D	42	E_	42
AL	40	RE	39	SI	38	IX	38	ON	37	_T	36
HS	35	HD	34	TO	34	SU	33	_R	32	T_	31
IM	30	_B	30	TA	30	HB	30	HF	30	HN	30
HC	30	HO	29	HR	29	HG	29	HU	29	HV	29
TI	29	HH	29	HL	29	AR	29	HJ	28	HT	28
_N	28	HM	28	HW	28	HX	28	HY	28	HZ	28
IA	28	CT	28	HI	28	IP	28	HP	28	HQ	28
HJ	28	L_	27	IO	26	_G	26	EQ	25	NY	25
_O	25	UB	25	IY	25	LE	24	_E	24	_P	23
AN	23	_	23	N_	23	ND	22	CO	22	SE	22
_A	22	Y_	21	AT	21	R_	20	S_	20	IS	20
RO	20	IC	20	NC	20	PR	20	ED	19	TR	18
G_	18	UR	18	ES	18	OT	17	ET	16	NG	16
NA	16	LY	16	TH	15	AC	15	PE	14	D_	14
PU	14	UM	14	NU	14	CH	14	BL	13	IV	13
LI	13	_J	13	FI	12	PF	12	GO	12	_K	12
OW	12	ST	12	_M	11	IL	11	SS	11	LA	11
AI	11	EP	11	NS	11	DA	11	EA	10	EC	10
TS	10	TY	10	FO	10	UE	10	F_	10	UN	10

Total combinations found: 4370

Note: __ represents a space character

In Table 3.11, the results of a similar analysis of a 20 465-character FORTRAN program is presented while Table 3.12 denotes the pairs encountered when a 54 417-character COBOL program was analyzed. In the FORTRAN program analysis, common pairs result from such frequently used statements as 'FORMAT', 'WRITE' and 'READ'. Similarly, common pairs encountered in the COBOL program are normally a result of the 'PICTURE IS' statement. Finally, Table 3.13 shows the results of an analysis of the merger of the individual BASIC, FORTRAN and COBOL programs into one entity. Here, the 230 paired characters represent 16 266 total combinations. Since the file contained a total of 84 204 data characters, diatomic compression of the 230 most frequently encountered pairs would result in a 19.3 per cent (16 266 / 84 204) data reduction. Note that the 12 most frequently encountered pairs represent a potential data reduction of 4388 characters or approximately 25 per cent of the theoretical reduction obtainable by diatomically encoding the 230 most frequently encountered pairs. From this, it is apparent that diatomic encoding can be effectively used in conjunction with other compression techniques by selecting only a portion of the most frequently expected pairs of characters for representation by special compression-indicator characters.

Table 3.12 Paired-character compression analysis, COBOL program containing 54 417 characters

Pair/count		Pair/count		Pair/count		Pair/count		Pair/count		Pair/count	
_P	542	_F	391	IC	342	AL	316	IN	309	RE	297
E_	286	_V	251	_X	243	_W	239	LE	235	R_	235
_T	231	IL	229	UE	229	TE	221	PG	212	_O	211
NT	204	M_	190	AR	186	RO	186	O_	182	UT	178
CN	164	_C	164	CT	156	LN	153	RI	152	_M	151
CH	149	_L	148	OV	144	CI	141	FO	139	TY	137
_B	136	OR	129	_S	129	_I	122	_A	118	TO	110
ER	109	G_	108	NG	106	RM	102	EF	101	CE	97
AD	91	__	91	VA	90	PA	88	ES	87	AC	84
NC	84	T_	82	F_	79	AN	79	TA	67	DV	66
FI	63	S_	61	WR	60	TI	59	ST	57	_E	55
Y_	54	PU	52	_R	50	BU	49	QU	48	OM	46
ON	44	OT	43	AT	43	OF	42	CO	40	RK	40
LS	36	CD	35	D_	35	NE	35	AS	34	OU	33
_Z	33	_G	33	ME	32	IV	30	RP	30	EN	30
ND	29	_U	28	BE	27	OP	27	L_	25	H_	24
EL	24	TP	23	SE	23	CA	22	_H	22	_D	22
TH	22	DD	21	TR	20	ET	20	VE	20	VI	20
EC	20	YI	20	_N	19	GS	19	IT	19	C_	19
GE	18	WA	18	UA	18	SH	18	_K	17	IM	17
RA	17	RS	17	MO	16	DE	16	GI	15	EX	15
ED	15	MP	15	CC	15	WO	15	EQ	15	UN	15
LI	14	IO	14	_Q	14	UR	14	DI	13	FL	13

Total combinations found: 12 509

Note: __ represents a space character

Table 3.13 Paired-character compression analysis, combined 84 204 character file

Pair/count		Pair/count		Pair/count		Pair/count		Pair/count		Pair/count	
__P	578	__F	510	IN	399	IC	362	AL	357	RE	336
E__	331	TE	328	__W	326	__I	297	UT	285	__T	279
RI	261	LE	259	R__	258	__V	255	__C	253	__X	252
O__	249	NY	242	IL	240	UE	239	__O	239	OR	231
AR	215	PG	212	RO	208	__S	196	M__	194	CT	185
__B	172	ER	170	CN	164	CH	163	__M	162	__L	159
LN	153	FO	149	TO	148	TY	147	__A	145	OV	144
CI	141	OU	135	G__	126	__	125	NG	124	T__	118
CE	107	ES	106	RM	105	TP	104	NC	104	AN	103
EF	102	AC	101	PA	98	TA	98	MA	94	F__	94
AD	91	VA	91	TI	89	__R	85	S__	84	__E	83
ON	83	EN	77	HA	77	C__	76	Y__	76	FI	75
IT	72	IR	71	ST	70	DV	66	PU	66	AT	66
__D	66	CO	63	OT	62	HE	62	RA	61	__G	60
WR	60	QU	56	ND	54	OF	4	BU	54	OM	53
L__	52	__N	51	D__	49	SE	48	IM	48	IO	44
IV	43	SI	41	NE	41	EQ	41	RK	40	N__	40
ET	39	IX	38	TH	38	TR	38	ME	38	HD	37
AS	37	LS	36	HR	36	UB	35	HS	35	CD	35
__U	35	ED	35	__Z	34	SU	33	HO	33	HP	32
HY	32	UR	32	IA	31	IS	31	HI	31	OP	31
HF	30	HB	30	HN	30	PR	30	HC	30	RP	30
__K	30	EC	30	LI	29	HV	29	HH	29	BE	29

Total combinations found: 16 266

Note: __ represents a space character

Communications hardware implementation

The use of a diatomic data-compression technique was implemented by Infotron Systems in combination with several other compression algorithms on their TL780 statistical multiplexer.

In a conventional time-division multiplexer, data from each input channel is assigned to a slot on the high-speed multiplexed output line, regardless of whether or not the bandwidth is used. Since each input line is assigned a corresponding time slot, implementing compression on the high-speed link will not increase any individual line efficiency. If compression is implemented on the low-speed line side, normally referenced as the channel side or level, the efficiency of only each low-speed compressed link will be increased, since each link is reserved a fixed slot on the high-speed side. This is illustrated in the upper portion of Figure 3.35.

In a statistical multiplexer, the bandwidth for a particular channel on the high-speed link is used only when the channel is transmitting data or control signals. Therefore, compression of one or more low-speed links permits the statistical multiplexer to utilize less of the bandwidth of the high-speed line for the low-speed link being compressed. The compression of the low-speed link at the channel side will then result in a lower, high-speed line rate or permit more low-speed channels to be added since compression reduces the total number of data characters transmitted over the high-speed line. Conversely, if compression is performed at the high-speed line level, the number of characters transmitted on that link will be reduced. This will permit a lower composite high-speed operating data rate or permit additional low-speed channels to be serviced. While some vendors have elected to compress the high-speed link, Infotron uses a diatomic encoding process combined with additional data-compression techniques on its low-speed channel adapters to perform compression at the channel level. This technique permits the user to select which channels, if any, should be compressed.

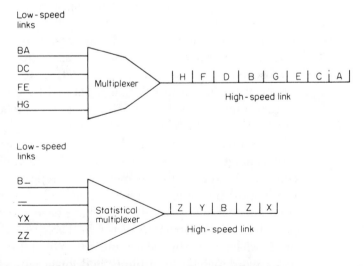

Figure 3.35 Multiplexing and compression. If compression occurs on one or more low-speed links, the effective information transfer ratio of those individual links will increase when a conventional time-division multiplexer is employed. When statistical multiplexers are employed, data may be compressed at the individual channel level or overall at the high-speed line level

In the Infotron technique, statistical multiplexer compression occurs through the use of multiple-space codes, repeated character codes, common character pair codes (diatomic encoding) and packed decimal codes (half-byte encoding). In addition, since the data must be queued at the channel level to compress it, it becomes necessary to transmit control signals through the data path of the high-speed link to preserve the time relationship between data and control signals. The addition of these signals reduces the overall compression efficiency. Since each channel adapter on the multiplexer requires a buffer area and a microprocessor to effect compression, compression of a large number of low-speed channels becomes more expensive from a hardware standpoint than compressing data at the high-speed line level where only one buffer area and a single microprocessor are required.

The Infotron channel adapter that performs compression only operates on asynchronous ASCII coded data. To obtain a sufficient number of special compression-indication codes, the parity bit in the normal 8-bit ASCII code is stripped for transmission. This results in 128 character codes that can be used to represent and indicate compressed information. The stripping of parity by the microprocessor within the multiplexer has no effect on errors since the multiplexer employs an HDLC-like frame transmission on the high-speed link level to include generating a cyclic redundancy check of transmitted frames.

In the Infotron system, codes are assigned to represent groups of 2 to 7 consecutive spaces for various multiple-space compression code schemes. These codes are most effective when transmitted data has been formatted in columns separated by groups of spaces or for textual information that contains paragraph indentations and margin justification through the use of spaces.

To represent repeated characters, 16 codes were assigned to represent groups of 3 to 18 consecutive identical characters. This code is followed by the character to be repeated, in a similar way to run-length encoding, and results in a 2-byte code. To represent common character pairs, 48 codes have been assigned. The characters pairs used by Infotron are listed in Table 3.14. With the exception of the decimal point, space and carriage return–line feed pairs, all other pairs include both upper and lower case characters.

Lastly, 16 codes are assigned to specify when 4 to 19 characters are in packed decimal (half-byte) format. Here, characters are represented by 4-bit codes packed two per 8-bit byte. In addition to numerics, the dollar sign, period, comma, per cent, diagonal sign

Table 3.14 Common character pair codes compressed by Infotron: both upper and lower case

S__	__T	IN	TE	AN
T__	__A	ED	ER	TI
E__	__N	AT	RE	ON
R__	__O	ES	TH	CRLF
D__	__I	SE	HE	
__				

Note: __ represents a space character. CRLF denotes carriage return followed by line feed

and space are stripped of the leading four bits if they occur in the string and are included in the packed format.

Although the effectiveness of the compression technique employed obviously depends upon the data to which the technique is applied, using multiple techniques increases the possibility of being able to use one technique effectively upon a portion of the data stream. During channel adapter compression tests, a compression ratio of up to 1.8 was noted by Infotron, indicating that only 55 per cent of the input data stream was actually transmitted.

Programming examples

The BASIC program PAIRC.BAS listed in Figure 3.36 was developed to perform diatomic compression based upon the Jewell character-combination pairing previously listed in Table 3.9. Although this example of diatomic compression was programmed to use the Jewell character-combination pairing, it is easily modified to compress data based upon the use of other character pairs that may more appropriately reflect the reader's data.

Similar to other compression routines previously presented in this chapter, the diatomic compression program was developed using subroutines linked together to provide distinct code modules that can be easily analyzed by the reader. After the data file is opened in line 100, the subroutine commencing at line 400 is invoked. This subroutine initializes the P$ array elements to the Jewell character-combination pairing, resulting in 25 character pairs assigned to the array P$. The reader can change the data pairs contained in lines 410 and 420 of the subroutine; however, if the number of data pairs is changed from 25, the appropriate indices in the program must be

```
10 REM PAIRC.BAS PROGRAM
20 DIM O$(132)
30 WIDTH 80:CLS
40 '***********MAIN ROUTINE***********************
50 '* THIS ROUTINE READS RECORDS FROM AN ASCII *
60 '* FILE INTO A STRING CALLED X$ WHICH IS     *
70 '* THEN PASSED TO SUBROUTINES FOR COMPRESSION
80 '**********************************************
90 PRINT "ENTER ASCII FILENAME. EG, PAIR.DAT"
100 INPUT F$: OPEN F$ FOR INPUT AS #2
105 OPEN "PAIRC.DAT" FOR OUTPUT AS #3
110 PRINT "PATIENCE - INPUT PROCESSING"
115 GOSUB 400                    'PAUSE TO SET UP TABLE
120 IF EOF(2) THEN GOTO 9000
130 LINE INPUT #2, X$
140 N= LEN(X$)
150 GOSUB 180
160 GOSUB 900
170 GOTO 120
180 '*****DIATOMIC COMPRESSION SUBROUTINE*******
190 '* THIS ROUTINE PROCESSES RECORDS FROM X$  *
200 '* AND COMPRESSES OUT COMMON PAIRS         *
210 '* USING O$ AS THE OUTPUT BUFFER.          *
220 '*********************************************
230 I=1                         'RESET INDICES
240 FOR J= 1 TO N-1             'STEP THRU RECORD
250 A$= MID$(X$,J,2)            'EXTRACT A PAIR
260 FOR K = 1 TO 25             'SETUP PAIR TABLE LOOP
270 IF A$=P$(K) THEN GOSUB 350  'IS INPUT PAIR IN TABLE?
280 NEXT K                      'NO - TRY NEXT
290 IF M = 1 THEN 310           'IF MATCH FLAG SET?
300 O$(I) = MID$(A$,1,1)        'NO-STUFF 1ST CHAR IN BUFFER
310 I=I+1                       'BUMP INPUT STRING INDEX
320 M=0                         'RESET MATCH FLAG
330 NEXT J                      'GO BACK FOR MORE
340 RETURN                      'DONE
350 M=1                         'SET PAIR MATCH FLAG
355 '*****************************************************
360 'INSERT COMPRESSION NOTATION IN OUTPUT BUFFER
365 V = K + 224                 'INDEX OUT TO SUBSTITUTE CHAR
370 O$(I)=CHR$(V)               'INSERT PAIR SUBSTITUTION
380 J=J+1                       'FORCE INPUT SHIFT 2 OVER PAIR
390 K = 25                      'FORCE END OF PAIR SEARCH
395 RETURN                      'GO BACK FOR MORE
400 DIM P$(25)                  'JEWELL CHAR. COMBINATION PAIRS
410 DATA "E "," T",TH," A","S ",RE,IN,HE,ER," I"," O","N ",ES,
420 DATA " B",ON,"T ",TI,AN,"D ",AT,TE," C"," S",OR,"R "
425 FOR I = 1 TO 25             'SETUP PAIR TABLE
430 READ Z$                     'GET COMMON PAIR
440 P$(I) = Z$: NEXT I          'AND STUFF INTO PAIR TABLE
450 RETURN                      'DONE - TABLE COMPLETE
```

Figure 3.36 PAIRC.BAS program listing

```
900 '*****TALLY THE COMPRESSION COUNT & WRITE BUFFER******
910 '* DISPLAY BEFORE & AFTER RESULTS OF COMPRESSION      *
920 '* AND SHOW THE NET RESULTS OBTAINED BY EACH METHOD   *
930 '*******************************************************
931 N1=N1+N                           'TALLY INPUT CHAR COUNT
932 T=N-I+1                           'NET DIFFERENCE IN BUFFERS
936 T1=T1+T                           'SAVE COUNT FOR SUMMARY
940 FOR I=1 TO J-1
950 PRINT #3, O$(I);
960 NEXT I
965 PRINT #3, ""
970 RETURN
1000 PRINT
1010 PRINT "**RUN-LENGTH ENCODING SAVED ";T;" CHARACTERS"
1020 RETURN
9000 CLOSE: OPEN F$ FOR INPUT AS #2
9010 PRINT "FILE ";F$;" BEFORE COMPRESSION:"
9020 LINE INPUT #2,X$
9030 IF EOF(2) THEN 9060
9040 PRINT X$
9050 GOTO 9020
9060 PRINT X$:OPEN "PAIRC.DAT" FOR INPUT AS #3
9070 PRINT "FILE ";F$;" AFTER COMPRESSION:"
9080 LINE INPUT #3,O$
9090 IF EOF(3) THEN 9998
9100 PRINT O$
9110 GOTO 9080
9998 PRINT O$:PRINT T1;" TOTAL CHARACTERS ELIMINATED FROM ";
9999 PRINT N1;"OR ";INT((T1/N1)*100);"%":CLOSE:END
```

Figure 3.36 (*continued*)

changed to reflect the actual number of pairs. In addition, the dimension size of the P$ array must be changed to reflect the new number of pairs to be used in the diatomic compression routine. Thus, lines 400 and 425 would require modification in the subroutine previously discussed when a new set of character pairs are entered in lines 410 and 420 whose sum differs from 25.

After a line of data is read in line 130, its length is determined in line 140. The subroutine invoked in line 150 processes the line of data read from the file commencing in line 230. After the indices are reset in line 230, the FOR-NEXT loop bounded by lines 240 to 330 steps through the record, extracting pairs of data in line 250. The inner FOR-NEXT loop bounded by lines 260 and 280 compares the pair extracted from the record in line 250 to the pairs contained in the pair table previously set up by the subroutine in line 400. The reader should note that the outer limit of 25 in line 260 should also be changed if the number of pairs used in the program changes from that value.

If a pair of characters extracted from the record matches a pair in the pair table, the subroutine in line 350 is invoked. Line 350 uses the variable M to denote that a match occurred. In line 365, the variable V is set to K + 224. Here the value of K is the position in the pair table where the pair extracted from the record matched a predetermined pair. The reason 224 was added to this value was for clarity of display of the results of this compression routine. That is, italics are printed from ASCII 225 upward on many printers including one printer used by the author. Thus, the pair 'E space' is represented by an italic 'a' when printed, and so on.

The pair substitution character is inserted into the appropriate element of the 0$ array as indicated in line 370. Note that J is incremented by 1 in line 380 to force a shift over the current position in the input record. Next, line 390 sets K to 25 to terminate the pair comparison in the FOR-NEXT loop bounded by lines 260 and 280, from which the compression routine was called and to which it returns upon execution of line 395.

Since the variable M was set to 1 to indicate a pair match occurred, the termination of the FOR K loop causes the execution of line 290 to result in a branch to line 310. Here the index used for the 0$ array is increased by one and the match flag is rest to zero prior to the loop terminating.

Figure 3.37 illustrates how the execution of the diatomic compression routine will appear on your monitor, while Figure 3.38 illustrates the screen image after it has been 'dumped' to a printer that outputs ASCII values from 225 upward as italics. Thus, some readers may prefer to use the execution illustrated in Figure 3.38 to compare the compression characters in italics with respect to the original data and the Jewell character combination pairs used in the program. Since an italic lower case 'a' represents the first combination pair while an italic 'b' represents the second pair and so on, it should be easier to use the second example of the PAIRC.BAS program execution for readers who wish to follow the logical flow of the program in detail.

Decompression

The program listing of PAIRD.BAS is listed in Figure 3.39. As indicated by the naming conventions used in this book, this program performs decompression upon previously compressed pairs of characters.

```
ENTER ASCII FILENAME. EG, PAIR.DAT
? PAIR.DAT
PATIENCE - INPUT PROCESSING
FILE PAIR.DAT BEFORE COMPRESSION:
1 TO BE OR NOT TO BE THAT IS THE QUESTION
2 THE RAIN IN SPAIN FALLS MAINLY IN THE PLAIN
FILE PAIR.DAT AFTER COMPRESSION:
1ΓΟΠß· NO±TOΠßπJΩσπßQUØ≥≡
2Γ§ RAτΩ∞SPAτ FALLσMAτLYΩ∞πßPLAτ
   30  TOTAL CHARACTERS ELIMINATED FROM  91 OR  32 %
Ok
```

```
ENTER ASCII FILENAME. EG, PAIR.DAT
? PAIR.DAT
PATIENCE - INPUT PROCESSING
FILE PAIR.DAT BEFORE COMPRESSION:
1 TO BE OR NOT TO BE THAT IS THE QUESTION
2 THE RAIN IN SPAIN FALLS MAINLY IN THE PLAIN
FILE PAIR.DAT AFTER COMPRESSION:
1ΓΟΠß· NO±TOΠßπJΩσπßQUØ≥≡
2Γ§ RAτΩ∞SPAτ FALLσMAτLYΩ∞πßPLAτ
   29  TOTAL CHARACTERS ELIMINATED FROM  86 OR  33 %
Ok
```

Figure 3.37 Sample execution of PAIRC.BAS program as displayed on a monitor

```
ENTER ASCII FILENAME. EG, PAIR.DAT
? PAIR.DAT
PATIENCE - INPUT PROCESSING
FILE PAIR.DAT BEFORE COMPRESSION:
1 TO BE OR NOT TO BE THAT IS THE QUESTION
2 THE RAIN IN SPAIN FALLS MAINLY IN THE PLAIN
FILE PAIR.DAT AFTER COMPRESSION:
1bOoay NOqTOoacujecaQUɴrp
2bh RAgjlSPAg FALLeMAgLYjlcaPLAg
   30  TOTAL CHARACTERS ELIMINATED FROM  91 OR  32 %
```

Figure 3.38 Sample execution of PAIRC.BAS program when printed using a printer that displays characters greater than ASCII 224 as italics

From an examination of the program coding listed in Figure 3.39, the reader will note that the construction of the code modules for decompression closely resemble the previously examined compression program. Although our programming goal was to do this to facilitate a comparison between programs, due to the relationship between compression and decompression such modular coding relationships will normally be the rule and not the exception.

After opening files for input and output, the subroutine beginning at line 500 is invoked by line 115 of the program. This subroutine

```
10 REM PAIRD.BAS PROGRAM
20 DIM O$(132)
30 WIDTH 80:CLS
40 '**********MAIN ROUTINE**********************
50 '* THIS ROUTINE READS RECORDS FROM AN ASCII *
60 '* FILE INTO A STRING CALLED X$ WHICH IS     *
70 '* THEN PASSED TO DECOMPRESSION SUBROUTINE   *
80 '*********************************************
90 PRINT "ENTER ASCII FILENAME. EG, PAIRC.DAT"
100 INPUT F$: OPEN F$ FOR INPUT AS #2
105 OPEN "PAIRD.DAT" FOR OUTPUT AS #3
110 PRINT "PATIENCE - INPUT PROCESSING"
115 GOSUB 500
120 IF EOF(2) THEN GOTO 9000
130 LINE INPUT #2, X$
140 N= LEN(X$)
150 GOSUB 180
160 GOSUB 900
170 GOTO 120
180 '*****DIATOMIC   DECODING SUBROUTINE********
190 '* THIS ROUTINE PROCESSES RECORDS FROM X$  *
200 '* AND DECOMPRESSES PAIR-ENCODED CHARACTERS*
210 '* USING O$ AS THE OUTPUT BUFFER.          *
220 '*********************************************
230 K=1:J=1:V=0                  'RESET INDICES
240 FOR I= 1 TO N                'STEP THRU RECORD
250 A$= MID$(X$,I,1)             'EXTRACT A CHAR
260 IF A$> CHR$(224) THEN 360    'COMPRESSED PAIR?
290 O$(J)=A$                     'STUFF IN OUTPUT BUFFER
300 J=J+1                        'BUMP BUFFER INDEX
310 NEXT I                       'GO BACK FOR MORE
320 RETURN                       'END OF STRING
355 '*********************************************************
360 'DECODE COMPRESSION NOTATION TO OUTPUT BUFFER
365 '*********************************************************
370 K= ASC(A$)                   'GET ORDINAL EQUIV.
380 K= K-224                     'SUBTRACT FOR INDEX
390 O$(J)= P$(K)                 'STUFF PAIR IN BUFFER
400 J= J+1                       'BUMP OUTPUT INDEX
405 V= V+1                       'SUM VARIABLE COUNT
410 GOTO 310                     'DONE
500 DIM P$(25)                   'JEWELL CHAR. COMBINATION PAIRS
510 DATA "E "," T",TH," A","S ",RE,IN,HE,ER," I"," O","N ",ES,
520 DATA " B",ON,"T ",TI,AN,"D ",AT,TE," C"," S",OR,"R "
530 FOR I = 1 TO 25              'SET UP PAIR TABLE
540 READ Z$                      'GET COMMON PAIR
550 P$(I) = Z$: NEXT I           'AND STUFF INTO PAIR TABLE
560 RETURN                       'DONE - TABLE COMPLETE
900 '*****TALLY THE DECOMPRESSION COUNT & WRITE BUFFER****
910 '* DISPLAY BEFORE & AFTER RESULTS OF DECOMPRESSION  *
920 '* AND SHOW THE NET RESULTS OBTAINED BY EACH METHOD *
930 '*********************************************************
931 N1=N1+N                      'TALLY INPUT CHAR COUNT
932 T=N-J+1+V                    'NET DIFFERENCE IN BUFFERS
936 T1=T1-T                      'SAVE COUNT FOR SUMMARY
```

Figure 3.39 PAIRD.BAS program listing

```
940 FOR I= 1 TO J-1
950 PRINT #3, O$(I);
960 NEXT I
965 PRINT #3, ""
970 RETURN
9000 CLOSE: OPEN F$ FOR INPUT AS #2
9010 PRINT "FILE ";F$;" BEFORE DECOMPRESSION:"
9020 LINE INPUT #2,X$
9030 IF EOF(2) THEN 9060
9040 PRINT X$
9050 GOTO 9020
9060 PRINT X$:OPEN "PAIRD.DAT" FOR INPUT AS #3
9070 PRINT "FILE ";F$;" AFTER DECOMPRESSION:"
9080 LINE INPUT #3,O$
9090 IF EOF(3) THEN 9998
9100 PRINT O$
9110 GOTO 9080
9998 PRINT O$:PRINT ABS(T1);" TOTAL CHARACTERS INSERTED"
9999 CLOSE:END
```

Figure 3.39 (continued)

simply builds the P$ table that will contain the Jewell character
combination pairs that the program will search for. In line 130, the
familiar LINE INPUT statement is used to obtain a record from
the input file. Next, line 140 is employed to determine the length
of the record while line 150 invokes the subroutine beginning at line
180 which performs the actual decompression of data.

The FOR-NEXT loop bounded by lines 240 and 310 searches
through the record previously extracted from the input file on a
character by character basis. This is accomplished by the use of the
MID$ function in line 250. If the character extracted from the
record exceeds a value of 224, it is assumed that diatomic or paired
compression has occurred. This assumption is based upon the
selection of each character beyond ASCII 224 to represent a pair of
characters in this coding example. If the character extracted from
the record equals or is less than ASCII 224, that character does not
represent a previously compressed pair of characters. Thus, line 290
simply places the extracted character into its appropriate position in
the output buffer.

When an ASCII character greater than 224 is encountered, the
branch to line 360 in the program results in the actual decompression
of a previously compressed pair of characters. In line 370, the
numerical value of the character that actually represents a pair of
characters is obtained. Next, line 380 subtracts 224 from the
numerical value of the character to obtain the appropriate index in
the paired table (P$(25)). Line 390 places the pair of characters that

was previously represented by one character into the output buffer while lines 400 and 405 increment the index position in the output buffer and the variable V which is only employed to compute the difference in size between the input and output buffers and is not required for decompression.

Figure 3.40 illustrates the execution of the PAIRD.BAS program as it would appear on our monitor using the data file PAIRC.DAT as input. PAIRC.DAT was created by the PAIRC.BAS program. Thus, it is of no surprise that the two compressed lines of data at the top of Figure 3.40 match lines 1 and 2 in the lower part of Figure 3.38, while lines 1 and 2 at the bottom of Figure 3.40 match those lines at the top of Figure 3.38.

```
ENTER ASCII FILENAME. EG. PAIRC.DAT
? PAIRC.DAT
PATIENCE - INPUT PROCESSING
FILE PAIRC.DAT BEFORE DECOMPRESSION:
1ΓΟΛß· NO±TOΛßπJΩσπßQUØ≥≡
2Γ§ RATΩ∞SPAT FALLσMATLYΩ∞πßPLAT
FILE PAIRC.DAT AFTER DECOMPRESSION:
1 TO BE OR NOT TO BE THAT IS THE QUESTION
2 THE RAIN IN SPAIN FALLS MAINLY IN THE PLAIN
 29  TOTAL CHARACTERS INSERTED
Ok
```

Figure 3.40 Sample execution of PAIRD.BAS program

Encoding considerations

The ability to perform diatomic compression is based upon the replacement of two characters with a special compression-indicating character. Thus, you must either use a character set from which undefined characters are available as substitutions for pairs of characters or you must consider the frequency of occurrence of pairs of characters versus the frequency of occurrence of the selected character using the insert and delete technique. Concerning the latter, assume you wish to apply diatomic compression and will transmit or store 8-bit ASCII characters. Since all characters in that character set are defined, the only way that diatomic compression can be effective is if the frequency of occurrence of a pair of characters exceeds twice the frequency of occurrence of the character selected to represent the character pair. The reason for this is that the insert and delete technique doubles the frequency of occurrence of the selected character, because each natural occurrence of the character selected to represent the pair is doubled, since the insert portion of the insert and delete technique adds an extra character whenever the selected character is encountered.

3.6 PATTERN SUBSTITUTION

This compression technique is basically a sophisticated form of diatomic encoding. Here, a special character code is substituted for a predefined character pattern. The employment of the pattern substitution compression technique can be highly advantageous when you are transmitting program listings and other types of data files containing known repeating patterns.

The advantage offered by pattern substitution is best understood by examining a higher-level language such as FORTRAN. In any FORTRAN program, a very high probability exists that one or more types of statements will be encountered containing common key words such as 'READ', 'WRITE' and 'FORMAT', among others. Instead of transmitting the characters of these key words on a character by character basis each time they appear, one of the unassigned characters from the employed character set can be substituted. When pattern substitution is applied to language text, common key words or phrases can similarly be replaced. For English text transmission, such commonly encountered words as 'and', 'the', 'that' and 'this' would be among the first candidates for substitution.

The pattern table

To employ pattern substitution, a pattern table is required. This table contains a set of list arguments and a set of function values. Each function value is a special compression-indicator character which represents the compressed value of a particular argument (Aronson, 1977). Figure 3.41 shows an example of the use of a pattern table. Although each list argument was of similar length, this table can be expanded to include many additional entries of various character length. Strings of four, five, six and more blanks, for example, could be assigned values represented by different special characters as well as patterns of alphanumeric data.

NOW IS THE TIME FOR ALL GOOD MEN

Pattern table

List arguments	Function values
THE	Sc_1
FOR	Sc_2
ALL	Sc_3

Compressed data stream

NOW IS Sc_1 TIME Sc_2 Sc_3 GOOD MEN

Figure 3.41 Pattern table utilization. Upon a portion of the original data stream matching the list argument, the appropriate function value is substituted. In the above example, special compression indicator characters Sc_1, Sc_2 and Sc_3 are substituted for the words 'the', 'for' and 'all' as they are encountered

Encoding process

To obtain the compressed data stream, the source data must be broken down into distinct search arguments, initially equal to the smallest-sized argument in the pattern table. The search argument is matched with those list arguments of equal character width. If a match is obtained, the function value associated with the list argument then replaces that portion of the original data stream and results in data compression. If no match is obtained, the width of the search argument is increased to the width of the next larger list argument or series of list arguments and the process is repeated. If after increasing the width of the search argument to the largest width of the list argument no match results, the first character of the original data string is passed to the compressed data string and the process is repeated, starting with the second character from the original data stream.

A second method of performing pattern substitution results from the use of blanks as delimiters. The binary or octal value of the characters between blanks can be generated and compared with the binary or octal values in the list argument portion of the pattern table. This process simplifies the searching of a long argument list and minimizes the processing time required to encode patterns.

Patterns in programming languages

Due to the utilization of keywords or reserved words in most programming languages, pattern substitution is often a very effective compression technique for storing or transmitting program files. Since the number of keywords or reserved words in a programming language can be as high as several hundred, a 2-byte sequence can be employed to represent each keyword pattern substitution. Here, the first byte or character would be used to indicate pattern substitution has occurred, while the following character would denote the actual pattern that was substituted for the keyword or reserved word. To illustrate this concept in additional detail, let us assume that the version of BASIC we are working with is limited to eight keywords. Table 3.15 lists these keywords and their equivalent function values contained in the pattern table that could be constructed.

Table 3.15 BASIC language pattern table

Keywords	Function values
END	$1
GOTO	$2
IF	$3
INPUT	$4
LET	$5
PRINT	$6
REM	$7
THEN	$8

For clarity of explanation the dollar sign ($) was employed as the compression-indicating character in Table 3.15, although obviously any character in the character set could be used. Preferably, one should select a character which is seldom or, better yet, never used. Since there is always the possibility that the character could occur in a BASIC program, one can replace each occurrence of the pattern compression-indicating character by duplicating that character when it is encountered. Then, the decompression routine would disregard each such duplication of a pattern compression-indicating character. The compression of a short BASIC program is illustrated in Figure 3.42 based upon the employment of pattern substitution, which in actuality is the replacement of BASIC keywords. Note that the

BASIC program	Compressed program
100 REM COMMISSION CALCULATION	100$7COMMISSION CALCULATION
110 PRINT "ENTER SALE PRICE"	110$6"ENTER SALE PRICE"
120 INPUT W	120$4W
130 PRINT "ENTER NUMBER SOLD"	130$6"ENTER NUMBER SOLD"
140 INPUT N	140$4N
150 LET C=W∗N∗.0875	150$5C=W∗N∗.0875
160 PRINT "COMMISSION=";C	160$6"COMMISSION=";C
170 PRINT "ANOTHER CALCULATION–Y/N"	170$6"ANOTHER CALCULATION–Y/N"
180 INPUT A$	180$4A$$
190 IF A$ ◇ "Y" THEN 210	190$3A$$◇"Y"$8210
200 GOTO 110	200$2110
210 END	210$1

Figure 3.42 Compressing a BASIC program

pattern table contained in Table 3.15 was used for the compression process. Since most BASIC languages require keywords to be delimited by spaces, we have assumed that the keywords entered in Table 3.15 contained leading and trailing blanks, enabling the functional value substituted for the keyword to be a more effective substitution. Using this method of substitution, 25 spaces as well as 26 other characters are eliminated from the program while two characters are added. The additional characters are due to the replacement of the natural occurrence of the $ character in the program by the special sequence $$ in lines 180 and 190.

Although the overall data reduction, which in this example was approximately 20 per cent, may not appear significant, it should be noted that the actual effort involved to compress data using pattern substitution may not be significantly demanding. To increase the data reduction resulting from compression usually requires the application of several compression techniques to one's data. In this particular example, one might first preprocess programming files through the utilization of pattern substitution compression. Then one could statistically encode the resulting compressed data. Since the statistical encoding process results in the replacement of frequently occurring characters by short bit sequences, statistically encoding data where keywords were previously replaced by short patterns is more effective than the statistical encoding of the original data. As an example, a 5-bit sequence might be required to represent the keyword PRINT; however, a short bit sequence would be required to represent the character sequence $6 that was substituted for the keyword. The reader is referred to Chapter Four for additional information concerning statistical encoding.

3.7 RELATIVE ENCODING

Relative encoding is a compression technique that is not normally applicable to the transmission of conventional data files. This type of compression is effectively employed when there are sequences of runs in the original data stream that vary only slightly from each other or the run sequences can be broken into patterns relative to each other. An example of the former is telemetry data while the bit patterns of digital facsimile machines represent a version of the latter.

Telemetry compression

In telemetry data generation, a sensing device is used to record measurements at predefined intervals. These measurements are then transmitted to a central location for additional processing. One example of telemetry signals is the numerous space probes which transmit temperature readings, colour spectrum analysis and other data, either upon command from earth stations or at predefined time intervals. Normally, telemetry signals contain a sequence of numeric fields consisting of subsequences or runs of numerics that vary only slightly from each other as illustrated in the top portion of Figure 3.43.

Original telemetry measurements

46 46 46.1 46.1 46.1 46 46 46 46.1 46.1 46.1 46.2

Relative encoding

46 0 .1 0 0 —.1 0 0 .1 0 0 .1

Figure 3.43 Relative encoding process. Telemetry signals often consist of a sequence of numerics that vary only slightly from each other during a certain time interval

Prior to actual data transmission, compression occurs to reduce the total amount of data necessary to represent the recorded measurements. Each measurement other than the first is coded with the relative difference between it and the preceding measurement, as long as the absolute value of the increment is less than some predetermined value. This is shown in the lower portion of Figure 3.43. If the increment should exceed this value, a special character is inserted to denote that the particular value at that location is not available or the special character could be followed by the measurement that is out of the boundary range for the relative encoding process. This limits wide fluctuations and is one disadvantage associated with the utilization of this technique. Another disadvantage is that if data values consistently vary both within and outside the relative encoding boundary range and a combination of a special character and actual value is transmitted, this will cause an expansion instead of a compression of the data stream.

Additional techniques may be employed to obtain a higher degree of compression depending upon the original telemetry measurements and the resultant data due to the relative encoding process. In the top portion of Figure 3.43, the original telemetry measurements illustrated consist of 38 characters to include numerics and decimal points. As a result of the relative encoding process, the number of numerics and decimal point characters has been reduced to 18. By the incorporation of a second compression technique, the number of characters used to represent the relative encoding process may be further reduced. One method that could be used is the half-byte packing process where each numeric digit is stripped of its first 4 bits and packed two per character. If we use a 4-bit representation for the decimal point and minus sign, half-byte packing will result in the transmission of nine 8-bit bytes of data. Thus, while the relative encoding process resulted in a 2.24 (38/17) compression ratio, recompressing the relative encoding results employing the half-byte packing technique approximately doubles the compression ratio to 4.223 (38/9).

While the half-byte packing process was illustrated as the combining or second compression technique, other techniques may be employed with results dependent upon the variability of the original telemetry measurements. If the original telemetry measurements indicated a stable 46 for the time interval sampled, the relative encoding process would result in a long string of zeros after the value indicator of 46. For this situation, run-length encoding would be more effective as the second compression technique.

Digital facsimile

Several relative encoding techniques can be employed to compress digital facsimile data. Prior to discussing these techniques, a review of the elements of facsimile technology is warranted.

Facsimile systems use the basic concept of scanning—normally on a line by line basis—to create a stream of information concerning the lightness or darkness of the small area being scanned at any given point in time. The resulting stream of information is then transmitted and used to drive an image-reproducing device at a facsimile receiver where the original information is reproduced. In general, the operation of a facsimile device is quite similar to the technology employed in television, where 525 lines on the US domestic television system are used to reproduce images. For facsimile systems, the clarity depends upon the fineness of the scan. Normally, approximately 100 scan lines per inch are required to successfully reproduce a page of typewritten material. Thus, a normal $8\frac{1}{2} \times 11$ sheet of paper, scanned longitudinally, would require approximately 850 scan lines. Each scan line in turn consists of approximately 1 730 picture elements (pixels, or pels), resulting in approximately 1 million bits for an $8\frac{1}{2} \times 11$ sheet of paper. To transmit this data at 4 800 bps without compression, 209 s or approximately 3.5 min are required.

For facsimile systems, the degree of compression theoretically obtainable is normally very large for the typical facsimile message. As an example, consider a typewritten memorandum containing 500 characters. In conventional data transmission, each character can be represented and transmitted by 8 bits. Thus, the entire message could be transmitted, ignoring control characters, by 500 * 8 or 4 000 bits of information. If transmitted at 4 800 bps, the total transmission time would be less than 1 s. In comparison, the same message sent by conventional facsimile requires the transmission of almost 1 million bits and takes about $3\frac{1}{2}$ min without data compression, a difference of approximately 270 to 1 between conventional facsimile code and character transmission.

Facsimile techniques

One of the earliest facsimile compression techniques was run-length encoding. Here, the transmission of the digital line scan is replaced by the transmission of a quantity count of each of the successive runs of black or white scanned pels.

Since the vast majority of documents to be scanned contains a much higher quantity of white pels than black ones, transmitting the difference between scans may significantly reduce the quantity of data to be transmitted. In this method of compression, one complete scan is held in a memory area of the device and compared with the subsequent scan. Transmitting only changes relative to the preceding scan results in the relative compression process. Once the differences between the first and second scans are transmitted, the first scan is removed from memory and replaced by the second scan. Next, a third scan is compared with the second scan now located in memory. A flow chart showing the required steps for this type of relative encoding process is illustrated in Figure 3.44.

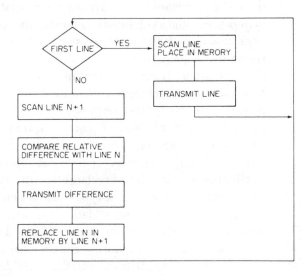

Figure 3.44 Facsimile relative encoding process

In Figure 3.45, a portion of the relative changes resulting from the comparison of two scan lines is shown. Several methods can be used to denote the relative changes between the Nth and Nth+1 scan lines. One method is to denote the position of the change by what is normally called a positional identification. Here, the position of each relative change is denoted with respect to the first pel of the line. If there are many consecutive changes, the transmission of each individual position could require more data bits than the transmission of the original line prior to comparison with the preceding line. To take advantage of successive relative changes between scanned lines, the position indicator can be followed by a quantity count which contains the number of successive relative changes. This is illustrated in Figure 3.46 where the table at the top of the figure tabulates the initial position of the relative change between line scans and the number of succeeding relative changes, while the transmission

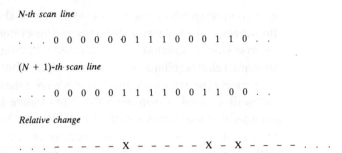

N-th scan line

. . . 0 0 0 0 0 0 1 1 1 0 0 0 1 1 0 . . .

(N + 1)-th scan line

. . . 0 0 0 0 0 1 1 1 1 0 0 1 1 0 0 . . .

Relative change

. . . – – – – – X – – – – – X – X – – – – . . .

Figure 3.45 Relative change. To denote the relative changes between scan lines several methods can be employed to include identification by position and displacement

Initial position of relative change	Number of successive relative changes
40	6
80	20
175	4
350	31
480	8
930	14
1250	16
1310	5
1340	4

Transmitted data

40	6	80	20	175	4	350	31	480	8	930	14	1250	16	1310	5	1340

Figure 3.46 Transmitting positional information. Using the positional relative process, the initial position of each relative change is followed by the number of successive relative changes

sequence is indicated at the lower portion of that figure. Under the Consultative Committee for International Telephone and Telegraph (CCITT) digital facsimile standards, there are 1 728 picture elements or points to be read by the scanner along the width of a document 215 mm wide. Due to the large number of positions, the transmission of positional information can rapidly increase in duration, especially when a number of relative changes occur at the far end of the scan line. One method used to alleviate this 'end of the line' increase is by the use of displacement notation. As with positional notation, the relative changes between scan lines are first computed. Then, instead of transmitting all of the initial positions of the relative changes and the number of successive changes as illustrated in Figure 3.46, only the first initial position is transmitted. Thereafter, the displacement between relative changes is transmitted. This displacement method can include the transmission of successive relative change information and is illustrated in Figure 3.47. This figure is based upon the data provided in the tabular portion of Figure 3.46. In comparing the illustrated positional and displacement methods, the positional method requires 41 numeric characters while the displacement method can be accomplished by the use of 35 such characters. If numerics are packed two per byte, then the displacement technique will result in 140 bits being required to represent the 1 728 points in the example while the positional method would require 164 bits.

Although the transmission of both positional and displacement information has been applied to various techniques used to compress facsimile information, a more efficient method is obtained by assigning predefined codes to different runs of black and white pixels. The codes are then substituted for each sequence of pixel runs encountered in each scanned line. This technique is based upon a modified version of Huffman encoding and is discussed in detail in Chapter 4.

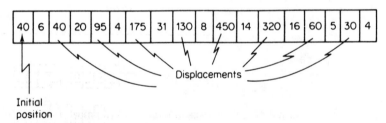

Figure 3.47 Transmitting displacement information. Another relative encoding technique results in the transmission of displacement information

3.8 FORMS-MODE OPERATION

Forms-mode operation is a method of compression that can be employed when data is to be communicated to and from a CRT display in a predefined series of formats. When operated in the forms mode, the display can be used for a fill in the blank type of operation. In this mode of operation, two basic types of data are displayed— protected information and variable information. Fixed or protected information corresponds to the preprinted information of a data field in a standard printed form such as name, address, social security number and similar types of information. Such information when the operation is in the forms mode is not cleared when the screen is erased, is not transmitted to the central processor and is not alterable by accidental keyboard entries. Each fixed field is one-half of a field pair, the other half being the corresponding variable field. Thus, in the forms mode the fixed field can be viewed as the question while the information entered into the corresponding variable field can be considered as the answer.

An example of forms-mode data entry is illustrated in Figure 3.48. Here, the blank spaces indicate the additional positions available for data entry into the variable fields.

In using the forms mode of operation, the operator denotes the form he or she wishes to complete and that form is transmitted from the computer to the terminal display or is locally generated from terminal memory or from a peripheral device attached to the terminal. Fixed fields are preceded by an 'FS' (start fixed field) character while variable fields are preceded by a 'GS' (begin variable field) character and a parameter character. The parameter character is used to define the allowable operations within the variable field such as numeric

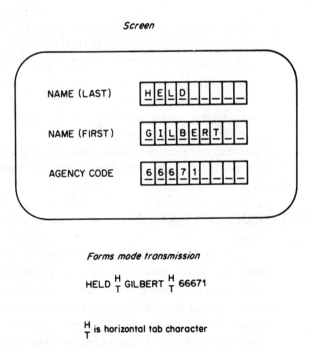

Figure 3.48 Forms-mode data entry

only, alphabetic only, alphanumeric, inhibit transmission and so on. The exact sequence of the GS and FS characters as well as the bit configuration of the parameter character to define allowable operations depends upon the terminal's program. When in forms mode, certain keyboard operations are usually changed from those of the normal mode of operation. As an example, the TAB key on most displays permits the operator to move the cursor (positioning data entry marker) to the first character position of the next sequential variable field, permitting rapid skipping-over of variable fields for which no data is to be entered (Peterson, Bitner and Howard, 1978).

Transmission

The transmission of data in the forms mode is normally performed on a screen basis. When the operator depresses the TRANSMIT key, only the data previously entered into the variable fields is transmitted, with all trailing blanks eliminated.

Here, transmission can occur on-line to the computer or it can be to one of the peripheral units of the terminal. In the case of the latter, a large number of terminal screens may be batched onto a peripheral device such as a cassette or floppy disc for transmission to the computer at one time. Using this combination of forms-mode encoding and off-line storage for transmission by batching screens of information, computer system resources in the form of computer ports and line requirements can be reduced or used more effectively. By reducing the amount of transmission time required to send batched screen information, a reduction in the number of computer ports required to support remote terminals may be possible. Concerning more effective line utilization, consider the situation where 10 terminals operate in a poll and select environment connected via a common modem sharing unit and modem to a central computer as illustrated in Figure 3.49. In the configuration illustrated, all terminals except the terminal transmitting or receiving data are locked out for the duration of the transmission. Normally, blocks of data up to the screen size, 1920 (80 × 24) characters or less, are transmitted. At 4800 bps, the transmission of a 1920 8-bit character block to completely fill a screen would require 3.2 s. If 10 terminals were connected to the modem sharing unit with a round robin polling sequence and each operator transmitted or received a full screen of data, it would take 32 seconds, ignoring transmission overhead, until the first terminal operator could again transmit or receive information.

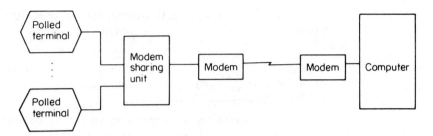

Figure 3.49 Forms-mode encoding increases line service. Forms-mode encoding reduces the poll and select time required per terminal, permitting more terminals to be connected on a shared line or an increase in throughput to existing terminals sharing the line

Thus, reducing the number of characters transmitted and received through the employment of forms-mode encoding can be used to decrease the response time of existing terminals or to permit additional terminals to be clustered without increasing overall response times.

Returning to the example in Figure 3.48, the 'HT' (horizontal tab) character is normally used as a variable field separator, resulting in the transmitted message indicated in the lower portion of that illustration. If a maximum of eight characters can be entered into each of the three variable fields shown in Figure 3.48, a maximum of 26 characters (24 data and 2 horizontal tab characters) will be transmitted to the computer for each form completed. This method of forms-mode data entry should be contrasted with conventional time-sharing as shown in Figure 3.50. Here, the message ENTER NAME (LAST), NAME (FIRST), AGENCY CODE serves as a variable field indicator, denoting to the terminal operator the data to be entered. The carriage return (C/R) character acts as a line termination character; however, if data was entered incorrectly, such as alphabetic characters in an all-numeric field, data must first be sent to the computer for processing to determine that such an error has occurred. In such cases, the computer would transmit an error message to the terminal operator who would then hopefully retype the entire line correctly and retransmit the data. In contrast, using an intelligent terminal and forms-mode operation the data entry operation can be preprocessed and such errors corrected prior to transmission.

In comparison with the operator depressing the TRANSMIT key on the display and having the forms-mode method of operation transmit and clear the variable fields so new data can be entered,

ENTER NAME (LAST), NAME (FIRST), AGENCY CODE

HELD, GILBERT, 6671 C/R

MORE? C/R
YES

ENTER NAME (LAST), NAME (FIRST), AGENCY CODE

Figure 3.50 Conventional time-sharing data entry. In conventional time-sharing, the prompt messages requesting data as well as the user responses are transmitted

conventional time-sharing requires the program to prompt the operater to determine if more data is to be entered. The MORE? and YES (C/R) sequence in Figure 3.50 add additional characters beyond the repeated message used as a variable field indicator. In comparing the sample forms-mode data entry with the conventional time-sharing data entry example, 18 characters are required for the former while 65 characters, excluding line feed and carriage return characters, are required for the latter.

Modified forms-mode method

We can implement a modified method of forms-mode compression by treating a screen display as a collection of forms. To do so we can subdivide a screen display into n segments or forms as illustrated in Figure 3.51. Then, we can operate upon each segment as if it

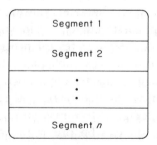

Figure 3.51 Treating the screen as a collection of forms. The screen display can be subdivided into n segments, with each segment operated upon as if it represents a form. Then, only if changes occurred to the segment will the contents of the segment be transmitted

were an individual form to reduce the transmission between a terminal device and a computer.

The key to the utilization of the previously described modified method of forms-mode operation is the assignment of a 'data tag' to each screen segment. Modifying the data tag each time a screen segment changes allows the data 'tag to serve as an indicator as to whether or not the screen segment must be transmitted. To illustrate the potential for this method to reduce the data required to update screen displays, assume the 80 × 25 character display of the typical IBM PC screen is subdivided into segments of 40 characters by 5 lines. Doing so would result in the screen being subdivided into a total of 10 segments that could be numbered as indicated in Figure 3.52.

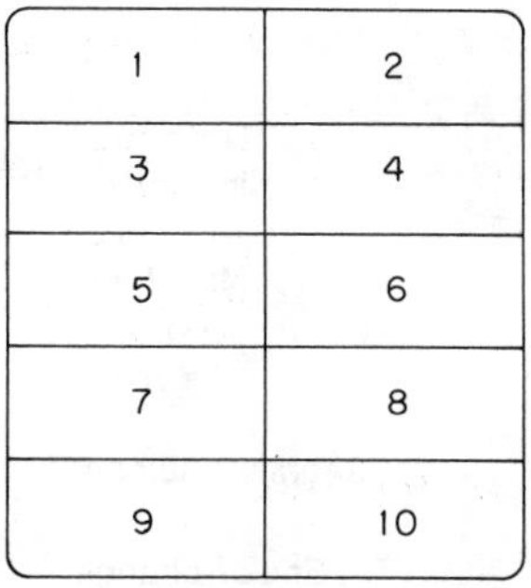

1	2
3	4
5	6
7	8
9	10

Figure 3.52   Screen Segmentation Example. By subdividing the terminal screen into 10 segments of 40 characters by 5 lines screen updates can be implemented in increments of 200 characters

When a terminal operator updates the screen, the terminal or personal computer keeps track of changes made to each segment but does not transmit any data until an ENTER, RETURN, program function (PF), or program assistance (PA) key is pressed. At that time the terminal or personal computer transmits a data tag for each segment which indicates whether or not the segment has been modified. If the segment has been modified the data tag is then followed by the 200 characters contained in the segment. Through the implementation of this compression technique it becomes possible to transmit full-screen updates in as little as one segment of a few hundred characters, including a modified data tag which indicates both the segment which was modified as well as the fact that only that segment was modified.

To illustrate one method by which a display screen can be seg-
mented, let us assume we are using a conventional 7-level ASCII
character set. We could set bit 8 to indicate it is a data tag character,
which, in effect, allows us to use up to 128 unique characters to
represent different information concerning screen segments.

Figure 3.53 illustrates one possible format for the construction of
a data tag character. Here the setting of bit position 7 would indicate
whether or not the segment that the data tag represents had been
changed since the last time the ENTER, RETURN, or a PF or PA
key was pressed. Bits 3 through 6 would identify the segment that
the data tag is associated with, while bit 1 would be used to indicate
whether or not the segment identified by the data tag was the last
segment changed.

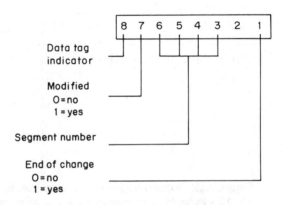

Figure 3.53 Possible data tag format

If the end-of-change bit is set to 0 the characters in the segment
would follow the data tag character. If the end-of-change bit is set
to 1 this would indicate that no additional characters would follow
the characters that define the changed segment identified by the data
tag character.

Although the previous discussion concerned the use of a character
set from which up to 128 characters could be defined to represent
data tag information, how could you accomplish a similar compression
scheme using EBCDIC, since most full-screen terminal operations
use that character set? As previously discussed in Chapter 2, there
are many EBCDIC 8-bit character representations that are undefined.
Thus, you could implement the previously described modified forms-
mode method of compression by selecting one undefined character

to represent a data tag character. Then, you could define a format in which the data tag character is followed by another character which indicates whether or not the segment was modified. If the segment was modified, you could then follow the character used to indicate a modified segment by the characters that represent the segment. Note that in using this method you might construct your format so that you would not transmit a segment number. Thus, if only segment 5 changed, you would have to transmit four data tags to represent segments 1 through 4 without each data tag character being followed by a character indicating that the segment was changed. In comparison, using the previous example you would transmit the data tag with bits 3 through 6 set to a value of 5 to indicate that segment 5 was changed. Regardless of the method used, the important aspect of this technique is that for most interactive terminal applications only a small portion of the screen is updated. Thus, subdividing the screen into segments, and only transmitting those segments that changed since a 'key' key was pressed, can significantly increase the efficiency of the transmission system.

4

STATISTICAL ENCODING

One common element of the eight data compression techniques discussed in Chapter 3 is that they all operate upon characters codes of a fixed bit size. In comparison with those compression methods statistical encoding takes advantage of the probabilities of occurrence of single characters and groups of characters, so that short codes can be used to represent frequently occurring characters or groups of characters while longer codes are used to represent less frequently encountered characters and groups of characters.

The statistical encoding process can be used to obtain a minimization of the average code length of the encoded data, in a manner similar to that in which Morse selected the dot and dash representations of characters so that a single dot was used to represent the letter E, which is the most frequently encountered character in the English language, while longer strings of dots and dashes were used to represent characters that appear less frequently. Included in the class of statistical compression methods is the Huffman coding technique, Shannon–Fano encoding and the Lempel–Ziv string encoding method, among others.

In this chapter we will focus our attention upon a variety of data-compression methods that are based upon the statistical encoding of characters and strings. Our examination will begin with the use of static compression tables and then investigate the construction and operation of dynamic tables. Prior to discussing these techniques in detail, a review of some basic information theory concepts is warranted. These concepts will provide an understanding of how redundancy can be statistically reduced.

4.1 INFORMATION THEORY

For a system capable of transmitting at n discrete levels at intervals of λ s, the number of different signal combinations in T s is $n^{T/\lambda}$.

Since information is proportional to the length of time of transmission, we can take the logarithm of $n^{T/\lambda}$, to obtain the information transmitted in T s being proportional to $(T/\lambda) \log n$.

The proportionality factor will depend upon the base of the logarithm used, the most common choice being the base 2. This results in the information unit H becoming

$$H = \frac{T}{\lambda} \log_2 n.$$

The unit of information defined in the preceding manner is known as the bit or binary digit. For the transmission of data over a 20 s period using two discrete levels (0 and 1) at 1 s intervals, the information content becomes:

$$H = \frac{20}{1} \log_2 2 = 20 \text{ bits.}$$

The capacity of a given system is defined as the maximum amount of information per second that a system can transmit and can be expressed in bits per second (bps). Thus, the capacity of the preceding example becomes:

$$C = \frac{H}{T} = \frac{1}{\lambda} \log_2 n = \frac{1}{1} \log_2 2 = 1 \text{ bps.}$$

The relative frequency of occurrence of any one combination or event is defined as the probability of occurrence, denoted symbolically as P, where

$$P = \frac{\text{number of times an event occurs}}{\text{total number of possibilities}}$$

If n possible events are specified to be the n possible signal levels, then $P = 1/n$ for events that are equally likely to occur. The information contained by the appearance of any one event in one time interval (H_1) becomes:

$$H_1 = \log_2 n = -\log_2 P \text{ bits/interval}$$

where P represents $1/n$. During t periods of time, consisting of periods λ s long, we should have t times as much information, or

$$H = tH_1 = -t \log_2 P \text{ bits in } t \text{ periods.}$$

Since the number of periods, t, equals the total time, T, divided by the number of intervals, λ, the information available in T s becomes:

$$H = -\frac{T}{\lambda} \log_2 P = \frac{T}{\lambda} \log_2 n \text{ bits in } T \text{ s.}$$

With the preceding serving as a foundation, we can consider the case where different events or signal levels do not have equal probabilities of occurrence. Let us assume just two levels are to be transmitted, 0 or 1, the first with probability P and the second with probability Q, where $P + Q = 1$. Then:

$$P = \frac{\text{number of times 0 occurs}}{\text{total number of possibilities}}$$

$$Q = \frac{\text{number of times 1 occurs}}{\text{total number of possibilities}}$$

The information content of a long message consisting of many 0s and 1s is thus dependent upon $P*\log_2 P + Q*\log_2 Q$ which is the information in bits per occurrence of a 0 or 1 times the relative frequency of occurrence of the bit value. We can let the frequency of occurrence of each possible signal level or signal be denoted by P_i, where $P_1 + P_2 + \ldots + P_n = 1$. Then each interval carries $-\log_2 P_i$ bits of information. In t periods of time, i will appear on the average $t*P_i$ times. By summing the information in bits contributed on the average by each symbol appearing $t*P_i$ times over the t intervals, we obtain:

$$H = -t* \sum_{i=1}^{n} P_i \log_2 P_i \text{ bits in } t \text{ periods.}$$

For the interval T, we then obtain:

$$H = -\frac{T}{\lambda}* \sum_{i=1}^{n} P \log_2 P_i \text{ bits in } T \text{ s.}$$

For a message with n possible symbols or levels with probability of occurrence P_i to P_n, the average information per single symbol interval of λ is:

$$H_{avg} = - \sum_{i=1}^{n} P_i \log_2 P_i \text{ bits/symbol interval.}$$

The above equation represents the mathematical definition of entropy, a term used in information theory to denote the average number of bits required to represent each symbol of a source alphabet.

Based upon the preceding, it becomes possible to compute the redundancy contained in information. Since the unit of information is $\log_2 n$ for a system capable of transmitting at n discrete levels, its redundancy becomes

$$R = \log_2 n - H_{avg}.$$

Then, when there is zero redundancy:

$$H_{avg} = \log_2 n.$$

Entropy examples

Since entropy represents the average number of bits required to represent each symbol of a source alphabet, let us probe deeper to verify its applicability to data compression. Let us first start with a simple coin toss experiment in which the probability of a head is equal to the probability of a tail. Then, $P_H = 0.5 = P_T$. How many bits are required to encode the result of this coin toss?

From the prior definition of entropy, $H_{avg} = -\Sigma_{i=1}^{n} P_i \log_2 P_i$. Here $\log_2 x$ for those that may have forgotten means $2^? = x$ or 2 to what power equals x. Substituting the probability of a head and the probability of a tail occurring into the equation for computing entropy we obtain:

$$H_{avg} = -[\tfrac{1}{2}\log_2\tfrac{1}{2} + \tfrac{1}{2}\log_2\tfrac{1}{2}].$$

One of the properties of logarithms is that $\log(1/X) = -\log X$. Thus $\log_2\tfrac{1}{2}$ is equivalent to $-\log_2 2$. Since $\log_2 2$ becomes -1, returning to our calculation of entropy for the one-coin toss, we obtain:

$$H_{avg} = -[\tfrac{1}{2}*(-1) + \tfrac{1}{2}*(-1)] = -[-1] = 1.$$

From the preceding, the computation of entropy tells us that one bit would be required to encode the results of a single-coin toss. Now let us expand the preceding to two coins.

The two sides of a coin, heads (H) and tails (T), correspond to members X_1 and X_2 from an alphabet X containing two symbols. If we toss two coins and encode the results so that T = 0 and H = 1, the coin toss result probabilities correspond to a four-symbol alphabet as tabulated in Table 4.1. The entropy or average number of bits required to represent each possible outcome or symbol from our four-symbol alphabet becomes:

$$H_{avg} = -\sum_{i=1}^{4} P_i \log_2 P_i = -4*0.25 \log_2 0.25.$$

Table 4.1 Coin toss representing four-symbol alphabet

Coin toss outcome	Alphabet symbol	Outcome probability	Representative code
TT	X_1	0.25	00
TH	X_2	0.25	01
HT	X_3	0.25	10
HH	X_4	0.25	11

Since $\log_2 0.25$ is -2, we can rewrite the preceding equation as follows:

$$H_{avg} = -4[0.25*(-2)] = 2.$$

For the coin toss experiment results listed in Table 4.1, two binary symbols were required to encode each alphabetic symbol. If for some reason the coin toss was fixed such that only tails (T) occurs, the only symbol required in our alphabet would be X_1. Under this condition, we would never have to do any coin tossing to determine the outcome since the result is always known in advance. The entropy of this one-symbol alphabet can be computed as follows:

$$H_{avg} = -\sum_{i=1}^{4} P_i \log_2 P_i = -\sum_{i=1}^{1} \log_2 1 = 0.$$

In this case, since the outcome is known in advance the symbol provides no information; hence, its entropy is zero.

We can again fix the coin toss experiment; however, this time we will fix it so the probability of tails (T) occurring is increased to 0.75, leaving a 0.25 probability of heads occurring. Under these circumstances, the tabular results of the coin toss outcomes representing a four-symbol alphabet would be as listed in Table 4.2. Although the representative code, number of coin toss outcomes and alphabet symbols have remained the same, the outcome probabilities have changed. Thus, the probability of two tails is now 0.75 times 0.75, or 0.5625, and so on. The entropy of this four-symbol alphabet is now:

$$H_{avg} = -\sum_{i=1}^{4} P_i \log_2 P_i = 0.5625 \log_2 0.5625 + 0.1875 \log_2 0.1875$$

$$+ 0.1875 \log_2 0.1875 + 0.0625 \log_2 0.0625 = 1.62 \text{ bits per symbol.}$$

Table 4.2 Fixed coin-toss representing four-symbol alphabet. Probability of head = 0.25; probability of tail = 0.75

Coin toss outcome	Alphabet symbol	Outcome probability	Representative code
TT	X_1	0.5625	00
TH	X_2	0.1875	01
HT	X_3	0.1875	10
HH	X_4	0.0625	11

Based upon the preceding, let us compute the redundancy in the fixed coin toss experiment. Since a two-symbol event results in four discrete levels

$$R = \log_2 n - H_{avg} = \log_2 4 - 1.68 = 2 - 1.68 = 0.38.$$

In comparison with the first coin toss experiment, the average number of bits required to represent a symbol from the four-symbol alphabet has been reduced by 0.38. This indicates that using another type of coding scheme to represent the four-symbol alphabet could result in an approximate 20 per cent reduction from the two bits per symbol previously used to represent the four-symbol alphabet. To obtain this reduction, we must assign short codes to the most frequently occuring symbols of the alphabet and longer codes to the less frequently encountered symbols. This method will result in a long string of data symbols having, on the average, fewer bits per symbol and is the foundation for what is known as Huffman coding (Dishon, 1977; Moilanen, 1978).

Huffman coding is one of several techniques where data is encoded based upon their probability of occurrence. Although the original method of Huffman coding was applied to characters, it can also be applied to strings of characters as well as previously compressed data, such as diatomic encoded pairs of characters. Due to Huffman coding forming the basis for a large number of data-compression techniques, we will examine this method as a separate entity in the next section of this chapter.

4.2 HUFFMAN CODING

Huffman coding is a statistical data-compression technique whose employment will reduce the average code length used to represent the symbols of an alphabet. The alphabet can be the English language alphabet or a type of data-coded alphabet such as the ASCII or EBCDIC character sets.

Prefix property of code

The Huffman code is an optimum code since it results in the shortest average code length of all statistical encoding techniques. In addition, Huffman codes have a prefix property which means that no short code group is duplicated as the beginning of a longer group. This means that if one character is represented by the bit combination 100, then 10001 cannot be the code for another letter since in scanning the bit stream from left to right the decoding algorithm would interpret the 5 bits as the 100-bit configuration character followed by a 01 bit configuration character.

The prefix property of the Huffman code ensures that the code is uniquely decipherable. To understand the importance of this property and how it relates to the construction of a Huffman code, consider a four-symbol alphabet X_1, X_2, X_3, X_4, which is to be encoded as follows:

$$X_1 = 0, \quad X_2 = 01, \quad X_3 = 11, \quad X_4 = 00.$$

If the received message is 0001, this bit sequence could represent $X_1X_1X_2$ or X_4X_2. Thus, the code is not uniquely decodable.

Using a decision tree diagram we can determine visually why the preceding encoded four-symbol alphabet is not instantly decodable. To construct a decision tree, let us start at an initial state and draw a branch to a node represented by the symbol X_1 and label the binary value assigned to the node on the branch. Next, since X_2 was assigned the value 01, let us draw a branch from the X_1 node to a node labeled X_2 and assign the value 1 to the branch between nodes X_1 and X_2. Similarly, we can route a branch from node X_1 to a node representing X_4 and assign that branch the binary value 0.

Since X_3 was assigned the value 11, we can draw a branch from the initial state to an intermediate node and another branch from the intermediate node to a node labeled X_3, assigning the binary value of 1 to each branch. Figure 4.1 illustrates the decision tree which corresponds to the assignment of values to the four symbol alphabet.

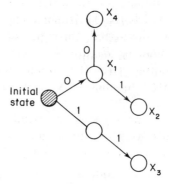

Figure 4.1 Decision tree to form the four-symbol alphabet $\mathbf{X_1}$, $\mathbf{X_2}$, $\mathbf{X_3}$, $\mathbf{X_4}$; where $X_1=0$, $X_2=01$, $X_3=11$, and $X_4=00$

In examining the decision tree illustrated in Figure 4.1, note that the route to node X_3 is through an intermediate node that is not necessary as there is no route from the intermediate node to another node other than node X_3. Also note that node X_1 is actually an intermediate node and the path to X_1 does not represent a unique bit combination. Now suppose in forming a decision tree we add the rules that each branch either ends with a node as a terminal state or functions as a decision point which allows a route to a terminal state. Following those rules, let us redraw the decision tree and assign binary values to each branch to develop codes for a four-symbol alphabet. Figure 4.2 illustrates the revised decision tree.

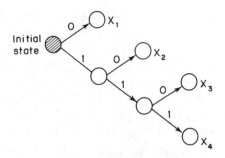

Figure 4.2 Revised decision tree. In constructing this tree each binary digit causes a branch, either to a terminal state or to a decision point

Note that X_1 still has the binary value of 0, but X_2 through X_4 are now assigned the values 10, 110, and 111, respectively. Also note that each bit is only examined once and each path represents a unique bit combination.

The rules we have just developed for constructing a decision tree that results in a code which is instantly decodable are the foundation from which the Huffman code is constructed. The Huffman code can be developed through the utilization of a tree structure as illustrated in Figure 4.3. Here, the symbols are first listed in descending order of frequency of occurrence. The groups with the smallest frequencies (X_3 and X_4) are combined into a node with a joint probability of occurrence of 0.25. Next, that node is merged with the next lowest probability of occurrence symbol or pair of symbols. In this illustration, the pair X_3X_4 is merged with X_2 to produce a node whose joint probability is 0.4375. Finally, the node

Character	Probability						Code
						0	0
X_1	.5625						0
				0			
X_2	.1875					⎯1.0	10
		0					
X_3	.1875				.4375	1	110
			.25	1			
X_4	.0625						111
		1					

Figure 4.3 Huffman code development employing a tree structure. Huffman codes can be developed by employing a tree structure. The Huffman code resulting from this construction method is derived by tracing from the 1.0 probability node to each source character (symbol), noting 1s and 0s encountered

representing the probabilities of occurrence of X_2, X_3 and X_4 is merged with X_1, resulting in a node whose probability of occurrence is unity. This master node represents the probability of occurrence of all four characters in the character set. By asssigning binary 0s and 1s to every segment emanating from each node, one can derive the Huffman code for each character. The code is obtained by tracing from the 1.0 probability node to each character symbol, noting the 1s and 0s encountered. If you construct the decision tree which represents the codes assigned to the characters X_1 through X_4 the tree is exactly the same as previously illustrated in Figure 4.2. Since each binary digit causes a branch to a terminal state or to a decision point, it represents a code that is uniquely decodable.

The average number of bits per symbol can be calculated by multiplying the Huffman code lengths by their probability of occurrence. Thus, the code uses:

$$1*0.5625 + 2*0.1875 + 3*0.1875 + 3*0.0625$$

or 1.63 bits per symbol. Note that the Huffman code result of 1.63 bits per symbol closely approaches the entropy of 1.62 bits per symbol (Dishon, 1977; Moilanen, 1978).

As previously explained, a key property of the Huffman code is that it can be instantaneously decoded as the coded bits in the compressed data stream are encountered. An example of the instantaneous decoding property is illustrated in Figure 4.4. Here, the compressed data stream can be decoded immediately by reading left to right without waiting for the end of the block of data to occur.

The substitution of a number of bits representing a particular data character or group of characters is a fairly simple process when the number of substitutions is limited. As the number of substitutions increases, the complexity of the substitution process increases. In

Encoded message	0	10	0	111	10	110	0
Decoded message	X_1	X_2	X_1	X_4	X_2	X_3	X_1

Figure 4.4 Instantaneous decoding property. One of the key properties of the Huffman technique is the fact that encoded data can be instantly decoded

Figures 4.5 and 4.6, the development of a Huffman code for the
English alphabet is illustrated. The tree structure used to develop
the code shown in Figure 4.5 is produced as follows:

A. The character set is arranged in a column on the left in order of
   decreasing frequency of occurrence with the frequency placed in
   a column next to each character.

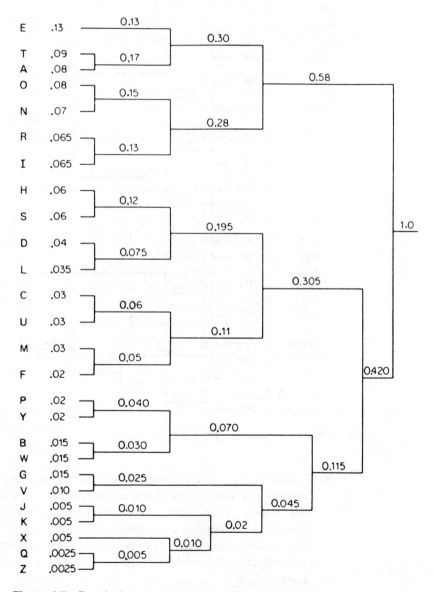

Figure 4.5 Developing a tree structure for the alphabet

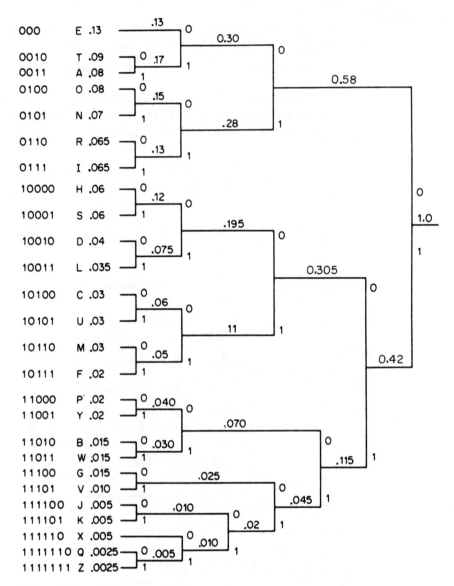

Figure 4.6 Assigning the Huffman code

B. Commencing at the bottom of the table, lines are drawn horizontally from each character frequency. The lines with the two lowest frequencies of occurrence are merged and their associated frequencies are added to obtain a composite frequency. This composite frequency is entered on a single new line and reflects the combined frequency of the previously paired characters.

C. The process of combining the two lowest frequency lines into a single line containing combined frequencies is continued until all the lines have been merged.

After the tree has been developed, the Huffman code for each character can be assigned by placing a 0 bit to one side of each nodal point and a 1 bit to the other path emanating from that point towards the left-hand symbol. The assignment of 0 and 1 bits is arbitrary. However, the assignment must be consistent. Thus, if a binary 0 is selected to represent one upper route then it must be used for all upper routes. The appropriate bit sequence assigned to each data character is then determined by tracing the route from the master nodal point where the probability of all character frequencies of occurrence is unity back to the starting node for the appropriate character, noting the bits assigned to the path. The assignment of bits to the paths and the resulting Huffman coded values for the English alphabet are illustrated in Figure 4.6.

The number of bits required to encode a letter using the Huffman technique can be determined from the following formula:

$$b = f(-\log_2 P)$$

where:

P = probability of occurrence of the letter

$f(x)$ = the closest integer greater than or equal to x.

Since the probability of E is 0.13 and $-\log_2 0.13$ is 2.94, then the integer greater than or equal to 2.94 is 3. Thus, 3 bits are required to encode the letter E (Peterson, Bitner and Howard, 1978).

Code construction considerations

When several characters have the same frequency of occurrence, you may be able to develop two or more codes to represent the Huffman code for a character set. This situation, which commonly occurs, provides us with an interesting problem—deciding which code to use. To illustrate how this problem can arise, as well as to provide a foundation for discussing the solution to the problem, let us first consider a five-character character set whose frequencies of occurrence are as indicated in Table 4.3.

Table 4.3 Sample five-character character set

Character	Frequency of occurrence
X_1	0.4
X_2	0.2
X_3	0.2
X_4	0.1
X_5	0.1

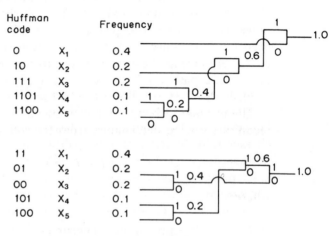

Figure 4.7 Developing different trees and codes

Figure 4.7 illustrates the development of two tree structures, each resulting in the construction of different Huffman codes for the characters listed in Table 4.3. In the top portion of Figure 4.7 note that X_4 and X_5 are combined exactly in the same manner as X_4 and X_5 are combined in the second tree structure illustrated in the lower portion of Figure 4.7. However, after X_4 and X_5 are combined, the resulting frequency of occurrence of the two characters is 0.2 and you have several options available in developing the Huffman code.

In the top portion of Figure 4.7, X_3 was next combined with the merger of X_3 and X_4 as X_3 had a probability of occurrence of 0.2, which exactly equalled the combined probability of occurrence of X_4 and X_5. In the lower portion of Figure 4.7, X_2 and X_3 were merged, resulting in a combined probability of occurrence of 0.4. Since we must merge lower frequencies of occurrences with higher frequencies of occurrence to form a Huffman code we combined the results of merging X_4 and X_5 with X_1 to produce a combined frequency of occurrence of 0.6. This was followed by merging the results of combining X_2 and X_3 with the results obtained from merging X_1 with the combination of X_4 and X_5.

In examining the resulting Huffman code at the top of Figure 4.7, how does it compare to the code at the bottom of that illustration? One way we can compare codes is by computing their average bit length, so let's do so. For the Huffman code at the top of Figure 4.7, its average length in bits is:

$$L = 0.4*1 + 0.2*2 + 0.2*3 + 0.1*4 + 0.1*4 = 2.2 \text{ bits.}$$

For the Huffman code at the bottom of Figure 4.7, its average length in bits is:

$$L = 0.4*2 + 0.2*2 + 0.2*2 + 0.1*3 + 0.1*3 = 2.2 \text{ bits.}$$

Note that both codes have the same efficiency expressed in terms of the average number of bits required to encode a character. However, the two codes do not have the same set of lengths for the characters in the character set. Although over a long period of time the use of either code should produce the same result in terms of efficiency expresssed as the sum of encoded bits, in actuality, a more appropriate choice is to select the code whose average length varies the least. To illustrate this, let us compute the variance for each Huffman code.

The variance of the Huffman code at the top of Figure 4.7 is:

$$Var(1) = 0.4(1-2.2)^2 + 0.2(2-2.2)^2 + 0.2(3-2.2)^2 + 0.1(4-2.2)^2$$
$$+ 0.1(4-2.2)^2 = 1.36.$$

The variance of the Huffman code developed in the lower portion of Figure 4.7 is:

$$Var(2) = 0.4(2-2.2)^2 + 0.2(2-2.2)^2 + 0.2(2-2.22)^2 + 0.1(3-2.2)^2$$
$$+ 0.1(3-2.2)^2 = 1.6.$$

As indicated, the second Huffman code has less variability and should be selected.

Returning to Figure 4.7, if we examine the construction of each tree, we note that the combined X_4 and X_5 frequencies of occurrence in the lower portion of the illustration were directly moved to the top. In comparison, the combination of X_4 and X_5 frequencies of occurrence in the upper portion of Figure 4.7 were gradually merged with other states to reach the top. When you move a combined state as high as possible it reduces the variability of the resulting Huffman code and can be considered as the key to construction of a minimum variability Huffman code.

Information requirements

To develop a Huffman code whose average code length will approach its entropy requires the frequency distribution of the characters or symbols to be encoded to be known in advance. Since the frequency distribution of a data stream is proportional to the end use of the stream, this factor can result in a preselected frequency distribution used to develop a Huffman code resulting in a code far from optimum during certain data transmission sequences. As an example, the frequency distribution of English text, such as that resulting from a data file used for computerized typesetting, may be quite different from the data file containing the results of a FORTRAN program compilation. In the first instance, the distribution of characters should follow the distribution of normal English, with E the most frequently occurring character while Z is one of the least frequent characters. For the FORTRAN compilation, special characters such as parenthesis, + for addition, − for substraction, * for multiplication and / for division have a high degree of occurrence not normally encountered in English text.

To compensate for frequency distribution differences, several encoding schemes can be considered. First, the analysis of mixed data files can be conducted employing the computer program listed in Appendix A (p. 249). This will enable one to ascertain the appropriate relationship between the frequency of occurrence of characters of different types of data.

A second method to consider is an adaptive Huffman encoding technique. Such a technique might first require a frequency analysis of a large block of data which would then be encoded based upon that distribution. Prior to the transmission of the encoded data, a table of the symbols and Huffman codes developed for each symbol must be transmitted to enable the encoded data to be successfully decoded. With a little imagination, one can visualize that frequently changing data streams would result in numerous tables as well as encoded data being transmitted. These tables can be considered as overhead, resulting in the compression frequency decreasing as the number of data-stream frequency distributions change per unit time.

Another problem encountered with some adaptive Huffman coding techniques is determining the size of the data stream to sample and the sample intervals. The larger the sample, the greater the processing requirement becomes. If the data is to be transmitted, a buffer area is required to place the sample in while the frequency analysis is conducted. Concerning the sample interval, if three FORTRAN jobs are followed by an English text job, all of equal size, T, sampling at T, $T + 2$ and $T + 4$ would result in the English text job being excluded from the sample. Since a remote batch terminal operator submits jobs and pulls system output, he or she knows ahead of time the type of job that will be transmitted to or received from the computer. For this type of operating situation, predefined frequency distributions can be selected by the operator and conveyed to the opposite end of the transmission link by the transmission of a special code.

To eliminate the previously described problems resulting from the generation of frequency tables, one can construct a truly adaptive or self-adapting Huffman encoding technique. This technique builds frequency tables at both ends of a transmission link as data transmission occurs and adaptively adjusts those tables during transmission. The reader is referred to Section 4.5 which discusses this technique in detail.

A third method of compensating for frequency distribution differences is by the use of a plain text code, which is used to indicate that the character following it should be reproduced exactly as received. This permits characters that rarely occur in the source data to be excluded from the encoding process and results in the development of one type of modified Huffman code. Here, one could group all characters of low frequency of occurrence into one probability of occurrence and assign a Huffman code to represent that summed probability. This would be the plain text code and would indicate that the next eight bits represent an actual non-encoded data character. Without the use of a plain text code, large strings of, say, 20 or more bits might result in the representation of low frequency of occurrence characters. If the plain text code were four bits in length, then a maximum of 12 bits would be required to represent any low frequency of occurrence character. The pre-emption of a 4-bit code to signify that the next eight bits are the plain text representation of an 8-bit character means that some relatively high frequency of occurrence character which would have had a 4-bit code as its Huffman representation will be represented by some longer code. Thus, although there will be no very long codes present, the mean number of bits per character will increase when a plain text code is employed.

4.3 MODIFIED HUFFMAN CODES

The representation of characters and symbols by an appropriate Huffman code is excellent in theory if one desires to have the average number of bits per symbol approach entropy. In practice, however, a number of difficulties can arise when Huffman coding is applied to certain applications, most particularly in the area of facsimile transmission.

When applying Huffman coding to facsimile transmission, each facsimile line can be viewed as consisting of a series of black or white 'runs', each run consisting of a series of similar picture elements. If the type of the first run is known, then the type of all successive runs will be known, as black and white runs must alternate. The probability of occurrence of each run of a given length of pels can be calculated and short code words can be used to represent runs that have a high frequency of occurrence while longer code words can be used to represent runs that have a low probability of occurrence. In a way similar to the changing of data processing jobs, statistics for the run-length probabilities associated with line scans change on a line-to-line and document-to-document basis. Thus, an optimum or near optimum code for a particular line or document may be far from optimum for a different line or document. A second major problem is the fact that the creation of the Huffman code on a real-time basis requires a large degree of processing power, normally in excess of the capabilities of facsimile machines where the cost of the scanner, transmitter/receiver, central logic and power supply results in a machine cost under a thousand dollars to remain competitive. To reduce some real-time processing requirements, a table look-up approach can be employed. Since CCITT standards require 1728 pels per line, the use of a table look-up technique would require storage for 1728 variable-length locations for each facsimile machine, each location containing a binary code word corresponding to a particular run length. The implementation problems associated with applying the full Huffman coding technique to facsimile applications resulted in the development of one modified Huffman coding scheme more suitable to the hardware cost constraints of the competitive facsimile marketplace.

In the development of a modified Huffman coding scheme for facsimile applications, a change was made which, while only rarely permitting the average symbol length to approach entropy, does permit significant compression while minimizing hardware and processing requirements. Here, the probability of occurrences of different run lengths of picture elements (pels) was calculated for all lengths of white and black runs based upon statistics obtained from the analysis of a group of 11 documents recommended by the CCITT as being typical. To reduce table look-up storage requirements, the Huffman code set was truncated by the creation of a base 64 representation of each run length and the utilization of two code tables to reduce the overall table size in comparison with the table size that would be required if only one table were used (McCullough, 1977).

Based upon the run-length probabilities of 11 typical documents, code tables were developed for run lengths ranging from 1 to 63 pels. Since the probability of occurrence of white runs differs from the frequency of occurrence of black runs, a table must be developed for both runs. This dual table set is listed in Table 4.4 for run lengths ranging from 0 to 63 pels. The codes in this table set

Table 4.4 Least significant digit codes for the modified Huffman process

White run length	Code word	Base 64 representation	Black run length	Code word
0	00110101	0	0	0000110111
1	000111	1	1	010
2	0111	2	2	11
3	1000	3	3	10
4	1011	4	4	011
5	1100	5	5	0011
6	1110	6	6	0010
7	1111	7	7	00011
8	10011	8	8	000101
9	10100	9	9	000100
10	00111	a	10	0000100
11	01000	b	11	0000101
12	001000	c	12	0000111
13	000011	d	13	00000100
14	10100	e	14	00000111
15	110101	f	15	000011000
16	101010	g	16	0000010111
17	101011	h	17	0000011000
18	0100111	i	18	0000001000
19	0001100	j	19	00001100111
20	0001000	k	20	00001101000
21	0010111	l	21	00001101100
22	0000011	m	22	00000110111
23	0000100	n	23	00000101000
24	0101000	o	24	00000010111

Table 4.4 (*continued*)

White run length	Code word	Base 64 representation	Black run length	Code word
25	0101011	p	25	00000011000
26	0010011	q	26	000011001010
27	0100100	r	27	000011001011
28	0011000	s	28	000011001100
29	00000010	t	29	000011001101
30	00000011	u	30	000001101000
31	00011010	v	31	000001101001
32	00011011	w	32	000001101010
33	00010010	x	33	000001101011
34	00010011	y	34	000011010010
35	00010100	z	35	000011010011
36	00010101	A	36	000011010100
37	00010110	B	37	000011010101
38	00010111	C	38	000011010110
39	00101000	D	39	000011010111
40	00101001	E	40	000001101100
41	00101010	F	41	000001101101
42	00101011	G	42	000011011010
43	00101100	H	43	000011011011
44	00101101	I	44	000001010100
45	00000100	J	45	000001010101
46	00000101	K	46	000001010110
47	00001010	L	47	000001010111
48	00001011	M	48	000001100100
49	01010010	N	49	000001100101
50	01010011	O	50	000001010010
51	01010100	P	51	000001010011
52	01010101	Q	52	000000100100
53	00100100	R	53	000000110111
54	00100101	S	54	000000111000
55	01011000	T	55	000000100111
56	01011001	U	56	000000101000
57	01011010	V	57	000000101100
58	01011011	W	58	000001011001
59	01001010	X	59	000000101011
60	01001011	Y	60	000000101100
61	00110010	Z	61	000001011010
62	00110011	*	62	000001100110
63	00110100	#	63	000001100111

represent the least significant digit (LSD) of the code word and are often referred to as the termination code. In order to permit the

Table 4.5 Most significant digit codes for the modified Huffman process

White run length	Code word	Base 64 representation	Black run length	Code word
64	11011	1	64	0000001111
128	10010	2	128	000011001000
192	010111	3	192	000011001001
256	0110111	4	256	000001011011
320	00110110	5	320	000000110011
384	00110111	6	384	000000110011
448	01100100	7	448	000000110101
512	01100101	8	512	0000001101100
576	01101000	9	576	0000001101101
640	01100111	a	640	0000001001010
704	011001100	b	704	0000001001011
768	011001101	c	768	0000001001100
832	011010010	d	832	0000001001101
836	011010011	e	836	0000001110010
960	011010100	f	960	0000001110011
1024	011010101	g	1024	0000001110100
1088	011010110	h	1088	0000001110101
1152	011010111	i	1152	0000001110110
1216	011011000	j	1216	0000001110111
1280	011011001	k	1280	0000001010010
1344	011011010	l	1344	0000001010011
1408	011011011	m	1408	0000001010100
1472	010011000	n	1472	0000001010101
1536	010011001	o	1536	0000001011010
1600	010011010	p	1600	0000001011011
1664	011000	q	1664	0000001100100
1728	010011011	r	1728	0000001100101
EOL	0000000000		EOL	00000000001

encoding of runs in excess of 63 pels, a second set of code tables must be employed to handle runs ranging in size from 64 pels to the maximum line scan length of 1728 pels. These codes are listed in Table 4.5. These represent the most significant digit of the code word and are known as the master code.

When a run of 63 pels or less is encountered, the appropriate type of LSD code set is accessed to obtain a single base 64 code word. To encode a run of 64 pels or more, two base 64 code words must be used. First, the most significant digit code word is obtained from the MSD code table such that $N*64$, $1 \leq N \leq 27$, does not exceed the run length. Here N cannot exceed 27 as when $N = 27$ the maximum of 1728 pels per line occurs. Next, the difference between the run length and $N*64$ is obtained and the least significant digit is accessed from the appropriate LSD code table. Figure 4.8 shows an example of the table look-up operations for a sample sequence of black and white runs of various pel sizes. In the upper portion of this illustration, the relationship between a series of original video data and its representation in the modified Huffman code is tabulated. Based upon the preceding you can consider the application of the described modified Huffman coding technique as a one-dimensional encoding scheme. This encoding scheme is applied on a line by line basis to each scanned line and represents the compressed horizontal correlation of pels within the same line.

To employ the modified Huffman coding scheme successfully, some rules must be developed and followed to alleviate a number of deficiencies inherent from employing a statistical encoding technique. In such techniques, code words do not contain any inherent positional information which is necessary for synchronization. This can be compensated for by making it a rule that the first run of each line must be a white run, even if it results in a run length of zero. Thereafter, runs must alternate between black runs and white runs. To denote the beginning and end of each scan line, a unique line delineation code, sometimes called an end-of-line code (EOL), can be employed. Once each line is encoded, fill bits of 0s may be

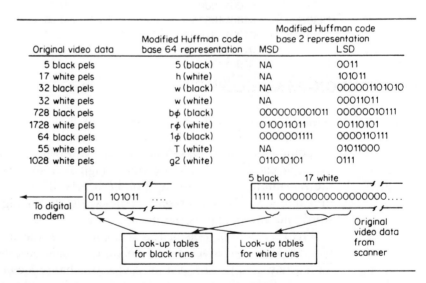

Original video data	Modified Huffman code base 64 representation	Modified Huffman code base 2 representation MSD	LSD
5 black pels	5 (black)	NA	0011
17 white pels	h (white)	NA	101011
32 black pels	w (black)	NA	000001101010
32 white pels	w (white)	NA	00011011
728 biack pels	bφ (black)	0000001001011	00000010111
1728 white pels	rφ (white)	010011011	00110101
64 black pels	1φ (black)	0000001111	0000110111
55 white pels	T (white)	NA	01011000
1028 white pels	g2 (white)	011010101	0111

Figure 4.8 Encoding using the modified Huffman code. By a sequence of tabular references for black and white runs the modified Huffman code is constructed

employed as pad bits prior to transmitting the EOL for timing purposes. The end result of the incorporation of theses rules permits a line format to be defined as shown in Figure 4.9. Through the incorporation of the modified Huffman coding technique, the transmission time of a typical business document has been reduced to under 20s at a transmission rate of 9600 bps.

The significance of the reduction becomes apparent when one considers that the resolution of 1780 pels per line and 96 horizontal lines per inch results in a total of 1410 048 pels for an $8\frac{1}{2} \times 11$ document. Without compression, a transmission time of approximately 2.5 minutes would be required for the data without considering the transmission of the end-of-line codes.

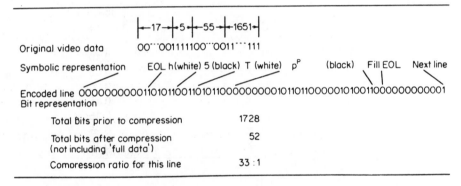

Figure 4.9 Rules define line format. To denote the beginning and end of each scan line an end-of-line code (EOL) is employed

4.4 SHANNON–FANO CODING

Similar to Huffman coding, Shannon–Fano coding results in a variable length code that is instantly decodable. Just like the development of a Huffman code, prior to developing the Shannon–Fano code for each character in your character set you must determine the probability of occurrence of each character. Then, you will arrange your character set in descending order based upon the probability of occurrence of each character.

Once your character set is arranged in descending order of its probability of occurrence, the set must be divided into two equal or almost equal subsets based upon the probability of occurrence of the characters in each subset. The first digit in one subset which represents a group of frequencies of occurrence is assigned a binary 0 value while a binary 1 is assigned as the first digit in the second subset. Here the second subset represents all remaining frequencies of occurrence. This process of forming subsets is repeated until the character set is completely subdivided. Then, a suffix bit is added to each character in a two-character subset as required to distinguish one character's binary composition from the other character in the subset.

To obtain an understanding of the Shannon–Fano coding procedure, let us assume our character set contains seven characters whose probabilities of occurrence are indicated in Table 4.6.

Table 4.6 Character set probability of occurrence

Character	Probability of occurrence
X_1	0.10
X_2	0.05
X_3	0.20
X_4	0.15
X_5	0.15
X_6	0.25
X_7	0.10

By arranging the characters in the character set in descending order based upon their probability of occurrence, we can begin to form our subsets. In our subset construction process, we will group the characters into each subset so that the probability of occurrence of the characters in each subset is equal or as nearly equal as possible. Then we will assign binary 1s to one subset and binary 0s to the other subset and continue to repeat the process until all possible subsets are constructed. Figure 4.10 illustrates this process.

Character	Probability	Code		
X_6	0.25	1		
X_3	0.20	1		
X_4	0.15	0	1	
X_5	0.15	0	1	
X_1	0.10	0	0	1
X_7	0.10	0	0	0
X_2	0.05	0	0	0

Figure 4.10 Initial Shannon–Fano coding process

Note that after the initial coding process is completed, the subsets represented by the character pairs X_6, X_3 and X_4, X_5 are not unique. Thus, a binary 1 and 0 must be added to the pairs in each subset. Doing so results in the completion of the variable-length coding process in which each character is represented by a unique bit combination that is instantaneously decodable. The completed code for each character in our character set is illustrated in Figure 4.11.

Character	Probability	Code			
X_6	0.25	1	1		
X_3	0.20	1	0		
X_4	0.15	0	1	1	
X_5	0.15	0	1	0	
X_1	0.10	0	0	1	
X_7	0.10	0	0	0	1
X_2	0.05	0	0	0	0

Figure 4.11 Completed Shannon–Fano coding process

Code ambiguity

One of the problems associated with the development of a Shannon–Fano code is the fact that the procedure to develop the code can be ambiguous. To illustrate this problem, consider the Shannon–Fano coding process illustrated in Figure 4.12. Note that the probability of occurrence of the characters in the eight-character character set is such that it is not clear whether the first division to

Character	Probability	Code development						Code
X_1	0.35	1	1					11
X_2	0.30	1	0					10
X_3	0.15	0	1					01
X_4	0.08	0	0	1				001
X_5	0.05	0	0	0	1			0001
X_6	0.03	0	0	0	0	1		00001
X_7	0.02	0	0	0	0	0	1	000001
X_8	0.02	0	0	0	0	0	0	000000

Figure 4.12 Ambiguous code development

create subsets should occur between X_1 and X_2 or between X_2 and X_3.

By making the first subdivision between X_2 and X_3 the resulting Shannon–Fano code has an average bit length of 2.43, computed as follows:

$$L = 0.35*2 + 0.3*2 + 0.08*3 + 0.05*4$$

$$+ 0.03*5 + 0.02*6 + 0.02*6 = 2.43.$$

In this particular example, making the first subdivision between X_2 and X_3 results in an optimum code whose average bit length is the same as that obtained by the Huffman code development process. If a different subdivision occurs, the Shannon–Fano code's average bit length will exceed that obtained by the Huffman code development process.

Efficiency comparison

To compare the efficiency of the Shannon–Fano coding process to the previously covered Huffman coding technique, let us develop the Huffman code for the character set whose probability of occurrence was previously listed in Table 4.6. Figure 4.13 (top) illustrates the construction of a Huffman code for the seven-character character set listed in Table 4.6. The lower portion of that illustration shows the assignment of binary 1s and 0s to each path member and the resulting Huffman code for each character when the binary digits in each path are recorded beginning at the unity or apex point in the coding tree.

Table 4.7 compares the codes generated by the Shannon–Fano coding procedure to the Huffman coding procedure for the seven-character character set used for each coding example. The average code length generated by each coding procedure can be computed by using the formula:

$$L = \sum_{i=1}^{7} L_i P_i$$

For the Shannon–Fano code, the average code length is:

$$L = 2*0.25 + 2*0.20 + 3*0.15 + 3*0.15$$

$$+ 3*0.10 + 4*0.10 + 4*0.05 = 2.7 \text{ bits.}$$

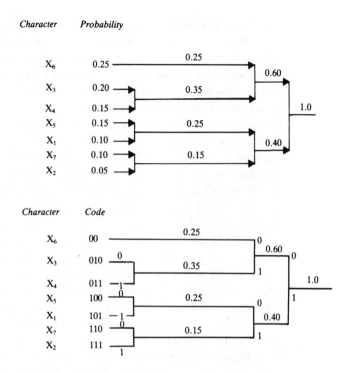

Figure 4.13 Huffman code construction

Table 4.7 Coding comparison

Character	Probability	Shannon–Fano code	Huffman code
X_6	0.25	11	00
X_3	0.20	10	010
X_4	0.15	011	011
X_5	0.15	010	100
X_1	0.10	001	101
X_7	0.10	0001	110
X_2	0.05	0000	111

For the Huffman code developed in Figure 4.13, the average code length is:

$$L = 2*0.25 + 3*0.75 = 2.75 \text{ bits.}$$

Although the Shannon–Fano code appears more efficient since its average code length is less than that of the Huffman code, in actuality, it cannot be more efficient. This is because the Huffman code will result in an optimum code when the code construction is efficient, which was purposely not the case in the construction illustrated in Figure 4.13. In that illustration the author purposely did not move groups of frequencies of occurrences as high as possible in an expedient manner. This was done as, upon occasion, it is easy to construct a Huffman code that does not represent an optimum code, and the creation of a Shannon–Fano code can be used as a method for verifying whether or not the Huffman code construction resulted in an optimum code. This is accomplished by comparing the average bit length of the Shannon–Fano code to the average bit length of the Huffman code. If the average bit length of the Huffman code exceeds the average bit length of the Shannon–Fano code, this fact should be used as an indicator that you should attempt to reconstruct your Huffman code. Since the Shannon–Fano average code length was less than the Huffman average code length, let us apply the insight just gained and reconstruct the Huffman code. This reconstruction is illustrated in Figure 4.14.

Note that in reconstructing the Huffman code, more combining steps occur for groupings of lower frequency of occurrence characters than higher frequency of occurrence characters in comparison to the original code construction illustrated in Figure 4.13. Although this results in an additional code bit being required to represent characters X_7 and X_2, it also results in one less bit required to represent X_3. Since the probability of X_3 exceeds the combined probability of X_7 and X_2, the reconstructed code will have a lower average bit length. To verify this fact, let us compute the average bit length for the Huffman code developed in Figure 4.14. Doing so, we obtain:

$$L = 2*0.25 + 2*0.2 + 3*0.15 + 3*0.15 + 3*0.10 + 4*0.10$$
$$+ 4*0.05 = 2.7 \text{ bits.}$$

Note that the average code length has been reduced by 0.05 bits and is now exactly equal to the average bit length of the Shannon–Fano code.

The previous illustrations were based upon one group of assigned probabilities of occurence to a seven-character character set. To illustrate how efficiencies between the two codes can change, let us assume that the probabilities of occurrence of the characters in the character set are now represented by the data listed in Table 4.8.

The top portion of Figure 4.15 illustrates the Shannon–Fano coding process while the lower portion of that illustration shows the Huffman coding process. Note that based upon the revisions in the

Character Probability

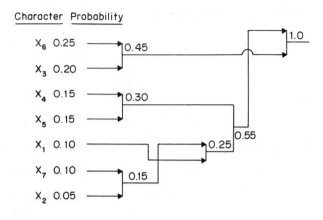

Character Code

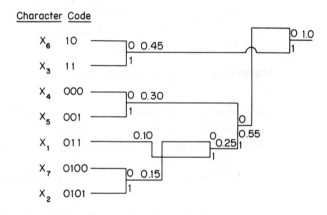

Figure 4.14 Huffman code reconstruction

Table 4.8 Revised character set

Character	Probability of occurrence
X_1	0.0625
X_2	0.0625
X_3	0.1250
X_4	0.1250
X_5	0.0625
X_6	0.5000
X_7	0.0625

A. Shannon–Fano coding

X$_6$	0.50	1						
X$_3$	·0.125	0	1	1				
X$_4$	0.125	0	1	0				
X$_5$	0.0625	0	0		1	1		
X$_1$	0.0625	0	0		1	0		
X$_7$	0.0625	0	0		0	1		
X$_2$	0.0625	0	0		0	0		

B. Huffman coding

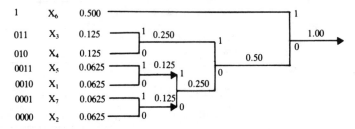

Figure 4.15 Recoding the new character set

probability of occurrence of the characters in the character set, the average code length for each coding technique is the same. That is, the average code length for the Shannon–Fano coding process is:

$$L = 1*0.5 + 3*0.125 + 3*0.125 + 4*(4*0.0625) = 2.25 \text{ bits}$$

which is exactly the same code length obtained from the Huffman coding process.

Now let us assume that the probability of occurrence of each character in the character set is again altered. Suppose the new probabilities of occurrence are as indicated in Table 4.9.

Table 4.9 New character set probabilities

Character	Probability of occurrence
X$_1$	0.10
X$_2$	0.10
X$_3$	0.10
X$_4$	0.10
X$_5$	0.40
X$_6$	0.10
X$_7$	0.10

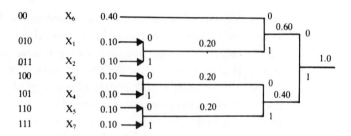

A. Shannon–Fano coding

X_6	0.40	1	1		
X_1	0.10	1	0		
X_2	0.10	0	1	1	
X_3	0.10	0	1	0	
X_4	0.10	0	0	1	
X_5	0.10	0	0	0	1
X_7	0.10	0	0	0	0

B. Huffman coding

Figure 4.16 Recoding the revised character set

The top portion of Figure 4.16 illustrates the Shannon–Fano coding process for the revised character set while the lower portion shows the Huffman coding process.

Now let us compute the average code length for each coding process. For the Shannon–Fano code, its average code length is:

$$L = 2*0.4 + 2*0.1 + 3*0.1 + 3*0.1$$
$$+ 3*0.1 + 4*0.1 + 4*0.1 = 2.7 \text{ bits.}$$

For the Huffman code, its average code length is:

$$L = 2*0.4 + 3*0.6 = 2.6 \text{ bits.}$$

Thus, in this instance the Huffman code results in a more efficient bit representation of the character set than the Shannon–Fano coding method.

In general, as the probabilities of each character in the character set approach probabilities that are negative powers of 2 both codes will have their average code length approach entropy. That is, if all the probabilities of the characters in the character set were negative powers of 2 the average code length would equal entropy and the efficiency of each code would be 100 per cent. If the probabilities of occurrence of the elements in a set have a large variance, the Shannon–Fano code will be more efficient while the Huffman code becomes more efficient as in the variance in probabilities decreases between elements in the set.

4.5 COMMA CODES

As previously discussed in this chapter, both Shannon–Fano and Huffman encoding methods have several advantages associated with their use. First, they produce codes whose average number of bits either represents or approaches an optimum code. Secondly, both encoding methods result in the absence of short code words that are prefixes of longer code words. This means that each code is instantaneously decodable. However, what can we say about the processing steps required to decode an instantaneously decodable code and the effect of a lost bit upon a received sequence of bits?

Concerning the decoding process, consider the Huffman code developed in Figure 4.16. The processing steps required to decode a received bit sequence into their appropriate character representations would require a significant series of bit comparisons as illustrated in Figure 4.17. Thus, we can state that Shannon–Fano and Huffman codes are processing-intensive codes.

Concerning a lost bit or sequence of lost bits, this occurrence would result in a loss of synchronization between the bit stream to be decoded and the decoding process. This situation would obviously result in decoding errors. Due to this, statistical encoding should always be encapsulated within an error detection and correction mechanism.

To alleviate a substantial amount of processing associated with statistical encoding as well as the effect of the loss of one or more bits, you can consider the use of a comma code. This code obtains its name from the fact that it contains a terminating symbol or comma at the end of each code word.

Figure 4.18 contains a comma code developed for the seven-symbol character set for which we previously constructed a Huffman code in Figure 4.16. In constructing the comma code we used a '1' bit as the comma or terminating symbol. When that bit is encountered, it informs the receiver that a new character code will begin, providing a method of synchronization within the code.

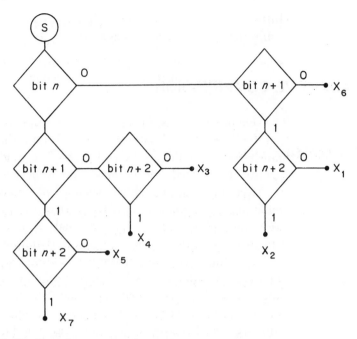

Figure 4.17 Decoding process for the Huffman code developed in Figure 4.16

X_6	.4	1
X_1	.1	01
X_2	.1	001
X_3	.1	0001
X_4	.1	00001
X_5	.1	000001
X_7	.1	0000001

Figure 4.18 Comma code for seven-symbol character set

In examining the comma code listed in Figure 4.18, let us compute its average bit length. Doing so, we obtain:

$$L = 0.4*1 + 0.1*2 + 0.1*3 + 0.1*4 + 0.1*5 + 0.1*6$$
$$+ 0.1*7 = 3.1 \text{ bits.}$$

Here the average number of bits per character has increased from 2.6 when the Huffman code was used to 3.1 bits for a comma code. This illustrates the key trade-off between a comma code and

Huffman and Shannon–Fano coding—synchronization and processing requirements are trade-offs against efficiency.

4.6 ADAPTIVE COMPRESSION

The examples of compression techniques previously covered in Chapter 3 and this chapter were based upon the assumption of prior knowledge of the data to be compressed. Using this prior knowledge permits us to predefine compression indicating characters and the character sequences which can then be substituted for strings of data containing predefined redundancy. In addition, we can construct a fixed compression table that will enable the statistical encoding of data to occur based upon the expected frequency of occurrence of the data. Run-length and diatomic encoding are examples of character sequence and character substitution where some prior knowledge or expectation of the composition of the data resulted in the definition of a single character or short sequence of characters to replace longer sequences of characters. Huffman and modified Huffman encoding are examples of data-compression techniques that would employ a fixed compression table whose construction is based upon prior knowledge or assumed knowledge of the data.

The fixed compression table

Figure 4.19 illustrates the general format of a fixed compression table. In actuality, this table can be two separate tables, with a relationship established between the elements in each table, or the table can consist of paired entries. Each character in the original data stream is compared to the entries in the 'data to compress' part of the compression table. When the character to be encoded matches an entry in the 'data to compress' portion of the table, the code that represents the character is extracted from the compression table.

data to compress	code
.	.
.	.
.	.
.	.

Figure 4.19 Fixed compression table format

Thus, the process required to replace each character with its statistical code is reduced to a table look-up operation.

To illustrate the utilization of a fixed compression table, let us assume that as a result of an analysis of a four-character character set $(X_1, X_2, X_3$ and $X_4)$ we have determined that the probability of occurrence of each character is 0.5625, 0.1875, 0.1875 and 0.0625 respectively. The Huffman code previously developed in Figure 4.3 for this character set results in the assignment of 0, 10, 110 and 111 to characters X_1 to X_4. Thus, based upon prior knowledge of the data we can develop the Huffman code for the character set which then enables us to construct the fixed compression table for this character set. This table is illustrated in Figure 4.20.

Data to compress	Resulting code
X_1	0
X_2	10
X_3	110
X_4	111

Figure 4.20   Resulting fixed compression table

The probability of occurrence of the characters in the character set must be determined prior to constructing a fixed compression table.

The use of a fixed compression table requires each character in the original data string to be compared to the 'data to compress' entries in the table. When a match occurs, the coded entry then replaces the character in the original data string. Thus, the sequence of characters

$$X_2 X_4 X_1 X_2 X_2$$

would be replaced by the Huffman code for each character, which would result in the binary sequence:

$$1011101010.$$

Efficiency

What happens to the efficiency of the predefined Huffman code when the probability of occurrence of the characters in the character set differs from the prior or expected knowledge of their frequency of occurrence? Since short codes are employed to represent frequently occurring characters while longer codes represent characters that occur less frequently, the predefined Huffman code's variance from entropy increases as the data varies from its prior or expected frequency of occurrence. One technique that can be used to maintain the efficiency of the resulting code obtained by compressing data statistically is the use of an adaptive or dynamic compression scheme, which is the main topic of this section.

Adaptive compression

When adaptive compression is performed, the data to be compressed is analysed in order to generate appropriate changes into a variable compression table.

Similar to the use of a fixed compression table, each character in the original data stream is first compared to the entries in the 'data to compress' portion of the compression table. When a match occurs, the corresponding entry in the 'resulting code' portion of the table is extracted and represents the statistically encoded character.

Where adaptive compression differs from fixed compression is in the employment of a count field in the compression table. This field is continuously updated and serves as a mechanism for the resequencing of the entries in the table. The updating of the field occurs after a character in the original data stream is matched with an entry in the 'data to compress' portion of the compression table and the 'resulting code' is extracted from the table. Then, a comparison of the entries in the count field occurs. Based upon the results of the comparison, the character and its count value may be repositioned in the compression table. This technique ensures that whenever the composition of the data changes, the compression table changes in tandem, resulting in a variable compression table that provides the most efficient statistical compression possible. Figure 4.21 illustrates how a variable compression table be resequenced based upon the composition of the data being transmitted.

Figure 4.21, part A, illustrates the initial composition of the variable compression table. Although this table was initially established based upon the frequency of occurrence of the characters in the character set, since the table is self-adjusting, we do not have to concern ourselves with the size of the sample used to initialize the entries into the table.

A. Initial table   Data transmitted

Data to compress	Count	Resulting Code
X₁	0	0
X₂	0	10
X₃	0	110
X₄	0	111

B. X₂ encountered   10

Data to compress	Count	Resulting code
X₂	1	0
X₁	0	10
X₃	0	110
X₄	0	111

C. X₄ encountered   111

Data to compress	Count	Resulting code
X₂	1	0
X₄	1	10
X₁	0	110
X₃	0	111

D. X₂ encountered   0

Data to compress	Count	Resulting code
X₂	2	0
X₄	1	10
X₁	0	110
X₃	0	111

Figure 4.21 The variable compression table

In Figure 4.21, part B, we assumed that the character X_2 was encountered. Since the binary code 10 is assigned to X_2 (Figure 4.21, part A), that bit string is transmitted, the count for X_2 is incremented by one and the variable compression table is resequenced. Similarly, at the receiver the bit sequence 10 is received, which is decompressed into the character X_2. The receiver then increments the count for X_2 in its compression table and its table is also resequenced.

In Figure 4.21, part C, we have assumed that the character X_4 is the next character encountered in the data to be compressed. Based upon the table then in use (Figure 4.21, part B), this character is encoded as the binary string 111. Next, the count of the frequency of occurrence of X_4 is incremented and the variable compression table is resequenced.

Figure 4.21, part D, assumes that the next character encountered in the original data string is X_2. Since the table illustrated in Figure 4.21, part C, was then in use, X_2 is encoded as the single bit 0. Then the count for X_2 is incremented by one; however, since X_2 was at the top of the compression table, the table is not resequenced.

As illustrated in Figure 4.21, adaptive compression dynamically changes the order of the entries in the compression table in tandem with the changes in the frequency of occurrence of the characters in the character set. Thus, this method of implementing a statistical compression technique should always be more efficient than the utilization of fixed compression.

Coded example

Figure 4.22 contains the ADAPTC.BAS program listing. This BASIC language program was developed to illustrate many of the programming concepts involved in adaptive compression. For simplicity of illustration only four characters—E,T,I and O—are considered to be in the character set suitable for adaptive compression. All other characters encountered in the data strings the program will operate upon will be passed 'as-is' to the output buffer.

In line 115, the program branches to the subroutine commencing at line 400 which initializes the character table P\$(I) to the characters E, T, I and O. Similar to the other coding examples presented in this chapter, line 130 obtains a line of up to 132 characters from a data file while line 140 obtains the length of the line.

The subroutine commencing at line 180 processes the records read from the data file. To illustrate the operation of adaptive compression, when the characters E, T, I and O are encountered they will be replaced by the characters, #, \$, % and &. For simplicity, the resulting Huffman table will be displayed on a line-by-line basis instead of on an individual character basis while the code changes

```
10 REM ADAPTC.BAS PROGRAM
20 DIM O$(132)
30 WIDTH 80:CLS
40 '***********MAIN ROUTINE***********************
50 '* THIS ROUTINE READS RECORDS FROM AN ASCII *
60 '* FILE INTO A STRING CALLED X$ WHICH IS    *
70 '* THEN PASSED TO SUBROUTINES FOR COMPRESSION
80 '**********************************************
90 PRINT "ENTER ASCII FILENAME. EG, ADAPT.DAT"
100 INPUT F$: OPEN F$ FOR INPUT AS #2
105 OPEN "ADAPTC.DAT" FOR OUTPUT AS #3
110 PRINT "PATIENCE - INPUT PROCESSING"
112 PRINT "SUBSTITUTION BASED ON ENTRY IN TABLE: 1=# 2=$ 3=% 4=&"
115 GOSUB 400                          'PAUSE TO SET UP TABLE
120 IF EOF(2) THEN GOTO 9000
130 LINE INPUT #2, X$
140 N= LEN(X$)
150 GOSUB 180
160 GOSUB 900
170 GOTO 120
180 '*****ADAPTIVE COMPRESSION SUBROUTINE*******
190 '* THIS ROUTINE PROCESSES RECORDS FROM X$  *
200 '* AND COMPRESSES WITH HUFFMAN CODES       *
210 '* USING O$ AS THE OUTPUT BUFFER.          *
220 '*******************************************
230 GOSUB 2120                         'PRINT HUFFMAN TABLE USED
235 I=1                                'RESET INDICES
240 FOR J= 1 TO N                      'STEP THRU RECORD
250 A$= MID$(X$,J,1)                   'EXTRACT A CHARACTER
260 FOR K = 1 TO 4                     'SETUP HUFFMAN LOOP
270 IF A$=P$(K) THEN GOSUB 350         'IS INPUT CHAR IN TABLE?
280 NEXT K                             'NO - TRY NEXT
290 IF M = 1 THEN 310                  'IS MATCH FLAG SET?
300 O$(I) = MID$(A$,1,1)               'NO-STUFF CHAR IN BUFFER
310 I=I+1                              'BUMP INPUT STRING INDEX
320 M=0                                'RESET MATCH FLAG
330 NEXT J                             'GO BACK FOR MORE
340 RETURN                             'DONE
350 M=1                                'SET CHAR MATCH FLAG
355 '***********************************************************
360 'INSERT COMPRESSION NOTATION IN OUTPUT BUFFER
365 V = K + 34                         'INDEX OUT TO SUBSTITUTE CHAR
370 O$(I)=CHR$(V)                      'INSERT SUBSTITUTION
380 P(K)= P(K) + 1                     'BUMP COUNT OF OCCURANCE
390 K = 4                              'FORCE END OF SEARCH
395 RETURN                             'GO BACK FOR MORE
400 DIM P$(4)                          'COMMON HUFFMAN CANDIDATES
410 DATA E,T,I,O
420 FOR I = 1 TO 4                     'SETUP CHARACTER TABLE
430 READ Z$                            'GET CHARACTER
440 P$(I) = Z$: NEXT I                 'AND STUFF INTO TABLE
450 RETURN                             'DONE - TABLE COMPLETE
```

Figure 4.22 ADAPTC.BAS program listing

```
900 '*****TALLY THE COMPRESSION COUNT & WRITE BUFFER******
910 '* DISPLAY BEFORE & AFTER RESULTS OF COMPRESSION      *
920 '* AND SHOW THE NET RESULTS OBTAINED BY EACH METHOD   *
930 '*******************************************************
931 N1=N1+N                          'TALLY INPUT CHAR COUNT
932 T=N-I+1                          'NET DIFFERENCE IN BUFFERS
936 T1=T1+T                          'SAVE COUNT FOR SUMMARY
940 FOR I=1 TO J-1
950 PRINT #3, O$(I);
960 NEXT I
965 PRINT #3, ""
966 GOSUB 2000                       'RESEQUENCE HUFFMAN TABLE
970 RETURN
2000 '*****RESEQUENCE & PRINT TABLE FOR ADAPTIVE COMPRESSION*****
2010 FOR J=1 TO 3                    'SETUP 1ST LOOP
2020 FOR K=J+1 TO 4                  'SETUP 2ND LOOP
2030 IF P(J) >= P(K) THEN 2100       'IS CURRENT ENTRY GREATER?
2040 TEMP= P(J)                      'NO-SAVE IN TEMP
2050 TEMP$= P$(J)                    'AND SAVE CHAR
2060 P(J)= P(K)                      'PICKUP GREATER COUNT
2070 P$(J)= P$(K)                    'AND ASSOC CHAR
2080 P(K)= TEMP                      'SWAP LESSER COUNT
2090 P$(K)= TEMP$                    'AND ASSOC CHAR
2100 NEXT K                          'FINISH 2ND LOOP
2110 NEXT J                          'FINISH 1ST LOOP
2115 RETURN                          'DONE-TABLE RESEQUENCED
2120 L= L + 1                        'REMEMBER LINE NO.
2130 PRINT "HUFFMAN TABLE USED FOR LINE";L;": ";
2140 FOR I=1 TO 4                    'SETUP PRINT TABLE LOOP
2150 PRINT P$(I);:PRINT P(I);        'PRINT CHAR AND COUNT
2160 NEXT I
2175 PRINT
2180 RETURN                          'DONE-TABLE PRINTED
9000 CLOSE: OPEN F$ FOR INPUT AS #2
9010 PRINT "FILE ";F$;" BEFORE SUBSTITUTION:"
9020 LINE INPUT #2,X$
9030 IF EOF(2) THEN 9060
9040 PRINT X$
9050 GOTO 9020
9060 PRINT X$:OPEN "ADAPTC.DAT" FOR INPUT AS #3
9070 PRINT "FILE ";F$;" AFTER SUBSTITUTION:"
9080 LINE INPUT #3,O$
9090 IF EOF(3) THEN 9998
9100 PRINT O$
9110 GOTO 9080
9998 PRINT O$
9999 CLOSE:END
```

Figure 4.22 (continued)

in the adaptive compression table will similarly occur on a line-by-line basis.

In line 230, the subroutine commencing at line 2120 is invoked. This subroutine prints the current values of the compression table. Next, lines 240 to 280 examine the extracted record from the data file on a line-by-line basis, comparing each character in the record to any of the characters in our compressible four-character character set (E, T, I, O). If a match occurs, the subroutine commencing at line 350 is invoked. Otherwise, the program simply places the character extracted from the input record into the output buffer.

The subroutine commencing at line 350 sets the character match flag to one and then adds 34 to the value of K in line 365. This action sets the ASCII value of V to either the #, $, % or & character which is used in this example to illustrate the substitution of a Huffman code for an appropriate character in the four-character character set we are using. Next, line 370 inserts the substituted character into the output buffer and the count is then incremented in line 380.

When the match flag is set, line 290 causes a branch to line 310, where the input string index is incremented by one, after which the match flag is reset to zero in line 320. If the match flag was not set, line 300 simply extracts one character from its appropriate position in the input record and places it into the output buffer.

Each time prior to a line of input being processed in this program, the subroutine call contained in line 230 will be invoked. This subroutine simply prints out the current status of the adaptive 'Huffman' compression table to include the character order and the frequency of occurrence of each character. Although this program was constructed to facilitate the visual observation of the changes in an adaptive compression table on a line-by-line basis, in developing an actual adaptive compression routine the tables would be subject to change on an individual character basis.

The actual resequencing of the adaptive compression table occurs in lines 2000 to 2115 of the program. This subroutine module sorts the characters in the adaptive compression table based upon their frequency of occurrence.

Figure 4.23 illustrates the sample execution of the ADAPTC.BAS program, with the status of the compression table displayed for each line of data in the file to be processed. In addition, the program displays the contents of the file prior to and after the substitution of characters from the previously defined four-character character set. As an example of the operation of the program, note that prior to line 1 being processed all entries in the compression table have a count of zero and the order of the entries is E, T, I and O.

The first line in the data file contains the string BEGIN, followed by many asterisks. Since the characters E and I will be replaced by the 'Huffman' codes # and %, after line 1 is processed the count for E and I should be one, while the adaptive compression table should be resequenced to account for the new frequency of occurrence.

```
ENTER ASCII FILENAME. EG, ADAPT.DAT
? ADAPT.DAT
PATIENCE - INPUT PROCESSING
SUBSTITUTION BASED ON ENTRY IN TABLE: 1=# 2=$ 3=% 4=&
HUFFMAN TABLE USED FOR LINE 1 : E O T O I O O O
HUFFMAN TABLE USED FOR LINE 2 : E 1 I 1 T O O O
HUFFMAN TABLE USED FOR LINE 3 : I 5 O 5 T 3 E 2
HUFFMAN TABLE USED FOR LINE 4 : O 9 E 7 T 5 I 5
HUFFMAN TABLE USED FOR LINE 5 : O 19 I 13 T 11 E 11
FILE ADAPT.DAT BEFORE SUBSTITUTION:
1 BEGIN*********************************
2 OVATION OVATION FOR THE MUSICIAN
3 ENCORE ENCORE FOR THE ACTOR
4 OOOOOOOOOO IIIIIIII TTTTT EEEE
5 ***************************************END
FILE ADAPT.DAT AFTER SUBSTITUTION:
1 B#G%N*********************************
2 &VA%$&N &VA%$&N F&R %H# MUS$C$AN
3 &NC$R& &NC$R& F$R %H& AC%$R
4 ########## &&&&&&&& %%%%% $$$$
5 ****************************************&ND
Ok
```

Figure 4.23 Sample execution of ADAPTC.BAS program

Examining the Huffman table used for line 2 in Figure 4.23, the reader will note that the count of E and I are set to 1, while the order of the characters in the table has been rearranged to take into consideration their new frequency of occurrence.

Examining line 2 in the ADAPT.DAT data file, the reader will note that OVATION contains four characters that can be substituted by the adaptive 'Huffman' code. Since the character O did not change its place in the compression table, the 'Huffman' code of & is substituted for that character. Next, the T in OVATION, which would have initially been replaced by the 'Huffman' code of $, is replaced by the 'Huffman' code of % since the adaptive table entries changed, which caused the 'Huffman' code substitutions to change. Table 4.10 summarizes the changes in the adaptive compression

Table 4.10 Adaptive compression table change

Initial table				
Character sequence	E	T	I	O
Code substitution	#	$	%	&
After line 1 processed				
Character sequence	E	I	T	O
Code substitution	#	$	%	&

table prior to and after the first line of data in the input file is processed. As an exercise, the reader may wish to follow the code substitutions for the four-character character set for the remaining lines in the ADAPT.DAT file that are processed by the ADAPTC.BAS program.

Count field considerations

Until now, we have assumed that the count field of a variable compression table is infinite. Obviously, the count field has a finite value based upon the size of the field which must be considered when developing an adaptive compression technique.

There are two easy-to-implement methods you can consider to eliminate the possibility of a count-field overflow occurring. Each of these methods is based upon the use of integer division to reduce the values previously assigned to the count field while maintaining the relative order of the frequency of occurrence of characters transmitted.

One method to eliminate the occurrence of a count-field overflow is to examine the values of the top field entry after a field update. Then, if the bits in that field are all set, you would implement an algorithm that would perform an integer division of 2 on each field entry. Implementing this technique would result in any remainder after division being discarded. As an example, 3/2 would equal 1, with the remainder being discarded.

A second method that can be used to prevent a count-field overflow would be to simply count transmitted characters and implement integer division by 2 each time the count equalled the maximum field value. Although this method obviously results in more frequent integer division operations, it eliminates the necessity of comparing the value of the highest-position count field to an all set bit condition each time a character is received.

4.7 MODERN STATISTICAL COMPRESSION METHODS

In concluding this chapter we will focus our attention upon several popular methods of data compression. Each of the methods to be examined in this section is related to one or more statistical compression techniques covered in this chapter. In addition, each method includes one or more unique properties which results in their examination providing us with additional information concerning the implementation and operation of data compression.

MNP Class 5

MNP Class 5 data compression is one of two methods of data compression supported by the Microcom Networking Protocol (MNP). The MNP protocol was developed by Microcom, Inc., to enhance the communications capability between modems and currently consists of 10 classes. Each class supports lower-class operations, providing downward compatibility between different products that support different MNP classes.

Operations defined by MNP include the adaptive packetization of data, conversion of asynchronous data into a synchronous format, different modulation schemes, as well as two types of data compression. MNP Class 5 data compression was the first method of compression incorporated into the protocol. As previously explained in Chapter 3, MNP Class 5 incorporates two manipulations to a transmitted data stream. The first manipulation is a version of run-length encoding in which sequences of three or more repeating characters are compressed by the insertion of a count after the third character and the removal of all repeating characters in excess of three. Under the MNP Class 5 version of run-length encoding, if the repeated character sequence is three characters in length, the sequence is followed by a repetition count of 0. The maximum repetition count supported is 250.

Both the run-length count and the three repetitions of a character, as well as any other characters in the data stream, are next compressed through the use of an adaptive frequency encoding technique.

The adaptive frequency encoding method employed by MNP Class 5 data compression results in the substitution of a compression token for each 8-bit data character. The token used changes with the frequency of occurrence of the actual data character so that shorter tokens are substituted for more frequently occurring data characters similar to the method described in Section 4.6 which covered adaptive compression.

The formation of tokens to represent 8-bit characters was based upon the fact that there are 2^8 or 256 different characters that can occur and each character must be mapped onto 256 different codes. Since conventional ASCII and non-eighth-bit-set EBCDIC represent a majority of characters used in data transmission, Microcom considered the fact that there are 128 characters that have fewer than 8 bits in developing tokens. The compression tokens were developed to recognize that fact by representing the more frequently occurring characters with codes that have leading zeros removed. To separate recoded data characters from each other, a two-part token was employed. The first part of the token, known as its header, is 3 bits in length as that enables a variable length of up to 8 bits to be defined. Thus, the token header can be viewed as a reverse comma code. The second part of the token is referred to as the token's body and is variable in length. The length of the token's body is defined by the bit composition of the header, which can range in value from binary 000 to 111.

Table 4.11 lists the relationship between the decimal value of each character and the substituted token at compression initialization. In examining the entries in Table 4.11, there are three special cases that do not follow the previously described relationships. First, there are two tokens with a header of 000 where the actual length of the body is 1. Lastly, when the header portion of the token indicates a length of 7 and the body is seven 1-bits, the actual length of the body is 8 bits. Otherwise, the header portion of the token indicates the length of the variable-length token body.

When MNP Class 5 compression is initiated, the frequency of occurrence of each of the 256 possible characters is zero. For purposes of character-to-token mapping, the character whose bit value represents decimal 0 (00000000 binary) is assumed to be the most frequently occurring character and is represented by the first of the shortest tokens in Table 4.11. Characters with increasing decimal values are represented by succeeding tokens, until the character whose decimal value is 255 (11111111 binary) is assumed to be the most infrequently occurring character.

As a character is processed, the token to which its decimal value is currently mapped is substituted for the character. After this substitution occurs, the frequency of occurrence of the character is incremented by one. If the frequency of occurrence of the character just encoded into a token is greater after incrementing than the frequency of the next most frequently occurring character, then the compression tokens of the current character and the next most frequently occurring character are exchanged. The frequency of the current character is then compared to the frequency of the character which is now the next most frequently occurring character. If the frequency of the current character is greater, then the compressed tokens are once again swapped. This process is repeated until no

Table 4.11 Character to token initial mapping

Data character decimal value	Token composition	
	Header	Body
0	000	0
1	000	1
2	001	0
3	001	1
4	010	00
5	010	01
6	010	10
7	010	11
8	011	000
9	011	001
10	011	010
11	011	011
12	011	100
13	011	101
14	011	110
15	011	111
16	100	0000
17	100	0001
18	100	0010
19	100	0011
20	100	0100
21	100	0101
22	100	0110
23	100	0111
24	100	1000
25	100	1001
26	100	1010
27	100	1011
28	100	1100
29	100	1101
30	100	1110
31	100	1111
32	101	00000
33	101	00001
34	101	00010
(35–246 continue in the same pattern)		
247	111	1110111
248	111	1111000
249	111	1111001
250	111	1111010

Table 4.11 (*continued*)

Data character decimal value	Token composition	
	Header	Body
251	111	1111011
252	111	1111100
253	111	1111101
254	111	1111110
255	111	11111110

more swaps are required, at which time the mapping of characters and compression tokens is correctly adapted based upon the relative frequency of occurrence of the characters processed.

The frequency of occurrence for each character is an 8-bit field which has a maximum value of 255 (11111111 binary). To prevent the field from overflowing, each time the character-compression token mappings are sorted by frequency the frequency count of the current character is compared to the maximum count value of 255. If the maximum count has been reached, the frequency of occurrence of each character is scaled downward by dividing each frequency by 2 using integer division.

As previously discussed in Chapter 3, as well as briefly mentioned in this section, sequences of three or more repeating characters are first placed into a four-character run-length encoded sequence. Here the first three characters are the actual repeated characters, while the fourth character is the repetition count. Although the repeated characters and count are mapped into tokens, the count character is not used to increase the frequency of occurrence of the character to which the token is mapped.

Flushing

During the compression process, 8-bit characters can be encoded into tokens ranging from 4 to 11 bits in length. Since computers operate upon 8-bit characters, it may be necessary to terminate a transmission sequence by inserting a number of 'pad' bits to fill an 8-bit boundary. To accomplish this under MNP Class 5 compression, the transmitter inserts a special token into the data stream after the last user data token. The special token is known as a flush token and has the bit composition 11111111111. After the flush token, '1' bits are appended by adding them to the low-order end of the body of the flush token as required to produce an integral number of 8-bit characters.

Efficiency

Although the efficiency of MNP Class 5 data compression, like all compression methods, is dependent upon the data stream it operates upon, we can note several characteristics with respect to its efficiency. First, discounting repeating strings of characters, its maximum compression ratio is 2. This is because the smallest token an 8-bit character can be mapped into is four bits. Secondly, only 32 out of 256 characters will be mapped into tokens that are seven bits or less in length. This means that this compression method will result in either no actual compression or expansion for 224 out of 256 8-bit character representations. In spite of these limitations, the use of run-length encoding, and the fact that the 15 most frequently occurring characters in most data streams cumulatively exceed 50 per cent of all data and can be encoded into six bits or less, can result in a compression ratio between 1.5 and 2.0. Thus, MNP Class 5 data compression can provide 2400 bps modems with an effective throughput between 3600 and 4800 bps. Similarly, 9600 bps modems that support MNP Class 5 data compression can be expected to provide an effective throughput between 14 400 and 19 200 bps when communicating with a compatible modem.

MNP Class 7 enhanced data compression

MNP Class 7 enhanced data compression is the second method of compression supported by the Microcom Networking Protocol. This method of data compression uses what is known as a first-order Markov model to predict the probability of character occurrence based upon the previous character and performs adaptive Huffman coding on the data stream. In addition, MNP Class 7 uses run-length encoding to compress streams of duplicate characters. However, the method of run-length encoding differs from that used by MNP Class 5 data compression.

MNP Class 7 enhanced data compression can be considered as a two-stage process. First, multiple consecutive copies of the same character or 8-bit pattern are compressed using run-length encoding. Under MNP Class 7, if the encoder has sent the same character three times it sends the count of the remaining identical consecutive characters as a single 4-bit nibble. Once a run-length encoding algorithm is applied to the data stream it is then compressed using a first-order Markov model for code selection.

The first-order Markov model used for code selection can be viewed as a two-dimensional 256 × 256 element matrix, which is illustrated in Figure 4.24. The top row of the matrix contains 256 entries that can be viewed as pointers to an appropriate column location within each row entry. Each pointer within the top row of the matrix corresponds to one of 256 8-bit character values while the column below the pointer can be considered as one of 256 coding tables.

```
pointers                    00000000    11111111

                       ⎡   00000000   . . . . . . . .  00000000
                       ⎪        .      . . . . . . . .       .
Coding                 ⎨        .      . . . . . . . .       .
tables                 ⎪        .      . . . . . . . .       .
                       ⎪                                     .
                       ⎣   11111111   . . . . . . . .  11111111
```

Figure 4.24   Initial Markov model

To encode a character for transmission the previous character is used to select the appropriate coding table by using the pointer entry to select the appropriate column. Next, the column is searched until the current character is encountered. In place of transmitting the 8-bit composition of the character the Huffman code developed for that character is used. In addition, the frequency of occurrence of the character is updated and the coding table may be adjusted based upon the frequency of the character transmitted being compared to the frequency of occurrence of other characters in that particular coding table. Thus, each of the coding tables previously shown in Figure 4.24 actually consists of three fields. One field contains the 8-bit composition of the character, while the other fields contain the frequency of occurrence of the character and its Huffman code. Similar to the previously described adaptive Huffman coding technique, the Huffman field is static and remains fixed. In comparison, each character's bit composition and count fields will be adjusted by location in the coding table based upon their frequency of occurrence.

The encoding process used by MNP Class 7 recognizes the fact that there is a high probability that many characters are followed by other characters. To illustrate this concept consider the English language. Here, the probability of a U following a Q is very high. Thus, the Q coding table will most likely have the character U move rapidly to the top of the table. Since Huffman coding is employed, normally U following a Q will be encoded as 1 bit. If we assume that only the letters of the alphabet are being encoded, a portion of the Markov model might appear as indicated in Figure 4.25.

Note that the letter T is in the top position in the coding table under the A pointer as the letter T frequently follows the letter A. Similarly, the letter L is illustrated at the top of the coding table under the B pointer as the letter L frequently follows the letter B.

pointers	A	B	C	D	E	...
character positions within coding tables	T	L	H	O	D	
	H	E	O	A	R	
	C	U	R	E	S	
	.	.	.	.	.	
	.	.	.	.	.	

Figure 4.25 First-order Markov model processing the alphabet

Efficiency

Unlike MNP Class 5 compression in which a minimum of four bits is required to represent a character, MNP Class 7 can represent a character with only one bit. In fact, the top character in each of 256 coding tables can be represented by one bit. Due to the use of adaptive Huffman coding, MNP Class 7 enhanced data compression can be expected to provide, as a minimum, a compression ratio between 15 and 25 per cent above that obtainable usiing MNP Class 7 compression.

CCITT V.42 bis

Prior to discussing CCITT V.42 bis data compression, it is important to make several observations concerning how the efficiency of statistical compression can be increased. Doing so will enable us to better understand why the Lempel–Ziv string-based compression technique upon which the CCITT V.42 recommendation is based can become more efficient than previously described data-compression techniques.

String compression efficiencies

To understand why string compression provides more efficiency than character-based compression methods, let us first examine the entropy of a two-character character set as the probability of occurrence of each character changes. If X_1 and X_2 represent our two-character character set, let us assume X_1 occurs 90 per cent of the time and X_2 occurs 10 per cent of the time. Then, the entropy is:

$$H = -[-0.9 \log_2 0.9 + 0.1 \log_2 0.1]$$
$$H = 0.9*(0.15) + 0.1*(3.3) = 0.47 \text{ bits.}$$

Now suppose X_1 occurs 80 per cent of the time, while X_2 occurs 20 per cent of the time. The entropy then becomes:

$$H = -[-0.8 \log_2 0.8 + 0.2 \log_2 0.8]$$
$$H = 0.8*(0.32) + 0.2*(2.31) = 0.72 \text{ bits.}$$

We can continue varying the frequency of occurrence of each character in our character set. Table 4.12 lists the resulting entropy for the two-character character set as X_1 decreased in frequency of occurrence from 90 per cent to 50 per cent, while X_2 increased from 10 per cent to 50 per cent.

Table 4.12 Entropy versus frequency of occurrence

Frequency of occurrence		
X_1	X_2	Entropy in bits
90	10	0.47
80	20	0.72
70	30	0.88
60	40	0.97
50	50	1.00

In examining the entropy column contained in Table 4.12, note that the greater the inequality in probability of occurrence the lower the theoretical average number of bits required to represent each character. This indicates that a compression method that recognizes common strings, which on a character basis constitute a large percentage of characters, offers the potential for representation by a low number of bits. Let us verify this observation by examining the effect of encoding groups of characters in place of single characters.

Suppose the frequency of occurrence of X_1 is 80 per cent and X_2 is 20 per cent. As previously calculated, the entropy for this character set is 0.72 bits. Using either Huffman or Shannon–Fano encoding would result in assigning a 0 to one character and a 1 to the other character. Here the average length is 1 bit per character, which is 28 per cent greater than the entropy. If we combine the characters in pairs we obtain four possible character sets whose resulting probabilities are indicated in Table 4.13..

Table 4.13 Character pair probabilities

Character pair	Probability of occurrence
X_1X_1	0.8*0.8 = 0.64
X_1X_2	0.8*0.2 = 0.16
X_2X_1	0.2*0.8 = 0.16
X_2X_2	0.2*0.2 = 0.4

Figure 4.26 illustrates the construction of a Huffman code for the character pairs listed in Table 4.13 based upon their probabilities of occurrence. Note that their average bit length is:

$$L = 1*0.64 + 2*0.16 + 3*0.16 + 3*0.04 = 1.56 \text{ bits.}$$

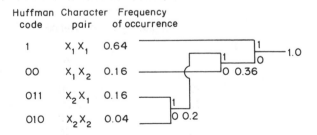

Figure 4.26 Huffman encoding of character pairs listed in Table 4.13

Since each character pair represents two characters, the average bit length per pair must be divided by 2 to find the average bit length per character. Doing so results in an average of 0.78 bits per character when characters are paired.

Now let us proceed one step further and encode three characters at a time. Table 4.14 lists the eight distinct tri-character combinations and their resulting probability of occurrence.

Table 4.14 Tri-character probabilities

Character pair	Probability of occurrence
$X_1X_1X_1$	$0.8*0.8*0.8 = 0.512$
$X_1X_1X_2$	$0.8*0.8*0.2 = 0.128$
$X_1X_2X_1$	$0.8*0.2*0.8 = 0.128$
$X_1X_2X_2$	$0.8*0.2*0.2 = 0.032$
$X_2X_1X_1$	$0.2*0.8*0.8 = 0.128$
$X_2X_1X_2$	$0.2*0.8*0.2 = 0.032$
$X_2X_2X_1$	$0.2*0.2*0.8 = 0.032$
$X_2X_2X_2$	$0.2*0.2*0.2 = 0.008$

Figure 4.27 illustrates the construction of the Huffman code for the tri-character groupings based upon their probability of occurrence listed in Table 4.14. Now let us examine the average bit length per tri-character group. The average bit length is:

$$L = 1*0.512 + 3*0.128*3 + 5*0.032*3 + 5*0.008 = 2.184 \text{ bits}.$$

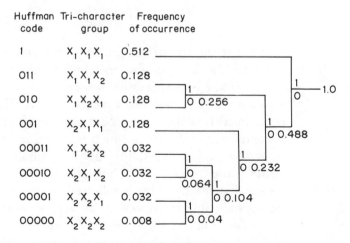

Figure 4.27 Huffman encoding of tri-character groupings listed in Table 4.14

Since the average number of bits per tri-character group is 2.184, dividing that number by 3 results in the average number of bits per character, which is 0.728. From the preceding computations, we note that as we combine more and more characters the average character bit length approaches entropy. In fact, the average length will equal entropy if all of the probabilities of occurrence are inverse powers of 2. As we combine additional characters into groups of strings their probabilities of occurrence approach inverse powers of 2, which is the reason why a compression technique based upon encoding strings should be more efficient than one based upon encoding characters and was one of the reasons for the selection of the Lempel–Ziv technique for use in the CCITT V.42 bis data-compression recommendation.

Lempel–Ziv string encoding algorithm

In 1975, Abraham Lempel and Jacob Ziv developed a string encoding algorithm which was published in *IEEE Transactions on Information Theory* in May, 1977. The string encoding algorithm, which has become more commonly known as the Lempel–Ziv technique, consists of a set of rules for parsing strings of symbols from a finite alphabet (A) into substrings, or words, whose lengths do not exceed a predefined integer L_S, and an encoding scheme which maps the resulting substrings into codewords of fixed length L_C. The relationship between the length of the codeword and substring is:

$$L_C = 1 + [\log (n - L_S)] + [\log L_S]$$

where n is the length of a buffer which stores the last n symbols.

Under the Lempel–Ziv encoding technique a string of symbols (S) is parsed into successive source words $S = S_1 S_2 \ldots S_n$, while a codeword C_i is assigned to each word S_i. To initiate encoding it is assumed that the output S of the source is preceded by a string Z containing $n - L_S$ zeros which is stored in the buffer as the string $B_1 = ZS$ $(1, L_S)$. Next, the first l_1 symbols are shifted out of the buffer while the next l_1 symbols are entered into the buffer to obtain a second string B_2. This is followed by an examination of the string for reproducible extensions to develop a codeword to represent the extension. The reader is referred to the article by Lempel and Ziv (1977) for detailed information concerning their algorithm.

The V.42 bis recommendation

The work of Lempel and Ziv was further refined by employees of IBM, British Telecom, Bell Laboratories, Unisys, and other companies and serves as the basis for the CCITT V.42 bis data-compression method which is designed to be used by modems. Under V.42 bis a string which typically averages between two and four characters in length is replaced by a codeword based upon the construction of a dictionary that will contain 512 or more text strings and associated codewords. The V.42 bis compression process includes construction of the dictionary and its search for entries that match non-compressed data, resulting in codewords being substituted for strings of data. At the receiver, codewords are looked up and decoded based upon the composition of strings in a dictionary maintained at the receiver.

The V.42 bis dictionary initially contains the basic character set and expands through the formation of new strings by adding single characters to existing strings. The dictionary is dynamic, with new strings being added and old strings being removed based upon the data being compressed.

Initially, all one-character strings are predefined in the table. Although this means that 256 one-character strings are defined, for illustrative purposes, let us focus our attention on the uppercase letters A through Z. Then, the dictionary at the transmitter and receiver would initially appear as a sequence of root nodes as illustrated in Figure 4.28.

The codeword for each string is initially set to the ASCII code for each character. That is, A would have the string number 65, B would be assigned the string number 66, and so on.

As data enters the encoder, it is examined against the contents of the dictionary. If a string is encountered that was not previously stored in the dictionary, it is then added to the dictionary and assigned a string number that functions as the codeword of the string. To illustrate this assume that the alphabet consisting of the

Figure 4.28   Initial dictionary state

letters A through Z is to be transmitted repetitively. The first new string that would be encountered would be AB, since A was known as it was previously defined when the dictionary was initialized. Thus, this new string would be stored in the dictionary and assigned the codeword 257 as A is known but AB represents a new string.

At the same time AB is entered into the encoder's dictionary the codeword for B is transmitted to the receiver. This enables the receiver to construct a mirror-image dictionary which matches the encoder's dictionary. Then, whenever the string AB is encoded, it will be transmitted as the codeword 257, which the receiver will both recognize and correctly decode. The next new string that would be identified as the alphabet is processed would be BC when the encoder encounters the character C. Now the dictionary is updated by the addition of C to the B node. At the same time the encoder transmits the codeword for C, which is 67, so that the receiver knows that the third character in the input data stream was a C. Both the encoding transmitter and the decoding receiver increment the codeword value by 1 to 258 and assign that value to the string BC in the dictionary. Thus, the next time the string BC is encountered it would be encoded and transmitted as the codeword 258.

As data is processed, the initial character set stored in the dictionary will expand into a tree-based structure. If we consider the initial set of characters as route nodes, expansion of the dictionary will result in the generation of leaf nodes. Figure 4.29 illustrates the leaves formed from nodes A and B based upon the previous example as well as a more complex leaf-node structure emanating from the root node T that has been added for illustrative purposes. The tree in Figure 4.29 represent the strings A, AB, B, BC, . . . , T, TH, THE and TO. Note that each leaf node is a dependent of a higher-level node (E dependent on H) or a root node.

In the encoding process, new strings always consist of a currently defined string in the dictionary plus one character. Thus a second

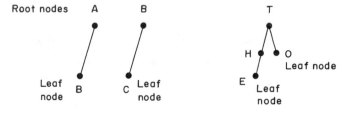

Figure 4.29 Dictionary evolution

sequence of the alphabet as original data would result in the addition of the string ABC to the dictionary since the string AB was previously known. When ABC is added by the formation of a new branch from leaf node B, the codeword of the string AB (257) is transmitted followed by the codeword for C which enables the receiver to update its dictionary. At the same time the next available codeword is assigned to the string ABC by the transmitter and receiver.

As can be noted from the previous discussion, the encoding of data into strings could result in an infinite number of strings and corresponding codewords. To prevent this from happening, the CCITT V.42 bis recommendation specifies a range of string lengths that is permitted and which can be negotiated between transmitter and receiver as well as a default value of 6 characters. The permitted maximum string length can be varied from 6 to 250. Similarly, the V.42 bis recommendation specifies a default value of 512 codewords, which is the minimum number of codewords or uniquely defined strings that can occur at one time. Although a maximum value is not specified in the current recommendation, you will probably want to increase the number of codewords by 256 for each expansion in the maximum string length by 3 characters above its default value of 6.

Dictionary functions

Under the V.42 bis recommendation each data-compression device maintains two dictionaries. One is maintained by the encoder for compressing data while the second dictionary is maintained by the decoder for decompressing received data. In addition to string matching and updating functions, the V.42 bis recommendation defines a procedure for deleting infrequently used strings. This function allows storage in the dictionary to be reused and occurs when the last available dictionary entry has been assigned. At that time a counter (C1) which indicates the codeword that would be assigned to the next empty dictionary entry is compared to the total number of codewords denoted as N2. If it exceeds N2−1, then C1 is set to the index number of the first dictionary entry used to store a string denoted as N5. If the node identified by the codeword with the value C1 is in use and is not a leaf node, counter C1 is incremented and its value again compared to N2−1. If the node identified by the codeword with value C1 is a leaf node, it is then detached from its parent, freeing an entry for reuse.

Although initial tests of V.42 bis compression indicate a level of efficiency between 10 and 20 per cent above MNP Class 7, to achieve this may require a significant investigation of modem parameters beyond what many end-users might normally consider. This is because the maximum string length and number of codewords allowed are proportional to the RAM memory contained in V.42 bis modems. Although all V.42 bis modems will support the default parameter settings, many modems are restricted by RAM memory to those settings and may not provide the additional compression efficiency you might anticipate from a perusal of trade literature.

SYSTEM CONSIDERATIONS AND DATA ANALYSIS

To obtain an effective data-compression routine or series of compression algorithms requires both an examination of the overall transmission system and an analysis and understanding of the composition of the data to be transferred. Both areas are the focus of the material contained in this chapter.

5.1 SYSTEM CONSIDERATIONS

An analysis of the complete transmission system is a prerequisite to maximizing the efficiency of communications. This analysis should examine not only hardware and software but must also consider the volume and type of data traffic expected to be communicated. An example of system considerations and their effect upon operational efficiencies can be obtained from an examination of the transmission requirement illustrated in Figure 5.1.

In this illustration, a remote batch terminal is interfaced to a magnetic tape unit and a communications line functioning as a stand-alone tape-to-tape transmission system. From an overall system standpoint, many factors affect the operational efficiency of the transmission. To investigate these factors, we can break up the system into its logical components—the magnetic tape subsystem, the remote batch terminal and the communications link.

Concerning the communications link, the protocol employed and the modem's data transfer rate govern the line utilization effectiveness.

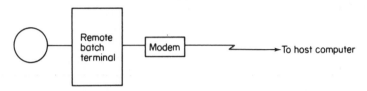

Figure 5.1 System considerations for tape-to-tape transmission. To investigate the operational efficiency of communications, the data transfer rates from the magnetic tape unit to the terminal and from the terminal to the communications line should be determined prior to examining the frequency distribution of data and its applicability to one or more compression routines.

If a higher-speed modem is employed or a more efficient transmission protocol utilized, an increase in the number of characters transmitted per unit time can be expected.

The remote batch terminal itself can affect the overall transmission efficiency. If we examine the remote batch terminal as a black box, we will note that it can accept input from the magnetic tape unit at a certain data transfer rate, process the data and then transfer the data to the communications line at another data transfer rate. The data transfer rate to the communications line will depend upon the channel adapter connecting the terminal to the modem, the modem's data transfer rate and the transmission medium employed. In addition, the processing performed by the terminal will determine whether the device can output data fast enough to use the communications facilities at their rated data transfer rate or at some average rate below the rated level. To produce an effective information transfer ratio (EITR) in excess of the communications line data transfer ratio, one or more compression routines must be employed, such that the overall transfer ratio exceeds unity. If this occurs, then the effective information transfer ratio will exceed the data transfer ratio. Key factors in determining the optimum compression routine or routines to employ will be based upon the processing power available to compress data and a data analysis of the information to be transmitted.

Compression ratio effect

Although you may wish to utilize a compression routine or group of routines that are most suited to the expected data traffic, in some cases processing limitations may preclude the use of the optimum technique. Thus, the user must determine if the higher compression ratio offered by one technique versus another will require additional processing time that could result in a lower overall effective information transfer rate. As an example, consider two compression routines, one resulting in a compression ratio of 1.52 while the second results in a compression ratio of 1.61. If we did not examine the processing effect of the two routines, our inclination would be to select the routine with the higher compression ratio. Let us assume that an investigation of the software required to implement the first routine shows no effect on the device delivering data to the line; therefore, the transmission protocol will govern the effective data rate of the line. If the line speed is 9600 bps and the information transfer ratio (ITR) of the transmission control sequence is 0.5, the data transfer rate would be 4800 bps while the EITR would be approximately 1.52*0.5, or 0.76, resulting in a transfer rate of information in bits (TRIB) of 0.76*9600 or 7296 bps.

For the second compression routine, assume that its sophisticated nature requires a larger amount of computational processing power, affecting the rate at which data can be transferred from the terminal to the communications line. Let us further assume that the ITR is lowered to 0.4 due to the additional processing delays. Then the 1.61 compression ratio of this routine would result in a TRIB of approximately 0.4*1.61*9600 or 6184 bps. In this particular illustration, increasing the compression ratio resulted in a decrease in the overall effective data transfer rate.

Device data transfer

Next, we can consider the effect of the data transfer rate of information on the magnetic tape unit to the remote batch terminal. Two factors govern the magnetic tape unit data transfer rate since the rate at which data can be transferred between the terminal's memory and the tape unit is equal to the number of characters per inch recorded on the tape times the number of those inches that pass the unit's read head each second. In addition, the number of characters recorded per inch of tape is dependent upon the record length and blocking factor originally employed to build the tape. From a systems standpoint, if DTR1 is the data transfer rate from the magnetic tape to the terminal and DTR2 is the data transfer rate from the terminal to the communications line, then, for DTR1 < DTR2, there is nothing to gain by introducing a compression routine or routines unless another modification to the hardware or software will be implemented to take advantage of the compression. These modifications could be in the generation of the magnetic tape to increase its blocking factor or the procurement of higher recording density and faster read/write head tape units would would permit a higher data transfer rate. From a communications standpoint, one may let DTR1 < DTR2 continue to exist but incorporate compression to lower DTR2 and thus save line and modem costs by reducing the communications data transfer rate while maintaining the overall effective information transfer ratio.

5.2 DATA ANALYSIS

After hardware and software have been analyzed with respect to the overall system, assume that the employment of one or more compression techniques indicates that the overall operational efficiency of communications will increase. At this point in time, a data analysis may be considered.

From the data analysis, you can structure one or more compression techniques to fit the data. The goal of this structuring should be to obtain the highest degree of compression consistent with the processing power available to compress the original data stream and structure or return it to its original form. However, you should note that you must also consider the skill level of the personnel that can be assigned to developing data-compression software, the period of time that might be required to implement different compression algorithms and the programming complexity of the devices upon which compression is to be implemented.

Although typesetters for centuries have taken advantage of the fact that some letters are used more frequently than others in stocking type, it was Samuel Morse who first applied the properties of frequency analysis to communications. When Morse decided to use an alphabetical system of signals for his newly invented telegraph, he consulted a Philadelphia newspaper's typecase. Morse desired to assign the shorter dot-and-dash symbols used for telegraph transmission to the more commonly used letters of the alphabet, while longer dot-and-dash symbols would be used for less frequently used characters. In counting type in each letter bin, he found 12 000 e's, 9000 t's, 8000 each of a, o, m, i and s, 6400 h's and so on. With few exceptions, Morse followed this list in developing his teletype code, assigning the shortest symbol, a dot, to the letter e which was the most common letter encountered. Another short symbol, a dash, was assigned to the letter t.

Using the Modern International Morse Code which differs slightly from the original Morse code, transmission of an English message consisting of 100 letters requires the transmission of approximately 940 units, where the duration of a dot equals one dot-unit, a dash equals three dot-units and the space between dots and dashes of a letter equals one dot-unit and the space between letters equals three dot-units. If instead of assigning symbols of the English language the symbols had been assigned at random, the same message would require the transmission of approximately 1160 dot-units, an increase of about 23 per cent. This encoding technique represents the earliest application of statistical compression for data transmission and permits almost one-quarter additional messages on a telegraph line during a rush period than if dot-and-dash assignments were done in a random manner.

Frequency considerations

For compression applications that will be applied to a specific type of data you should first determine the frequency of individual characters and patterns of characters in the original data stream to be compressed. Although this preprocessing of data may not be possible in many situations, you can estimate the anticipated frequency based upon the category of information expected in the data stream. Table 5.1 contains a frequency table developed from an examination of a string of 10 000 letters of normal English taken at random from a book. If we anticipate transmission or storage of normal English text, we can use the anticipated frequency of occurrence of each letter from that table to appropriately set up a statistical compression scheme.

One problem associated with a frequency analysis by itself is that seldom does the nature of data storage or transmission remain static. Thus, the transmission of normal English text at one point in time might have been preceded by the transmission of a FORTRAN program compilation and execution. This type of data is normally heavily oriented toward scientific notation and numeric characters. In addition, the English text could be followed by a COBOL program execution, usually oriented toward alphanumeric characters and such special symbols as dollar signs, commas and decimal points. To maximize compression performance, it sometimes becomes necessary

Table 5.1 Normal English frequency table

Letter	%	Occurrence	Letter	%	Occurrence
A	8.0	800	N	7.00	700
B	1.5	150	O	8.00	800
C	3.0	300	P	2.00	200
D	4.0	400	Q	0.25	25
E	13.0	1050	R	6.50	650
F	2.0	200	S	6.00	600
G	1.5	150	T	9.00	900
H	6.0	600	U	3.00	300
I	6.5	650	V	1.00	100
J	0.5	50	W	1.50	150
K	0.5	50	X	0.50	50
L	3.5	350	Y	2.00	200
M	3.0	300	Z	0.25	25

to recognize the changing frequency patterns of data and employ a different compression technique more suitable to the new data structure. In other cases, a simple examination of data will permit the analyst to recognize that the addition of one simple compression technique to another technique already being utilized will permit additional operational efficiencies. Conversely, if a data analysis process identifies significant variances you will probably want to consider the development of an adaptive data-compression technique similar to those discussed in Chapter 4.

Since the analysis of data files can be a long and tedious process, a computer program called DATANALYSIS is listed in Appendix A to assist readers in determining the susceptibility of their data to one or more compression algorithms. Through the use of the DATANALYSIS program, you may examine the consistency of your typical data files and plan the implementation of one or more compression routines with a predefined expectation of results. As we review the program execution against a system output 'SYSOUT' data file, we will be able to predetermine the effect of different compression algorithms.

The SYSOUT file chosen for the analysis is representative of typical large computer system data files. Here only upper case characters were contained in the file which is representative of an accounting report, payroll file or another typical computer-generated document other than word-processing output.

Table 5.2

DATANALYSIS
EXECUTION REPORT SUMMARY
FILE ANALYZED: SYSOUT

SEGMENT	DESCRIPTION
I	SYSTEM STANDARD FREQUENCY OF OCCURRENCE
II	SORTED FREQUENCY OF OCCURRENCE
III	REPEATED CHARACTER STRING ANALYSIS
IV	RUN-LENGTH ENCODING SUSCEPTIBILITY
V	HALF-BYTE ENCODING SUSCEPTIBILITY
VI	PAIRED-CHARACTER COMPRESSION ANALYSIS
VII	ENTROPY ANALYSIS

DATANALYSIS analysis

Table 5.2 contains the heading or summary sheet of the DATANA-LYSIS program. As indicated, the program is divided into seven segments, ranging from a system standard frequency of occurrence tabulation through an entropy analysis. Table 5.3 lists the output from segment I of the program. This segment lists in ASCII character of occurrence the count of each character found in the analyzed file as well as its frequency of occurrence in per cent. From Table 5.3, it should be noted that out of the 99 132 characters in the SYSOUT file analyzed, 73 509 were spaces, representing 74.15 per cent of the file.

Segment II of the DATANALYSIS program is listed in Table 5.4. Here, the characters are printed by sorted frequency of occurrence.

Table 5.5 presents the results of the repeated character string analysis performed by the execution of Segment III of the DATANALYSIS program upon the sampled SYSOUT file. Here, the number of occurrences of numeric strings to include imbedded commas, decimal points, dollar signs and asterisks, strings of spaces or strings containing any repeated character are tabulated. From this table, it is apparent that spaces are the predominant repeated character in the file analyzed.

Table 5.6 shows the results of segment IV of the DATANALYSIS program. In this segment of the program, the actual number of characters that can be saved by the employment of run-length

Table 5.3

SYSTEM STANDARD FREQUENCY OF OCCURRENCE
TABLE OF CHARACTERS FOUND IN SYSOUT FILE

SEGMENT I			CHAR.	COUNT	%	CHAR.	COUNT	%	DATANALYSIS		
CHAR.	COUNT	%							CHAR.	COUNT	%
SH	0.	0.	EP	13.	0.01	A	713.	0.72	a	0.	0.
EX	0.	0.	"	201.	0.20	B	252.	0.25	b	0.	0.
SX	0.	0.	#	2.	0.00	C	427.	0.43	c	0.	0.
ET	0.	0.	$	2.	0.00	D	290.	0.29	d	0.	0.
EQ	0.	0.	%	7.	0.01	E	928.	0.94	e	0.	0.
AK	0.	0.	&	105.	0.11	F	279.	0.28	f	0.	0.
BL	0.	0.	'	1.	0.00	G	192.	0.19	g	0.	0.
BS	0.	0.	(	542.	0.55	H	1095.	1.10	h	0.	0.
HT	0.	0.	)	542.	0.55	I	1223.	1.23	i	0.	0.
LF	0.	0.	*	1055.	1.06	J	97.	0.10	j	0.	0.
VT	0.	0.	+	74.	0.07	K	121.	0.12	k	0.	0.
FF	0.	0.	,	1327.	1.34	L	355.	0.36	l	0.	0.
CR	0.	0.	-	135.	0.14	M	332.	0.33	m	0.	0.
SO	0.	0.	.	135.	0.14	N	644.	0.65	n	0.	0.
SI	0.	0.	/	60.	0.06	O	694.	0.70	o	0.	0.

DE	0.	0.	0	1066.	1.08	P	432.	0.44	p	0.	0.
D1	0.	0.	1	905.	0.91	Q	98.	0.10	q	0.	0.
D2	0.	0.	2	1427.	1.44	R	813.	0.82	r	0.	0.
D3	0.	0.	3	405.	0.41	S	573.	0.58	s	0.	0.
D4	0.	0.	4	354.	0.36	T	1022.	1.03	t	0.	0.
NK	0.	0.	5	353.	0.36	U	511.	0.52	u	0.	0.
SY	0.	0.	6	248.	0.25	V	95.	0.10	v	0.	0.
EB	0.	0.	7	281.	0.28	W	197.	0.20	w	0.	0.
CN	0.	0.	8	312.	0.31	X	196.	0.20	x	0.	0.
EM	0.	0.	9	242.	0.24	Y	190.	0.19	y	0.	0.
SB	0.	0.	:	21.	0.02	Z	62.	0.06	z	0.	0.
EC	0.	0.	;	4.	0.00	[	1.	0.00	{	0.	0.
FS	0.	0.	<	1.	0.00	\	1.	0.00	|	0.	0.
GS	0.	0.	=	152.	0.15	]	1.	0.00	}	0.	0.
RS	0.	0.	>	1.	0.00	^	53.	0.05	~	0.	0.
US	0.	0.	QM	5.	0.01	_	0.	0.	DL	0.	0.
SP	73509.	74.15	@	2.	0.00				**	99132.	100.00

** DENOTES TOTAL CHARACTERS IN FILE

Table 5.4

SEGMENT	SORTED FREQUENCY OF OCCURRENCE TABLE OF CHARACTERS FOUND IN SYSOUT FILE								DATANALYSIS		
CHAR.	COUNT	%	CHAR.	COUNT	%	CHAR.	COUNT	%	CHAR.	COUNT	%
SP	73509.	74.15	"	201.	0.20	SX	0.	0.	a	0.	0.
2	1427.	1.44	W	197.	0.20	ET	0.	0.	b	0.	0.
,	1327.	1.34	X	196.	0.20	EQ	0.	0.	c	0.	0.
_	1223.	1.23	G	192.	0.19	AK	0.	0.	d	0.	0.
H	1095.	1.10	T	190.	0.19	BL	0.	0.	e	0.	0.
0	1066.	1.08	=	152.	0.15	BS	0.	0.	f	0.	0.
*	1055.	1.06	—	135.	0.14	HT	0.	0.	g	0.	0.
T	1022.	1.03		135.	0.14	LF	0.	0.	h	0.	0.
E	928.	0.94	K	121.	0.12	VT	0.	0.	i	0.	0.
1	905.	0.91	&	105.	0.11	FF	0.	0.	j	0.	0.
R	813.	0.82	¢	98.	0.10	CR	0.	0.	k	0.	0.
A	713.	0.72	J	97.	0.10	SO	0.	0.	l	0.	0.
O	694.	0.70	V	95.	0.10	SI	0.	0.	m	0.	0.
N	644.	0.65	+	74.	0.07	DE	0.	0.	n	0.	0.

Char	Count	%
S	573.	0.58
(	542.	0.55
)	542.	0.55
U	511.	0.52
P	432.	0.44
C	427.	0.43
3	405.	0.41
L	355.	0.36
4	354.	0.36
5	353.	0.36
M	332.	0.33
8	312.	0.31
D	290.	0.29
7	281.	0.28
F	279.	0.28
B	252.	0.25
6	248.	0.25
9	242.	0.24
Z	62.	0.06
/	60.	0.06
|	53.	0.05
..	21.	0.02
EP	13.	0.01
%	7.	0.01
QM	5.	0.01
.;	4.	0.00
#	2.	0.00
$	2.	0.00
@	2.	0.00
∧	1.	0.00
∨	1.	0.00
[	1.	0.00
_	1.	0.00
]	1.	0.00
~	1.	0.00
`	1.	0.00
D1	0.	0.00
D2	0.	0.00
D3	0.	0.00
D4	0.	0.00
NK	0.	0.00
SY	0.	0.00
EB	0.	0.00
CN	0.	0.00
EM	0.	0.00
SB	0.	0.00
EC	0.	0.00
FS	0.	0.00
GS	0.	0.00
RS	0.	0.00
US	0.	0.00
SH	0.	0.00
EX	0.	0.00
@	0.	0.00
o	0.	0.00
p	0.	0.00
q	0.	0.00
r	0.	0.00
s	0.	0.00
t	0.	0.00
u	0.	0.00
v	0.	0.00
w	0.	0.00
x	0.	0.00
y	0.	0.00
z	0.	0.00
{	0.	0.00
|	0.	0.00
}	0.	0.00
~	0.	0.00
DL	0.	0.00
**	99132.	100.0

** DENOTES TOTAL CHARACTERS IN FILE

Table 5.5

SEGMENT III   DATANALYSIS
REPEATED-CHARACTER STRING ANALYSIS FOR SYSOUT FILE

STRING LENGTH	NUMBER OF OCCURRENCES			
	NUMERICS	SPACES	OTHER	TOTAL
3	12	93	36	141
4	0	6	7	13
5	1	22	755	778
6	0	160	1	161
7	0	472	5	477
9	0	13	0	13
12	0	2	0	2
14	0	498	0	498
15	0	90	0	90
16	0	12	0	12
22	0	0	3	3
23	0	0	5	5
24	0	0	4	4
25	0	0	2	2
26	0	0	1	1
27	0	2	1	3
28	0	2	3	5
29	0	2	0	2
30	0	7	0	7
31	0	6	0	6
32	0	5	2	7
33	0	3	0	3
34	0	5	1	6
35	0	1	1	2
36	0	2	0	2
37	0	1	0	1
38	0	6	2	8
39	0	2	0	2
40	0	1	0	1
41	0	1	0	1
43	0	1	0	1
44	0	3	0	3
45	0	2	0	2
46	0	3	0	3
47	0	4	0	4
48	0	4	0	4
49	0	1	0	1
50	0	2	0	2
51	0	3	0	3
52	0	82	0	82

Table 5.5   (*continued*)

SEGMENT III   DATANALYSIS
        REPEATED-CHARACTER STRING ANALYSIS FOR SYSOUT FILE

STRING LENGTH	NUMBER OF OCCURRENCES			
	NUMERICS	SPACES	OTHER	TOTAL
53	0	3	0	3
54	0	4	0	4
55	0	3	0	3
56	0	4	0	4
57	0	3	0	3
58	0	3	0	3
60	0	4	0	4
61	0	6	0	6
62	0	1	0	1
63	0	11	0	11
64	0	1	0	1
65	0	5	0	5
66	0	1	0	1
67	0	8	0	8
68	0	4	0	4
69	0	4	0	4
71	0	7	0	7
72	0	4	0	4
73	0	16	0	16
74	0	3	0	3
75	0	4	0	4
76	0	24	0	24
77	0	9	0	9
78	0	10	0	10
79	0	19	0	19
80	0	7	0	7
81	0	14	0	14
82	0	6	0	6
83	0	31	0	31
84	0	17	0	17
85	0	52	0	52
86	0	27	0	27
87	0	12	0	12
88	0	21	0	21
89	0	12	0	12
90	0	12	0	12
91	0	32	0	32
92	0	4	0	4
93	0	21	0	21

Table 5.5   (*continued*)

SEGMENT III   DATANALYSIS
REPEATED-CHARACTER STRING ANALYSIS FOR SYSOUT FILE

STRING LENGTH	NUMBER OF OCCURRENCES			
	NUMERICS	SPACES	OTHER	TOTAL
94	0	8	0	8
95	0	10	0	10
96	0	15	0	15
97	0	6	0	6
98	0	10	0	10
99	0	23	0	23
127	0	82	0	82

ANALYSIS SUMMARY:
  RECORDS PROCESSED 751
  TOTAL REPETITIONS 76750
  TOTAL CHARACTERS IN FILE 99132.
  PER CENT REPETITIOUS 77.42

Table 5.6

SEGMENT IV   DATANALYSIS
RUN-LENGTH ENCODING COMPRESSION SUSCEPTIBILITY
FOR REPEATED CHARACTER STRINGS IN SYSOUT FILE

STRING LENGTH	REPEATED CHARACTERS				CHAR. SAVED BY COMPRESSION			
	NUMERICS	SPACES	OTHER	TOTAL	NUMERICS	SPACES	OTHER	TOTAL
3	36	279	108	423	0	0	0	0
4	0	24	28	52	0	6	7	13
5	5	110	3775	3890	2	44	1510	1556
6	0	960	6	966	0	480	3	483
7	0	3304	35	3339	0	1888	20	1908
9	0	117	0	117	0	78	0	78
12	0	24	0	24	0	18	0	18
14	0	6972	0	6972	0	5478	0	5478
15	0	1350	0	1350	0	1080	0	1080
16	0	192	0	192	0	156	0	156
22	0	0	66	66	0	0	57	57
23	0	0	115	115	0	0	100	100
24	0	0	96	96	0	0	84	84
25	0	0	50	50	0	0	44	44
26	0	0	26	26	0	0	23	23

Table 5.6   (*continued*)

SEGMENT IV   DATANALYSIS

RUN-LENGTH ENCODING COMPRESSION SUSCEPTIBILITY
FOR REPEATED CHARACTER STRINGS IN SYSOUT FILE

STRING LENGTH	REPEATED CHARACTERS				CHAR. SAVED BY COMPRESSION			
	NUMERICS	SPACES	OTHER	TOTAL	NUMERICS	SPACES	OTHER	TOTAL
27	0	54	27	81	0	48	24	72
28	0	56	84	140	0	50	75	125
29	0	58	0	58	0	52	0	52
30	0	210	0	210	0	189	0	189
31	0	186	0	186	0	168	0	168
32	0	160	64	224	0	145	58	203
33	0	99	0	99	0	90	0	90
34	0	170	34	204	0	155	31	186
35	0	35	35	70	0	32	32	64
36	0	72	0	72	0	66	0	66
37	0	37	0	37	0	34	0	34
38	0	228	76	304	0	210	70	280
39	0	78	0	78	0	72	0	72
40	0	40	0	40	0	37	0	37
41	0	41	0	41	0	38	0	38
43	0	43	0	43	0	40	0	40
44	0	132	0	132	0	123	0	123
45	0	90	0	90	0	84	0	84
46	0	138	0	138	0	129	0	129
47	0	188	0	188	0	176	0	176
48	0	192	0	192	0	180	0	180
49	0	49	0	49	0	46	0	46
50	0	100	0	100	0	94	0	94
51	0	153	0	153	0	144	0	144
52	0	4264	0	4264	0	4018	0	4018
53	0	159	0	159	0	150	0	150
54	0	216	0	216	0	204	0	204
55	0	165	0	165	0	156	0	156
56	0	224	0	224	0	212	0	212
57	0	171	0	171	0	162	0	162
58	0	174	0	174	0	165	0	165
60	0	240	0	240	0	228	0	228
61	0	366	0	366	0	348	0	348
62	0	62	0	62	0	59	0	59
63	0	693	0	693	0	660	0	660
64	0	64	0	64	0	61	0	61
65	0	325	0	325	0	310	0	310
66	0	66	0	66	0	63	0	63

Table 5.6   (*continued*)

SEGMENT IV   DATANALYSIS

RUN-LENGTH ENCODING COMPRESSION SUSCEPTIBILITY
FOR REPEATED CHARACTER STRINGS IN SYSOUT FILE

STRING LENGTH	REPEATED CHARACTERS				CHAR. SAVED BY COMPRESSION			
	NUMERICS	SPACES	OTHER	TOTAL	NUMERICS	SPACES	OTHER	TOTAL
67	0	536	0	536	0	512	0	512
68	0	272	0	272	0	260	0	260
69	0	276	0	276	0	264	0	264
71	0	497	0	497	0	476	0	476
72	0	288	0	288	0	276	0	276
73	0	1168	0	1168	0	1120	0	1120
74	0	222	0	222	0	213	0	213
75	0	300	0	300	0	288	0	288
76	0	1824	0	1824	0	1752	0	1752
77	0	693	0	693	0	666	0	666
78	0	780	0	780	0	750	0	750
79	0	1501	0	1501	0	1444	0	1444
80	0	560	0	560	0	539	0	539
81	0	1134	0	1134	0	1092	0	1092
82	0	492	0	492	0	474	0	474
83	0	2573	0	2573	0	2480	0	2480
84	0	1428	0	1428	0	1377	0	1377
85	0	4420	0	4420	0	4264	0	4264
86	0	2322	0	2322	0	2241	0	2241
87	0	1044	0	1044	0	1008	0	1008
88	0	1848	0	1848	0	1785	0	1785
89	0	1068	0	1068	0	1032	0	1032
90	0	1080	0	1080	0	1044	0	1044
91	0	2912	0	2912	0	2816	0	2816
92	0	368	0	368	0	356	0	356
93	0	1953	0	1953	0	1890	0	1890
94	0	752	0	752	0	728	0	728
95	0	950	0	950	0	920	0	920
96	0	1440	0	1440	0	1395	0	1395
97	0	582	0	582	0	564	0	564
98	0	980	0	980	0	950	0	950
99	0	2277	0	2277	0	2208	0	2208
127	0	10414	0	10414	0	10168	0	10168
****	41	72084	4625	76750	2	65778	2138	67918

Table 5.6   (*continued*)

_____

SUMMARY INFORMATION: TOTAL CHARACTER IN DATA FILE: 99132
PERCENTAGE SEQUENTIAL REPEATED CHARACTER:
   NUMERIC: 0
   BLANK (SPACES)   72
   NON-NUMERIC NON-BLANK: 4
   TOTAL REPEATED: 77

POTENTIAL COMPRESSION REDUCTION (%):
   NUMERIC: 0
   BLANK (SPACES):   66
   NON-NUMERIC NON BLANK: 2
   TOTAL: 68

_____

encoding are computed and tabulated. Note that the potential compression reduction was computed to be 68 per cent by the use of a run-length encoding technique.

Table 5.7 shows the results of segment V of the DATANALYSIS program. In this program segment, the susceptibility of the data file to half-byte packing is computed and the number of characters that could be saved based upon occurrences of different string lengths

Table 5.7

_____

SEGMENT V   DATANALYSIS
     HALF-BYTE ENCODING COMPRESSION SUSCEPTIBILITY
       FOR SEQUENTIAL (NON-REPEATING) NUMERICS
            IN SYSOUT FILE

_____

| | NUMBER OF | | | |
| STRING | OCCURRENCE | TOTAL | COMPRESSED | CHARACTERS |
LENGTH	S	CHARACTERS	CHARACTERS	SAVED
4	655	2620	2620	0
5	43	215	215	0
6	17	102	85	17
8	34	272	204	68
11	11	121	88	33
14	6	84	54	30

ANALYSIS SUMMARY:
   TOTAL CHARACTERS IN FILE 99132
   TOTAL CHAR. SUSCEPTIBLE TO COMPRESSION 3414
   TOTAL CHARACTERS SAVED BY COMPRESSION 148
   PER CENT FILE COMPRESSION REDUCTION 0.15

_____

containing numerics and predefined characters is listed. Although only a 0.15 per cent file reduction results from half-byte packing, it is cumulative and can result in 68.15 per cent file reduction when this technique is added to the run-length encoding technique.

Table 5.8 contains a paired or diatomic analysis of the data file, resulting from Segment VI of the DATANALYSIS program. Although 4528 paired combinations were encountered, this figure was based upon a total of 138 different paired characters. To save 4528 characters through the transmission of a special character in place of each encountered pair would require the employment of 138 special characters. Since this quantity is beyond the number of unused and available characters in most character sets, one must select a subset to encode. If the 24 most commonly encountered

Table 5.8

SEGMENT VI										DATANALYSIS
		PAIRED-CHARACTER COMPRESSION ANALYSIS								

Pair/count		Pair/count		Pair/count		Pair/count		Pair/count		Pair/count	
_I	156	TE	149	RI	110	UT	108	PU	96	_W	85
E_	80	TI	75	IN	75	_C	72	OR	70	_F	68
RE	68	N_	66	AT	66	MA	60	ER	59	SE	56
_D	55	AL	55	IR	53	FO	53	T_	52	O_	52
ON	50	L_	48	R_	46	D_	46	HA	46	S_	45
EN	45	SU	45	CO	43	AR	42	IS	40	_T	39
NT	39	LA	39	SI	38	_S	37	TH	37	AN	35
IT	34	_E	33	PA	33	IO	33	_R	33	HE	31
RA	30	RM	30	IA	30	TO	29	WE	29	ME	28
UB	28	LE	27	EQ	26	IM	26	H_	25	OU	25
AC	25	GE	24	CH	24	NE	24	_O	24	NU	24
LI	24	CT	23	OM	23	PR	23	ND	22	IL	22
TA	22	_P	22	DA	22	NA	21	_A	21	AI	21
NG	21	RO	20	MP	20	HS	20	AB	20	NO	19
CE	19	LY	19	RS	19	HC	19	YS	19	BE	18
RD	18	HG	18	IX	18	HI	18	HO	18	FI	18
IP	18	HU	18	ST	18	HQ	17	_B	17	DI	17
HW	17	HY	17	HK	17	HM	17	GO	17	_N	16
PI	16	CU	16	HD	16	G_	16	UE	16	UN	16
AP	16	EG	16	WO	16	CS	15	MI	15	ED	15
HN	15	EL	15	HH	14	PE	14	RR	14	TR	14
TS	14	HB	14	X_	14	HV	14	UR	14	_G	14
ES	14	OS	14	EP	14	HR	13	HF	13	HT	13

TOTAL COMBINATIONS FOUND: 4528

pairs of characters were encoded, this would result in the saving of 1839 characters, providing an additional 1.85 per cent data reduction. Thus, when combined with run-length and half-byte encoding, an averall data reduction of 70 per cent can be expected. Finally, Table 5.9 shows the results of segment VII of the program. In this program segment, the entropy of the data file is computed to denote its theoretical statistical compression. Many transmission sequences operate upon $8*N$ bit boundaries requiring the padding of dummy bits at the end of a word for the transmission of statistically encoded data blocks. This will result in the actual statistical compression data reduction approaching but never reaching the theoretically calculated data reduction. The degree of variation will be a function of the transmission block size and the sum of the number of bits per character for each character in the encoded block. It is interesting to note that the theoretical 75.77 per cent data reduction is closely approached by the use of the three easily combined data-compression techniques previously discussed. As shown, the execution of this program serves as a valuable guide. Here, it has provided information which indicates that the combination of three fixed-length, easily implemented techniques will approximate the data reduction obtainable from a variable-length technique that requires a lot of processing power and whose use could result in data expansion under certain conditions.

Table 5.9

SEGMENT VII	DATANALYSIS
ENTROPY ANALYSIS FOR SYSOUT FILE	

ENTROPY: 1.94 BITS/CHARACTER
FILE CONTAINS:
    99132 CHARACTERS
    793056 BITS
THEORETICAL STATISTICAL COMPRESSION: 75.77%
FILE WOULD REQUIRE:
    24016 CHARACTERS
    192130 BITS

6

SOFTWARE-LINKAGE
CONSIDERATIONS

Many factors must be taken into consideration when developing software to perform compression. These factors include the type of device the software will operate on, the method used to link the compression software to other software, the transfer rate of the compressed data, either internally to or from peripheral storage units or to and from a transmission medium, and the number of instructions required for coding the appropriate software. In this chapter we will examine the software-linkage considerations applicable to the application of data compression to on-line teleprocessing systems.

6.1 COMPRESSION ROUTINE PLACEMENT

In general, compression software will be written as a modular routine whose relationship in the overall system software structure will depend upon the ultimate application—for the storage or transmission of compressed data.

The software structure for transmission compression is illustrated in general form in Figure 6.1. Here, the compression/decompression routine will be at the same level as other communications routines, such as automatic baud recognition and code conversion, with the transmission handler acting as an overall routine controller or traffic policeman, similar to the way the operating system is the controller of application programs. Upon an interrupt occurring on the line, the automatic baud detection routine might be invoked by the transmission handler to determine the operating speed of the incoming transmission. Next, assuming the baud rate was detected and proper

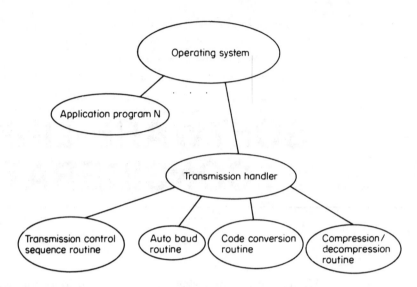

Figure 6.1 Software structure for transmission compression

buffering set up, the transmission control sequence routine might be invoked.

If transmission follows the BISYNC protocol, blocks of data have their block check character recomputed at the receiving location and compared with the transmitted block check character. When both the computed and transmitted check characters match, a positive acknowledgement is sent to the transmitting station. As part of the transmission control sequence, the special control characters appended to the data block for transmission purposes can be stripped, resulting in a data block of compressed data. At this point, the decompression routine can be invoked to bring the data back to its original format. Although the preceding description makes the placement of the compression routine appear to be a simple matter, careful study of the routine must precede its placement into the system's software.

Software considerations

The compression routine, like all software routines, will require both processor memory and program execution time. The amount of memory and program execution time required by the routine will determine whether or not compression can be performed in addition to the other functions on a particular machine. For buffer requirement analysis, let us assume we are considering run-length encoding. If the transmission protocol is BISYNC, we must first look at the existing data-block size handled by the protocol. If we assume that our block is 240 characters in size, compressed data will also occur in blocks of 240 characters unless we change the transmission block size. To determine the buffer area required for decompression, let us examine the worst case requirement as illustrated in Figure 6.2. Here, the received data-block buffer is first filled with 240 characters from a transmitted data block.

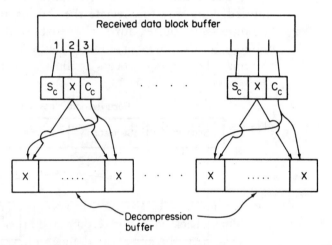

Figure 6.2 Memory requirements. When compresed data is transmitted, buffer areas must be available to restore the data to its orginal form. S_C = special character indication compression, C_C = compressed character count

If the run-length encoding is completely effective, the data block will be filled with 80 three-character sequences, consisting of a special character indicating compression followed by the repeated character of a string that was compressed and the character count that indicates the number of repeated characters. If each character count indicates that the original string consisted of 64 similar characters, a compression buffer of 5120 characters (64 × 80) becomes necessary. Although this may appear to be an excessive buffer size since the probability of encountering such a degree of compression is remote, you must consider allocating this space unless you perform decompression in stages cycling through the received data. Conversely, shortening the decompression buffer will result in additional data transfer time as we will shortly see.

If the decompression buffer is reduced to 2560 characters in size while all other conditions remain the same, two cycles will be required to complete the return of the compressed data into its original format to satisfy worst case conditions. In the first cycle, one-half of the received data-block buffer is processed, which will result in the 2560 character decompression buffer being filled. At this point, either an I/O transfer or DMA cycle transfer must be initiated to empty the buffer and transfer its contents to a peripheral storage unit. While the transfer is set up and executed, the decompression process cannot continue; therefore, reducing the buffer size results in two wait states while the smaller buffer is emptied. One way to alleviate the waiting process is to reduce the decompression buffer further in size while employing two such buffers. In this manner, double buffering can occur which will minimize the waiting process as illustrated in Figure 6.3.

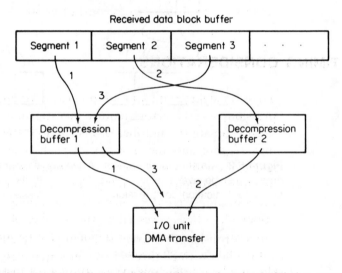

Figure 6.3 Double buffering—this can be employed to minimize transmission waiting times

When double buffering is employed, the received data-block buffer is processed in variable-length segments. The end of the first segment occurs when the first decompression buffer is filled while the end of the second segment occurs when the second decompression buffer is filled.

After the first decompression buffer is filled and while the second buffer is being filled, a DMA transfer can occur in order to empty the first buffer. Once the second decompression buffer is filled, another DMA transfer can occur and this buffer will be emptied while the first buffer is being filled again. At this point, the end of the third segment of the received data-block buffer will occur when the first decompression buffer is again filled. This concurrent filling and emptying of the dual decompression buffers will continue until the received data-block buffer is completely processed, at which time a second transmitted block will overlay the previously processed block. The size of the decompression buffers as well as the received data-block buffer will depend upon the transmission block format as well as available processor memory. While the received data-block buffer should equal the size of the transmitted block, the decompression buffers as previously explained can be set to any size; however, the smaller the size the larger the processing and the I/O transfer time required to decompress the received data block. Thus, the programmer must also investigate the program timing prior to selecting a final decompression buffer size.

6.2 TIMING CONSIDERATIONS

To estimate the amount of processor timing required for decompression, several factors require investigation. First, the programmer must estimate the number of instructions the decompression routine may require and the quantity of each type of instruction, such as single or double word, memory reference, shift instruction by number of shift positions and so on. From the computer manufacturer's programming reference manual, the timing per instruction can be obtained, either expressed by the number of machine cycles required to execute the program or denoted as a period of time and normally expressed in microseconds or 10^{-6} s. If expressed as a function of the number of machine cycles, timing per instruction can be obtained by multiplying the machine's cycle time by the number of cycles required for the instruction. Next, the sum of the product of the number of instructions of each type times the execution time per instruction is obtained. This becomes the estimated decompression time per block, less waiting time and data transfer time. The data transfer time can be estimated by examining the coding required to set up and initiate a DMA transfer. If double buffering is employed, the actual transfer time one must consider may be zero or a very minimal value. This is because one decompression buffer is being filled while the second decompression buffer is emptied as shown in Figure 6.4. In this illustration, if one decompression buffer is emptied before the second is filled, there is no waiting time and the

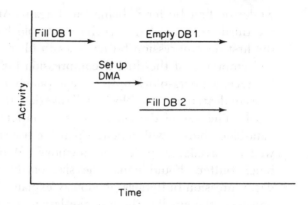

Figure 6.4 Timing considerations using double buffering. After the first buffer is filled, subsequent buffers are emptied and filled with minimal waiting time since only a DMA transfer set-up is required for each operation to occur concurrently with processing

only extra time in addition to the normal buffer processing time is the DMA set-up time. Although this set-up time varies from computer to computer, the total time required is normally less than 20 μs. For most machines, the buffer starting and ending address are loaded into certain registers along with a peripheral address code and a DMA transfer request is then initiated. Since a DMA set-up is required to empty buffers, two such DMA set-up times are required to empty the two decompression buffers.

Total time

The total decompression time for the received data blocks will depend upon the data contained in the blocks. This can be estimated for the worst case condition where the most efficient type of run-length encoding has been conducted as previously explained. If double decompression buffers are employed, 40 segment cycles as listed in Table 6.1 will be required if each decompression buffer is 64 characters in size. By obtaining the time for the process cycle listed in Table 6.1 and multiplying by 40, the total decompression time can be estimated based upon the previous assumptions. If data is being received at 9600 bps, then 1200 cps (characters/s) are being received. At that data rate, ignoring control characters and retransmission time due to line errors, the received data-block buffer of 240 characters will be filled once every 0.2 (240/1200) s. This

Table 6.1 Processing cycle

A.	Process received data-block buffer. Move pointer through buffer as decompression buffer 1 is filled.
B.	Set up DMA transfer. Decompression buffer 1 → storage.
C.	Process received data-block buffer. Move pointer through buffer as decompression buffer 2 is filled.
D.	Set up DMA transfer. Decompression buffer 2 → storage.

means that all of the previously discussed decompression processing as well as line handling and other communications functions must occur in that time or buffer queues must be employed to permit the processing of non-worst case conditions to be encountered which will then permit the processing to catch up with the data. By trade-offs of buffer size and timing and the employment of double buffering, most compression routines, other than some of the Huffman and modified Huffman coding techniques, can be easily adapted to on-line processing.

As an alternative to determining timing, one can compute the number of processing instructions available for operating upon the data prior to compression resulting in degraded performance. As an example, consider a data concentrator servicing 1200 bps terminals and connected via a 56 000 bps high-speed data link to a host computer. If there are 8 data bits per character, the 1200 bps terminals are communicating at 150 cps while the concentrator is communicating at 7000 cps.

If the terminals connected to the concentrator are used for time-sharing, their typical message length is 32 characters which takes 32/150 or 0.213 s to reach the concentrator from the terminal. To send that message from the concentrator to the host computer requires 32/7000 or 0.004 57 s. The difference between the time it takes the concentrator to receive the message and transmit the message is 0.208 76 s and can be considered a 'window of operation'. This is the amount of time available for all concentrator processing to include data compression prior to a message transmission delay resulting.

If we assume a 2 μs cycle time and 4 cycles per instruction, then a time of 8×10^{-6} s is required to execute an instruction. Dividing that figure into the previously computed window of operation results in 26 095 instructions which can be performed upon the data prior to a message transmission delay occurring. If one knows the current number of programmed instructions in the concentrator software, that number can be subtracted from 26 095 to determine the number of data-compression instructions that can be written prior to causing a message transmission delay.

Flow control

During periods of heavy transmission activity, buffers may become filled to capacity and subsequent data transfers will cause data to overflow such buffers, in effect becoming lost. To prevent such an occurrence, one can incorporate a number of flow-control procedures via software. These procedures are designed to selectively inhibit and enable data sources and, thus, prevent data buffers in memory from overflowing.

The most common method of flow control is obtained by the transmission of XON and XOFF characters to terminals and computers built to recognize such data characters. Transmitting an XOFF character can be used to tell a data source to inhibit all future transmission activity while one processes the data buffer contents residing in memory. Once the data buffer is emptied or has reached a certain percentage of occupancy, one can transmit an XON character to tell the data source to resume transmission. We must ensure that these two characters are not compressed if they are to be recognized and acted on by hardware which is unaware that the data is compressed.

A second method of selectively enabling and inhibiting the transmission of data can be obtained by raising and lowering the clear-to-send (CTS) signal interface lead on the RS-232 interface connection between a compression-performing device and a data source. The raising and lowering of the CTS signal would function in a way similar to the transmission of XON and XOFF characters previously discussed.

An XON, XOFF sequence and the raising and lowering of the CTS signal are normall used for asynchronous data-flow control. For synchronous data-flow control one should consider selectively altering a clock generator rate. As an example, using this method one could clock data initially at 19.2 kbps into a compression device for transmission at 9.6 kbps. As the compression buffers build up, one can lower the input clocking rate to prevent buffers from overflowing. Conversely, one can raise the clock rate if the data is susceptible to compression and buffer occupancy is minimal.

Routine linkage

When data compression is added to a front-end processor or programmable communications controller, several methods can be considered to link the compression module to existing software. The compression software can be added to an existing module or it can be coded as a separate module. For the latter situation, several methods can be used to invoke its operation. If the compression routine is to reside on a minicomputer, a 'jump and store return address' instruction or subroutine call are the two most frequently used methods for one routine to invoke another. At the completion of the routine, a return to the invoking instruction plus one location occurs and the instruction following the jump or the call instruction is executed next. If compression is to be employed with microcomputers, hardware and software differences may preclude the use of a jump or call statement. Many microprocessors are designed so that complete functions, such as a data-compression routine, may be burned into chips which are connected to the microprocessor's I/O or DMA bus. Since these coded chips are then considered part of the microprocessor's memory, linkage becomes a memory access problem. For these microprocessors that lack a 'jump and store return address' or subroutine call instruction, the address of the chip can be stored in one of the processor registers. Then an indirect address through the register will result in the processor fetching the chip address to initiate the compression routine.

7

USING COMPRESSION-PERFORMING HARDWARE AND SOFTWARE PRODUCTS

Many times you can obtain the benefits of data compression while avoiding the efforts required to analyze actual or potential data traffic and develop software to perform compression. This can be accomplished by leasing or purchasing data-compression-performing devices that are specifically designed to be used in a particular networking environment. In this chapter, we will examine the utilization of several hardware and software products to obtain a better understanding of the use of compression-performing devices. The products covered in this chapter were selected for illustrative purposes only and should not be construed as an endorsement of any device.

The utilization of a compression-performing hardware device or the use of a software program eliminates the necessity of analyzing data transmission traffic and developing the software routines required to compress data. However, readers are cautioned that many devices and compression performing software programs are designed to be most efficient when operating upon a particular type of data traffic that may not match the data consistency one actually transmits. Thus, such devices and programs may not generate a compression ratio level equivalent to the level that could be obtained from the development of a customized system tailored to operate based upon an analysis of the consistency of the user's data traffic.

In the first section in this chapter we will focus our attention upon the operation and utilization of several commercially available compression-performing hardware products. This will be followed by a second section focusing upon several types of compression-performing software packages. Included in this section are operational reviews of software programs used to enhance the efficiency of teleprocessing monitors operating on mainframe computers, programs that can be used to compress database files on mainframes, and programs that can be used to compress MS-DOS and PC-DOS files on IBM PC and compatible personal computers.

7.1 HARDWARE PRODUCTS

In examining hardware compression-performing products, we will distinguish such products by their functionality. First, we will examine devices that are restricted to compressing asynchronous data streams. Next, we will examine the operation and utilization of several multifunctional compression performing hardware products.

Asynchronous data compressors

Since asynchronous terminals outnumber synchronous operating terminals by a factor of ten or more, it should be of no surprise that many vendors have developed products for use with asynchronous transmission. Such products can normally be used for transmission occurring on both leased lines and the switched telephone network; however, their primary use is for transmission on the public switched telephone network. When used on this transmission facility, the primary advantage of the compression device is its ability to reduce the duration of the transmission session. Since the cost of a long-distance call is approximately proportional to its duration, decreasing the duration of the transmission session reduces the cost of the call. Two products specifically designed to compress asynchronous data that will be examined for illustrative purposes are RAD Computers' CompressoRAD-1 and Chung Telecommunications' turboMUX.

CompressoRAD-1

The CompressoRAD-1 is a stand-alone compression unit that also performs   asynchronous-to-synchronous/synchronous-to-asynchronous

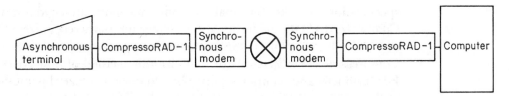

Figure 7.1 Using the CompressoRAD-1. The CompressoRAD-1 accepts asynchronous data at 1200, 2400, 4800 and 9600 bps. Data is compressed by the device, converted into a modified HDLC protocol and output to the attached modem according to the modem's clock rate setting

conversion and provides error detection and correction capability to one's data flow. Figure 7.1 illustrates how the CompressoRAD-1 could be utilized for transmitting data via the switched telephone network.

The CompressoRAD-1 accepts asynchronous data at 1200, 2400, 4800 or 9600 bps. the asynchronous data can consist of seven or eight bits per character, with either one or two stop bits and odd, even, mark, space or no parity. Utilizing an automatic adaptive algorithm, data compression ratios from 2 : 1 to 4 : 1 are obtainable according to RAD Computers, Inc.

In addition to compressing data, the device converts the asynchronous data flow into a synchronous modified higher-level data link control (HDLC) protocol. By adding a cyclic redundancy check character to each transmitted data block end-to-end error detection and correction capability is added to the data transmission.

The output data rate of the CompressoRAD-1 is determined by the clock of the attached modem, with the device capable of operating between 600 and 4800 bps. A buffer in the device is used to compensate for the differences in the compressibility of input data. Thus, when data input into the CompressoRAD is compressed, and represents a data flow greater than the rate at which data is output to the attached synchronous modem, the buffer fills, serving as a temporary storage area. Since the buffer is finite in size, the CompressoRAD employs two methods to inhibit additional data input once the buffer is filled to a predefined level. Known as flow control, data is regulated into the device by the transmission of XOFF and XON characters and the raising and lowering of the RS-232 clear-to-send control signals. When buffer storage fills to a predefined level, the CompressoRAD will either transmit an XOFF character or drop the CTS signal on the RS-232 interface. The choice of which method one selects is based upon the operational specifications of the terminal or computer port attached on the CompressoRAD. Some terminals and computer ports recognize XON and XOFF as flow control character signalling, enabling the CompressoRAD to be configured to use this method of flow control. For terminals and computer ports that do not recognize this method of flow control the CompressoRAD can be configured to enable and inhibit transmission to the device via the CTS control signal. Thus, after data is inhibited from transmission into the device by the CompressoRAD dropping CTS, it will raise this control signal once the buffer is emptied to another predefined level. The issuance of flow control signals based upon the quantity of data in the device's buffer is illustrated in Figure 7.2.

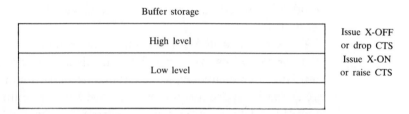

Figure 7.2 Buffer control. To prevent buffer storage overflow and the loss of data flow control occurs through the raising and lowering of the clear-to-send (CTS) control signal or the generation of XOFF and XON characters

The use of XOFF and XON characters and the raising and lowering of the CTS control signal are used by most compression-performing products that operate upon asynchronous data. When synchronous data is compressed, flow control is normally accomplished by reducing the clocking rate signal passed from a modem attached to the compression device to a synchronous operating terminal, computer port or similar device. One common method used by hardware manufacturers is to halve the clock rate several times until the buffer empties to a predefined level. Once this occurs, the clock rate is then doubled several times until the original data rate is restored.

To understand the economics associated with the utilization of the CompressoRAD and similar compression-performing products, assume that the daily cost for communicating on the switched telephone network between a remote terminal and a central computer facility is $5, a cost representing a long-distance call duration of under 30 min. Assuming one call per day and 22 working days per month, the cost of using the switched telephone network is $110 per month or $1320 on an annual basis. Now, let us assume that the use of two asynchronous data-compression devices reduces the transmission session duration by half, resulting in the ability to reduce the cost of communications by $660 during one year of operation. To what should one then compare this potential cost saving?

In using the CompressoRAD illustrated in Figure 7.1 or a similar compression-performing product, one must obtain two synchronous modems as well as two compression devices. In comparison, one would use two lower-cost asynchronous modems when transmitting data without the use of asynchronous compression devices. Thus, from an economic perspective:

$$(\triangle M)*2 + 2*C \leq 660*EL$$

where:

$\triangle M$ = cost difference between synchronous and asynchronous modems

C = unit cost of each compression-performing device

EL = expected life or use of the compression-performing devices in years.

turboMUX

The Chung Telecommunications' turboMUX is an asynchronous data compressor that has two modes of operation, of which one mode offers a significantly different network operation from the previously discussed CompressoRAD device. The turboMUX supports one input asynchronous data source at 2400 bps or two asynchronous data sources operating at 1200 bps. In its latter mode of operation, the device supports two data transmission sessions over one public switched telephone network call as illustrated in Figure 7.3.

As illustrated in Figure 7.3, two asynchronous data input sources are supported by the turboMUX. Designed to work with the commonly used Bell System 212A modem operating synchronously, the compression unit, in essence, permits a 1200 bps modem to operate at double its rated speed. Other than its dual data source support, the turboMUX operates similar to the CompressoRAD, containing a buffer area which is controlled via the previously discussed flow control process while an automatic error detection

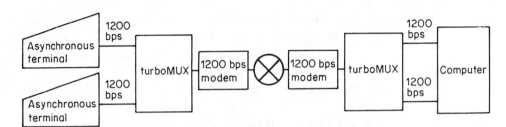

Figure 7.3 Typical turboMUX network utilization. The turboMUX permits two asynchronous data transmission sessions to occur over one public switched telephone network session

and retransmission mechanism is incorporated into data flowing between the two turboMUX's, providing end-to-end error-free transmission.

Multifunctional compression devices

One of the more popular uses of compression-performing devices is to reduce the quantity of data to be multiplexed, increasing the servicing capacity of multiplexers. A natural evolution of the development of compression devices was to include both statistical multiplexing and data compression in one hardware device. Two products representing this multifunctional capability are the Racal-Vadic Scotsman III and the Datagram Corporation Streamer product line which, upon that company's acquisition by Memotec Data, has been relabeled as the MC series of products.

Scotsman III

The Racal-Vadic Scotsman III is a stand-alone data compressor that can be configured in a variety of ways to include the addition of an optional four-channel multiplexer. Figure 7.4 illustrates the utilization of the Scotsman III as a multiplexer, compressing four bisynchronous data streams onto a single transmission line.

The utilization of the Scotsman III illustrated in Figure 7.4 should be compared to the employment of a statistical multiplexer. Since most statistical multiplexers do not perform data compression, significant time delays would occur in attempting to multiplex four 9600 bps bisynchronous data sources onto one 9600 bps transmission

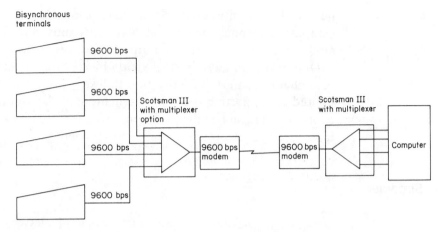

Figure 7.4 Using the Scotsman III as a multiplexer. An optional four-channel multiplexer can be added to the Racal-Vadic Scotsman III, resulting in the ability to transmit four high-speed bisynchronous data sources on a single transmission line

line. In other situations, statistical multiplexers may service bisynchronous data through the use of band-pass channels. When this occurs, only asynchronous data is actually statistically multiplexed, while bisynchronous data is time division multiplexed onto a predefined time slot on the composite multiplexed link as illustrated in Figure 7.5.

When bisynchronous data is multiplexed via a band-pass channel, the data rate of the bisynchronous input data reduces the portion of the composite channel bandwidth available for multiplexing other data sources. As an example, one bisynchronous data source operating at 4800 bps would reduce the bandwidth of the composite channel for multiplexing other data sources by 4800 bps when the bisynchron-

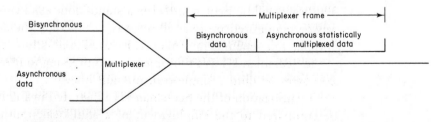

Figure 7.5 Band pass multiplexing. When data is multiplexed using a bandpass channel the size of the band-pass channel proportionally reduces the capacity of the multiplexer frame for multiplexing other data

ous data is multiplexed via a band-pass channel. Thus, if the composite channel operates at 9600 bps, only 4800 bps would be available for the statistical multiplexing of other data sources.

Due to the limitations of servicing bisynchronous data with band-pass channels, most statistical multiplexers using this technique are limited to supporting only one bisynchronous data source. Thus, the Scotsman III can be effectively employed for situations where several high-speed bisynchronous data sources transmit to a common location.

Streamer

Datagram Corporation's Streamer series of devices, which were renamed as the MC 504 and MC 508 when that company was acquired by Memotec Data, are statistical multiplexers that incorporate data compression, resulting in an overall statistical efficiency of up to 4 : 1 according to the company. In comparison to many similar products, the Streamer series of devices supports a wide variety of bit-oriented protocols to include synchronous data link control (SDLC), X.25, HDLC, Univac data link control (UDLC) and character-oriented protocols to include asynchronous and bisynchronous transmission.

Each Streamer, now marketed as the MC 504 and 508 data-compression multiplexer, analyzes incoming data on an individual port basis and employs an adaptive string compression algorithm to compress the more frequently occurring strings into shorter strings. Since the data transmitted in each direction can vary in composition, each compression-performing multiplexer maintains both inbound and outbound compression tables for each port, that are independent of each other. Once each port's data stream is compressed, the data stream of all ports is then multiplexed.

Due to the ability of the Streamer series of devices to support numerous data link protocols, this compression-performing communications device can be used in a large variety of network applications. Figure 7.6 illustrates one potential application that shows the versatility of the Streamer. The Streamer first performs typical statistical multiplexer functions to include stripping start and stop bits from asynchronous transmission and passing data only from active terminals. After the device's compressor uses an adaptive compression table to encode the data, the resulting compressed data is statistically multiplexed, resulting in overall statistical and compression efficiencies of up to [4 : 1]. One of the more interesting

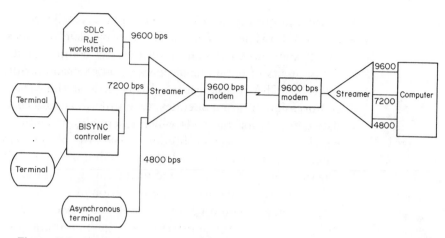

Figure 7.6 Using the Streamer. Datagram's Streamer series of compression performing multiplexers supports a large number of bit- and character-oriented protocols

characteristics of the Streamer is its analysis and construction of adaptive compression tables for each direction of data flow on a port-by-port basis. This approach maximizes the potential efficiencies obtained by compressing data as it ensures different data characteristics flowing in one direction as promptly recognized.

7.2 SOFTWARE PRODUCTS

In this section we will examine three types of data-compression software products. First we will focus our attention upon teleprocessing monitor compression software designed to reduce terminal response time by reducing the quantity of data transmitted between a mainframe application and a terminal device. This will be followed by an overview of a few mainframe database compression-performing products and software designed to compress personal computer files.

Teleprocessing monitor compression products

A large number of software vendors have developed data-compression products to enhance the efficiency of a variety of IBM teleprocessing monitor systems. Some products are designed to work with specific IBM teleprocessing monitor systems, such as CICS, IMS, and TSO. Other vendors have developed products that operate at the Virtual

Telecommunications Access Method (VTAM) level. When operating at the VTAM level the compression package provides compression for all applications operating on the host computer which eliminates the necessity of obtaining a separate compression-performing product for each VTAM application. Regardless of the location where the compression program operates, each program uses a core of equivalent data-compression methods which essentially make their performance equal. Compression techniques used by teleprocessing monitor enhancement software include the elimination of all consecutive repetitive characters, outbound image-saving, and inbound mirroring.

To illustrate the effect of the operation of a teleprocessing monitor system compression program consider the network segment illustrated in Figure 7.7. In this illustration a large mainframe operating CICS, IMS and TSO is accessed by 32 terminals located at a remote site. If each terminal operator pressed a Program Function (PF) key to display a new screen image the number of bits that would be transmitted to each terminal exclusive of the protocol overhead would be 80*25*8 or 16 000 per terminal. Assuming a worst case scenario where 32 terminal operators simultaneously press a screen PA, PF, or Enter key, 16 000*32 or 512 000 bits would require transmission. If the line connecting the remote location to the central computer site operates at 19.2 kbps it would require 512 000 / 19 200 or approximately 27 s to transmit all screen images. Since the preceding calculation did not consider the processing time required by the host to interpret the key request and retrieve a required screen, nor the

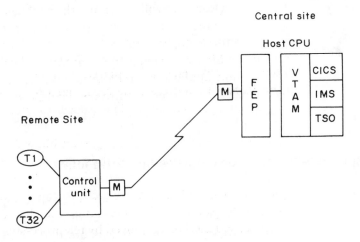

Figure 7.7 Network segment to illustrate benefits of teleprocessing monitor compression software

effect of the overhead associated with the transmission protocol, the actual time would be considerably more. Even if it were not, waiting 27 s for a response would clearly be an unacceptable level of response time. Thus, any technique that can reduce response time will boost terminal operator productivity. In fact, although 32 terminal devices are illustrated in Figure 7.7 as being connected to the control unit, normally a lesser number are connected to preclude excessive response times. For large organizations with hundreds of terminals located at different offices remote from the host computer, the reduction in the number of terminals connected to each control unit will normally result in the use of additional control units, each requiring modems and a communications line. Thus, any method that reduces terminal response time can also allow more terminals to be connected to a control unit, which can result in a reduction in the cost of communications.

Compression methods

In many applications character strings that contain a letter or character are repeated several times in succession. For example, the character string '− − − . . . −Page n' is used as a page separator in many applications. This string may have a run of 60 to 70 dashes followed by a page number. In other applications a string of equal signs '= = = = = =' may be used to underscore a field or separate it from other fields. Although not visible, some applications commonly use a string of blanks to delete the contents of an existing field on a screen.

Teleprocessing monitor compression products examine outbound data streams for consecutive repetitive characters. When found, repetitive characters are replaced by a four-byte sequence which uses the Repeat-to-address code recognized by terminals as the first byte in a four-byte sequence. The Repeat-to-address code is followed by a two-byte screen address which identifies where the repeated character is repeated to. This is then followed by the actual character to be repeated. Figure 7.8 illustrates the format used to compress repetitive strings. Note that each character is encoded in a hexadecimal. Thus, 3C, which is the hexadecimal code for the Repeat-to-address code, represents one character.

A second method employed by teleprocessing monitor compression-performing software is commonly referred to as outbound image-saving or suppressing redundant data images. To accomplish this

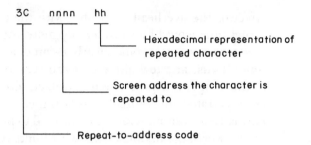

Figure 7.8 Repeated character compression format

the compression program intercepts outbound screen images and compares the current screen image to the previously transmitted image, suppressing the transmission of common fields or portions of fields. Figures 7.9 and 7.10 illustrate the operation of image-saving. Figure 7.9 shows a typical terminal screen when an operator is using a customer maintenance mailing list program. Figure 7.10 shows how the next screen might appear. Note that only the first name, date, and amount fields changed. Thus, transmitting only those

```
                    FRED UNGER HARDWARE CORP
            ======================================
               CUSTOMER MAINTENANCE MAILING LIST

     Customer Name

            Last.............:   Held
            First............:   Beverly

     Customer Address

            Street..........:   4736 Oxford Road
            City, State ....:   Macon, GA
            Zip..............:   31210

     Last Purchase

            Date.............:   6/18/89
            Amount..........:   $3.27


     Help: F1          Add: PF2        Update: PF3        Delete: PF4
     Fwd: F5           Back: PF6       Search: PF8        Return: PF12
```

Figure 7.9 Initial screen

changes in place of an entirely new screen can significantly reduce the number of characters required to update the screen.

A third method used by many teleprocessing monitor compression-performing programs involves increasing the efficiency of an application program. As previously discussed in Chapter 3 in which forms-mode compression was described, when an operator enters data into a screen field, the data tag associated with that field is modified. The modified data tag (MDT) can also be turned on by an application when data is transmitted to a terminal. If this is done, the field will be transmitted back from the terminal even if the field is not changed by the operator.

To obtain inbound mirroring the compression program turns off all MDTs as the transmission flows to terminals, which results only in the fields modified by the operator being transmitted. By keeping an image of the screen in memory the compression program knows which fields had their associated MDTs set on. If those fields are not transmitted back from the terminal they are inserted into the

```
                    FRED UNGER HARDWARE CORP
               ========================================
                  CUSTOMER MAINTENANCE MAILING LIST


        Customer Name

              Last............:   Held
              First.......... :   Gilbert

        Customer Address

              Street .........:   4736 Oxford Road
              City, State    :    Macon, GA
              Zip.............:    31210

        Last Purchase

              Date ...........:   7/19/91
              Amount..........:   $43.27


         Help: F1        Add: PF2      Update: PF3      Delete: PF4
         Fwd: F5         Back: PF6     Search: PF8      Return: PF12
```

Figure 7.10 Subsequent screen. Only the first name, date, and amount fields are transmitted since all other fields are the same as contained in the previously transmitted screen

downstream by the compression program prior to that program passing the data to the application program.

Two popular teleprocessing monitor enhancement compression programs are Datapacker/II marketed by H&M Systems Software of Maywood, NJ, and VTAM-EXPRESS marketed by SofTouch Systems of Oklahoma City, OK. The first program is a CICS product, while the second program supports CICS, IMS, and TSO applications.

Database compression

InfoTel Corporation of Tampa, FL, markets a series of data-compression software programs for compressing different types of databases. Programs marketed under the INFOPAK label include INFOPAK DB2, INFOPAK VSAM, INFOPAK IMS, INFOPAK IDMS, and INFOPAK SEQ.

INFOPAK DB2 reduces the amount of direct access storage device (DASD) storage required for DB2 databases. According to the company, disk space recovery rates between 50 and 75 per cent are typically obtainable with a minimum of CPU overhead. In addition, since disk storage requirements are considerably reduced, the number of input/output (I/O) operations required for DB2 applications is also reduced.

INFOPAK DB2 uses a modified Huffman encoding technique in which a scanning program module performs a three-dimensional analysis of data and then makes compression decisions based upon the nature of the data. The scanning program uses artificial intelligence to determine which of several different compression methods to use for optimum performance. Most data is compressed using the Huffman encoding technique but other compression techniques, including repeating character substitution, bit represen-tation of blank and zero fields, and a proprietary algorithm for certain kinds of data, are also used.

InfoTel's INFOPAK VSAM allows compression of KSDS or ESDS data sets running under IBM's MVS or MVS/XA operating systems. This program is CICS compatible and is completely transparent to the application program.

To maintain application program transparency, the compression program ensures that each key retains its exact record position. To accomplish this the uncompressed keys are saved in a separate work area during compression. After compression the keys are inserted into the compressed record in the exact positions they occupied prior to compression. Then, the new compressed record is provided to VSAM for physical storage. If the compressed data does not fill out the record after the insertion of the keys in their exact record positions the record is lengthened by the addition of bytes of binary zeros to obtain a minimum record length. This serves to maintain application program transparency.

Figure 7.11 illustrates the operation of INFOPAK VSAM on a record that has KSDS primary and alternate keys located in positions 12 and 40, respectively. Note that when the record is compressed, its compressed length depends upon the susceptibility of the data to compression.

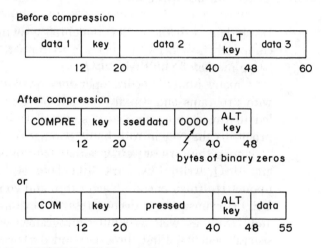

Figure 7.11 INFOPAK VSAM operation

INFOPAK IMS enables IMS databases to be compressed while INFOPAK IDMS enables compression of IDMS databases. Both compression programs result in compressed databases that are totally transparent to application programs. InfoTel's INFOPAK SEQ operates upon files that are processed sequentially. The resulting compressed sequential files are identified by a special suffix appended to the dataset name. Other than this suffix, INFOPAK SEQ is transparent to the job control language (JCL) and is completely transparent to all applications.

Due to the high cost of DASD, the INFOPAK series of products has gained wide acceptance by numerous private industry and government agencies. INFOPAK users include several US Department of Defense agencies, large universities, health care organizations, insurance companies, and many other organizations that maintain a variety of large databases. Since the reduction of just one IBM 3380 or 3390 disk system can essentially recover the cost of the program, its payback can be instantaneous. In fact, many firms can obtain savings significantly exceeding the cost of the software while obtaining additional storage capacity through the use of storage space freed from the use of the program. This can provide large data processing organizations with years of expansion capacity through the use of existing equipment.

Personal computer file compression

In tandem with the near exponential growth in the use of personal computers has been an increase in both the number of programs being marketed and their complexity. As software products prolifer-ated many bulletin board operators quickly filled their hard disks with programs and rapidly ran out of storage space. This problem led to the development of a series of public domain compression programs that began to achieve popularity in the mid-1980s.

Among the earliest public domain compression programs were SQ and USQ, written by Dick Greenlaw. SQ (for squeeze) was based upon a Huffman encoding algorithm and compressed PC files, while USQ (for unsqueeze) decompressed previously compressed files. SQ and USQ, as well as similar programs, provided PC users with several benefits. First, program and data files could be stored using less disk storage. This, in turn, allowed bulletin boards to store more programs. In addition, it provided software vendors and end-users with the ability to distribute more software on a smaller number of diskettes. Another significant benefit was a reduction in communi-cations time and cost, since compressed files could be downloaded quicker than uncompressed files.

ARC—the archive utility that compresses data

Building upon the initial development of PC file compression and decompression programs, System Enhancement Associates of Wayne, NJ, developed an archive utility for personal computers running under DOS and OS/2 that compresses data. This program, called ARC, performs an archive operation by grouping a series of specified files together into one file in such a way that the individual files may be recovered intact. In addition, ARC automatically compresses the files being archived so that the resulting archive takes up a minimum amount of space.

When ARC is used to add a file to an archive it analyzes the file to determine which of three storage methods will result in the greatest savings. These three methods are:

1. No compression; the file is stored as is.
2. Repeated-character compression; repeated sequences of the same byte value are collapsed into a three-byte code sequence.
3. Dynamic Lempel–Ziv compression; the file is stored as a series of variable-size bit codes which represent character strings and which are created 'on the fly'.

Note that since one of the three methods involves no compression at all, the resulting archive entry will never be larger than the original file.

Using ARC

ARC is invoked with a command of the following format:

ARC ⟨x⟩ ⟨arcname⟩ [⟨template⟩. . .]

where

⟨x⟩ is an ARC command letter (see below), in either upper or lower case.
⟨arcname⟩ is the name of the archive to act on, with or without an extension. If no extension is supplied, then .ARC is assumed. The archive name may include path and drive specifiers.

⟨template⟩ is one or more filename templates. The 'wildcard' characters * and ? may be used. A filename template may include a path or drive specifier, though it is not always meaningful.

If ARC is invoked with no arguments (by typing ARC and pressing Enter), then a brief command summary is displayed.

Following is a brief summary of the available ARC commands:

a	=	add files to archive
m	=	move files to archive
u	=	update files in archive
f	=	freshen files in archive
d	=	delete files from archive
x,e	=	extract files from archive
r	=	run files from archive
p	=	copy files from archive to standard output
l	=	list files in archive
v	=	verbose listing of files in archive
t	=	test archive integrity
c	=	convert entry to new storage method.

Following is a brief summary of the available ARC options, which may alter how a command works:

m	=	move files to archive
z	=	include subdirectories in archive
v	=	verbose mode
b	=	retain backup copy of archive
s	=	suppress compression (store only)
w	=	suppress warning messages
n	=	suppress notes and comments
o	=	overwrite existing files when extracting
5	=	produce only level-5 compatible archives
g	=	encode or decode archive entry.

To illustrate the operation of ARC commands, let us examine the use of the A (Add), U (Update), and F (Freshen) commands which allow files to be added to an archive:

Add always adds the file

Update differs from Add in that the file is only added if it is not already in the archive, or if it is newer than the corresponding entry in the archive.

Freshen is similar to Update, except that new files are not added to the archive; only files already in the archive are updated.

For example, if you wished to add a file named TEST.DAT to an archive named MY.ARC, you would use a command of the form:

ARC a my test.dat

If you wanted to add all files with a .C extension and all files named STUFF to an archive named JUNK.ARC you could type:

ARC a junk*.c stuff.*

If you had an archive named TEST.ARC and you wanted to add to it all of your files with an extension of .TXT which have been created or changed since they were last archived, then you would type:

ARC u text*.txt

If you have a bunch of files in your current directory with backup copies being stored in an archive named SAFE.ARC, then if you wanted to make sure that every file in the archive is the latest version of that file, you would type:

ARC f safe

A word about Update and Freshen—these are similar in that they look at the date and time of last change on the file and only add it if the file has been changed since it was last archived. They differ in that Update will add new files, while Freshen will not.

In other words, Update looks for the files on disk and adds them if they are new or have changed, while Freshen looks in the archive and tries to update the files which are already there.

To illustrate the potential efficiency of ARC, let us examine its main executable file named ARC602.EXE, which, when copied to a user's personal computer, unpacks itself. Figure 7.12 illustrates the sequence of operations performed by the author to copy ARC602.EXE to his personal computer's hard disk under the directory \ARC that he created, list his hard disk directory structure, unpack ARC602.EXE, and take a second directory listing to observe the effect of the unpacking. Note that after ARC602.EXE was copied to the author's hard disk the directory listing shows that this file contains 85 527 bytes. After entering the command ARC602 the program unpacks or uncrunches itself into four files: ARC.DOC, ARC.EXE, ARC.TXT, and ARCORDER.TXT. Note that the second directory listing indicates that these four files require 136 102 bytes of storage. Thus, ARC obtained a compression ratio of 1.59

```
C>md\arc

C>cd\arc

C>copy d:arc602.exe c:
        1 File(s) copied

C>dir

  Volume in drive C is GILSGARBAGE
  Directory of  C:\ARC

  .              <DIR>      4-23-90    5:37p
  ..             <DIR>      4-23-90    5:37p
  ARC602   EXE    85527     6-22-89    3:39p
         3 File(s)   1986560 bytes free

C>


C>arc602
SARC  Copyright 1986-89 by Wayne Chin and Vernon D. Buerg.  /H gives help
Archive self-extractor, Version 1.10, 03/06/89. ALL RIGHTS RESERVED.

  Archive:  C:\ARC\ARC602.EXE
  UnCrunching > ARC.DOC
  UnCrunching > ARC.EXE
  UnCrunching > ARC.TXT
  UnCrunching > ARCORDER.TXT
C>dir

  Volume in drive C is GILSGARBAGE
  Directory of  C:\ARC

  .              <DIR>      4-23-90    5:37p
  ..             <DIR>      4-23-90    5:37p
  ARC602   EXE    85527     6-22-89    3:39p
  ARC      DOC    64321     6-22-89    3:33p
  ARC      EXE    65339     3-13-89   10:30a
  ARC      TXT     2299     3-14-89    9:57a
  ARCORDER TXT     4143     6-22-89    3:39p
         7 File(s)   1845248 bytes free

C>
```

Figure 7.12   Installing ARC602.EXE

when operated upon itself. To appreciate its compression efficiency, readers should note that ARC.EXE is an executable file while ARC.DOC, ARC.TXT, and ARCORDER.TXT are ASCII files.

Readers should also note that ARC is a copyrighted proprietary program of System Enhancement Associates, Inc., which has granted permission to the author to include it and several associated programs on the convenience disk you can obtain from John Wiley & Sons. Purchasers of the convenience disk are granted a LIMITED LICENSE to use ARC and to copy it and distribute it, provided that the following conditions are met:

1. No fee may be charged for such copying and distribution.
2. ARC may *only* be distributed in its original, unmodified state.

3. ARC may *not* be distributed, in whole or in part, as part of any commercial product or service without the express written permission of System Enhancement Associates, Inc.

Contributions for the use of this program will be appreciated and should be sent to: System Enhancement Associates, Inc., 21 New Street, Wayne, NJ 07470, USA.

In addition to ARC602.EXE the convenience disk contains several additional programs, including ARCE.COM, ARCE.DOC, ARCP.EXE, MARC.EXE, MARCP.EXE, MKSARC.EXE, and PACKING.LST. ARCP.EXE is a program which is used to extract files from an archive in a highly optimized manner and can be quicker than using ARC.EXE. ARCE.DOC contains the documentation for the program.

MARC.EXE can be used to merge archives previously created by ARC. MKSARC.EXE is used to create an archive into a self-unpacking program similar to the concept used to create ARC602.EXE. PACKING.LST as its name may imply is an ASCII file which describes the files contained on the ARC program disk. Figure 7.13 illustrates the list of PACKING.LST. Readers should note that all of the files listed in Figure 7.13 are contained in the directory \ARC on the convenience disk.

Readers shsould note that each of these programs are user-supported software. This means that you may copy it freely and give the copies away to anyone you wish, at no cost. Those recipients are, in turn, requested to send in a contribution if they decide to use it.

The user-supported software concept (often referred to as 'shareware') is an attempt to provide software at low cost. The cost of offering a new product by conventional means is staggering and, hence, dissuades many independent authors and small companies from developing and promoting their ideas. User-supported software is an attempt to develop a new marketing channel where products can be introduced at low cost.

If user-supported software works, then everyone will benefit. The user will benefit by receiving quality products at low cost and by being able to 'test drive' software thoroughly before purchasing it. The author benefits by being able to enter the commercial software arena without first needing large sources of venture capital.

But it can only work with your support. We're not just talking about ARC here, but about *all* user-supported software. If you obtain a user-supported program from a friend or colleague and are

Following is a list of what is contained on the ARC 6.02 program disk:

Filename	Description
ARC602.EXE	This is ARC version 6.02 for MS-DOS (plus documentation) in the form of a 'self-unpacking archive.' It unpacks itself when you run it.
ARCE.COM	This is a small archive extractor by Vern Buerg and Wayne Chin which is included on the ARC disk as a service to our customers.
ARCE.DOC	This is the full documentation for ARCE.
ARCP.EXE	This is the protected mode version of ARC for use with the OS/2 operating system.
MARC.EXE	This is an archive merge/split utility. It is described in the ARC documentation.
MARCP.EXE	This is the protected mode version of MARC for use with the OS/2 operating system.
MKSARC.EXE	This is the program that creates self-extracting archives. It is described in the ARC documentation.
PACKING.LIST	This file, of course!
README	This file contains directions on how to install ARC on your system.
README.BAT	This is a batch file to print out the README file.

Figure 7.13 PACKING.LST file contents. This file lists and describes the files contained on the ARC program disk and which are also contained in the \ARC directory on the convenience diskette available from the publisher of this book

still using it after a couple of weeks, then it is obviously worth something to you, and a contribution should be sent.

PKWARE file compression system

In concluding this chapter we will examine a second popular set of file-compression programs developed for MS-DOS and PC-DOS compatible personal computers. Collectively referred to as PKWARE, which represents the name of the firm marketing this software, the system consists of one main file which, when executed, decomposes into a series of programs. Similar to ARC, PKWARE can be used to both compress and store files together under one filename. In addition, PKWARE provides users with the ability to recreate files previously compressed as well as to view technical information concerning compressed files, delete files from within a compressed file, and perform many additional functions.

To illustrate the use of PKWARE, let us examine the contents of its distribution diskette and the execution of its main program which 'explodes' the program into a series of programs.

Figure 7.14 illustrates the contents of the PKWARE distribution diskette upon its transfer to the author's hard disk. Note that the executable file PKZ110.EXE contains 140 116 bytes. The file labeled README contains installation instructions and is not affected by the execution of PKZ110.

```
C>dir

    Volume in drive C is GILSGARBAGE
    Directory of  C:\TEMP

    .               <DIR>       3-21-90   11:08p
    ..              <DIR>       3-21-90   11:08p
    PKZ110   EXE   140116       3-15-90    1:10a
    README          1825        3-15-90    1:10a
            4 File(s)    1560576 bytes free

C>
```

Figure 7.14 PKWARE diskette contents

By entering the command PKZ110 the program functions as a self-extraction utility, in effect, exploding a series of previously compressed files into their original format. Figure 7.15 illustrates the self-extraction process performed by PKZ110 which results in the formation of 13 files.

By performing a directory listing you can easily obtain first-hand information concerning the compression capability of the program. Figure 7.16 contains the directory listing after PKZ110 was executed. If you add the file size of each file with the exception of PKZ110 and README you obtain a total of 292 541 bytes of storage. Thus, the compression ratio of PKZ110 obtained when compressing several executable and document files is 292 541 / 140 116 or approximately 2.09.

PKZIP is the main compression program, while PKUNZIP is the main extraction program. Similar to ARC, PKWARE provides a program that can be used to create self-extracting files. This program is labeled ZIP2EXE.

```
C>pkz110

PKSFX (R)   FAST!   Self Extract Utility   Version 1.1.   03-15-90
Copr. 1989-1990 PKWARE Inc. All Rights Reserved. PKSFX/h for help
PKSFX Reg. U.S. Pat. and Tm. Off.

Searching EXE: C:/TEMP/PKZ110.EXE - Thanks for using PKWARE!
   Exploding: WHATSNEW.110
   Exploding: README.DOC
   Exploding: MANUAL.DOC
   Exploding: ADDENDUM.DOC
   Exploding: DEDICATE.DOC
   Exploding: LICENSE.DOC
   Exploding: ORDER.DOC
   Exploding: APPNOTE.TXT
   Exploding: OMBUDSMN.ASP
   Exploding: PKZIP.EXE
   Exploding: PKUNZIP.EXE
   Exploding: ZIP2EXE.EXE
   Exploding: PKZIPFIX.EXE

   C>
```

Figure 7.15 PKWARE self-extraction process

```
             Directory of  C:\TEMP

   .                   <DIR>      5-15-90   8:08p
   ..                  <DIR>      5-15-90   8:08p
   PKZ110    EXE     140116      3-15-90   1:10a
   README              1825      3-15-90   1:10a
   WHATSNEW  110       2916      3-15-90   1:10a
   README    DOC        534      3-15-90   1:10a
   MANUAL    DOC     140355      7-21-89   1:01a
   ADDENDUM  DOC      21473      3-15-90   1:10a
   DEDICATE  DOC        720      3-15-90   1:10a
   LICENSE   DOC       9366      3-15-90   1:10a
   ORDER     DOC       4701      3-15-90   1:10a
   APPNOTE   TXT      25811      3-15-90   1:10a
   OMBUDSMN  ASP        595      3-15-90   1:10a
   PKZIP     EXE      32880      3-15-90   1:10a
   PKUNZIP   EXE      22540      3-15-90   1:10a
   ZIP2EXE   EXE      21426      3-15-90   1:10a
   PKZIPFIX  EXE       9224      3-15-90   1:10a
        17 File(s)   18569216 bytes free

   C:\TEMP>
```

Figure 7.16 Directory listing after completion of self-extraction process

Other files included in PKWARE include README.DOC which contains general information, DEDICATE.DOC which is a dedication of file format and extensions to the public domain, ORDER.DOC which includes registration information and an order form, LICENSE.DOC which contains information on site and distribution licenses, MANUAL.DOC which is the reference manual for PKWARE, APPNOTE.TXT which contains technical background material, PKZIPFIX.EXE which is a program that can be used to recreate corrupted program files, and OMBDSMAN.ASP which contains information on the Association of Shareware Professionals.

Similar to ARC, PKWARE is a shareware program. PKWARE, Inc., as a firm believer in shareware, has consented to the distribution of their software on the convenience diskettes that you can obtain from the publisher of this book. If you find the software fast, easy, and convenient to use, a registration of $25 would be appreciated. If you send $47 or more, you will receive a diskette with documentation for the next version of the software, when available. Please state the version of the software that you currently have. Send registrations to: PKWARE, Inc., 7545 N. Port Washington Rd., Suite 205, Glendale, WI 53217–3422, USA.

Program features

PKWARE includes a large number of features that warrant discussion, including password encryption, automatic detection and utilization of Intel 80386 microprocessor-based personal computers, and the ability to display a significant level of information about compressed files.

The password encryption feature provides users with the ability to scramble sensitive data files, while the automatic detection and utilization of 80386 microprocessors enables the program to use 32-bit instructions and extended addressing modes for improved performance when that CPU is available for use. One of the nicest features of the program is obtained by the use of its (v) view command, which displays technical information several ways based upon the specification of an optional suffix added to the v option. Table 7.1 indicates the basic information about each file that will be listed through the use of the v command.

In examining the entries in Table 7.1 the reader should note that the CRC-32 functions as a data integrity check appended to each file when compressed and which the program checks upon explosion. Both PKZIP and PKUNZIP follow a similar command execution format and are essentially very easy to use. For example, to compress files using PKZIP you would enter a command according to the following command syntax:

PKZIP ZIPFILE [options] [files]

where:

Table 7.1 PKWARE file information displayed by using the v command

Length	Original length of the file
Method	Type of file compression used
Size	Size of the compressed file
Ratio	Percent reduction in file size
Date	Actual date of the file
Time	Actual time of the file
CRC-32	The CRC-32 value of the file
Attribute	The attribute of the file (s = System, h = Hidden, w = Writable, r = readonly file, and * = encrypted)
Name	Name of the file

PKZIP is the program name of the executable file that compresses data files.

ZIPFILE represents the name you assign to the resulting compressed file.

options represent commands that effect the operation of PKZIP, such as −a to add files.

files represents the files to be compressed into the ZIPFILE.

Although space does not permit an examination of the use of PKWARE options, the reader is referred to the convenience diskettes that contain both ARC and PKWARE file compression programs as well as the other programs referenced in this book. By trying each program you can select one that is best suited to the types of files you use on your personal computer. In doing so, please remember that each program is a shareware program and the companies depend upon satisfied users to send in an appropriate fee if you intend to use the software.

APPENDIX A

DATANALYSIS PROGRAM DESCRIPTIONS AND LISTINGS

A.1 FORTRAN PROGRAM: OPERATIONAL DESCRIPTION

The original data-compression analysis program was written in industry standard FORTRAN IV for execution on a Honeywell 66/80 computer system. It consists of one main routine which performs all file handling. Twelve independent subprograms are called by the main routine to perform specific functions such as string analysis, sorting and report formatting.

Included in this documentation are narrative descriptions of each subprogram. The reader should refer to the program listing when reading the following operational description of the main routine, subprograms and the discussion concerning program transferability and variable assignments.

A.2 MAIN ROUTINE

The routine first builds two symbolic arrays filled with those characters associated with the frequency counters. The first array contains the 127 ASCII characters followed by a summary symbol and a temporary work slot used while sorting the array. The second array contains all the ASCII character pairs normally encountered. The array, although structured in one dimension, can be viewed as a two-dimensional array directly proportional to the paired-integer array IP(28, 26). The DATA statement was chosen to minimize external I/O.

The routine then asks three questions prior to performing the actual analysis:

ENTER FILE TYPE—Up to seven characters which identifies the file to be analyzed. This is displayed on each report for future reference.

ENTER INPUT LINELENGTH—Up to 132 characters is 'strings' of data to be read. A card-type file would be 80 versus a print file of 132. This conserves run time by reducing unnecessary iterations. Longer strings can be accommodated by increasing dimensions.

TO SUPPRESS TRAILING SPACES ENTER 1—This is useful for variable line lengths, such as a BASIC program entered from a terminal. Blanks or spaces trailing the last printable character are ignored. Any other entry will cause the entire fixed line length to be used.

A record or string is then read. Each character is converted to its ordinal decimal value and the value is used to subscript into an array of tallies. Before the next record is read, three subprograms are called and the alphanumeric string is passed to each subprogram for further analysis. These subprograms are: SUB-1 to resolve purely numeric strings, SUB-7 to resolve repetitious strings, and SUB-9 to resolve pair combinations.

The remaining subprograms are called upon encountering the end-of-file to sort and print the eight reports.

Subprogram 1

This calculates sequential numeric strings which are susceptible to half-byte encoding. The following special characters normally found in financial programs are also included as part of the string:

$$044_8 = \$ = 36_{10}$$
$$052_8 = * = 42_{10}$$
$$054_8 = , = 44_{10}$$
$$055_8 = - = 45_{10}$$
$$056_8 = . = 46_{10}$$
$$057_8 = / = 47_{10}$$

Half-byte numeric packing would permit compression of:

$***1,234.56
12/12/80-2/11/81
026-36-1048
800-555-1212
45, 675, 109, 210.86
1941/1945/1952-1954

Subprogram 2

This prints the execution report summary.

Subprogram 3

This prints the frequency of occurrence table first in ordinal sequence, then, after sorting by SUB-6, in descending frequency of occurrence for ease of analysis. The array is folded into a table consisting of 4 columns and 32 rows to fit on a single page.

Subprogram 4

This prints the repeated character string analysis report. Only strings of *identical* characters are included. Void string lengths are omitted to conserve printing.

Subprogram 5

This prints a further analysis of that displayed by SUB-4 in that it derives the actual savings achieved by employing data-compression encoding techniques. For example, $4 \leqslant R \leqslant 256$ when compressed as:

SPECIAL CHARACTER	COUNT	COMPRESSED CHARACTER

Subprogram 6

This performs an internal parallel sort of the frequency array, with its associated ASCII symbol, in descending order of frequency. Simply stated, for every movement of an IR(N) value there is a corresponding of a B(N) symbol.

Subprogram 7

This calculates the sequential repeating characters displayed by SUB-4 and SUB-5. Three separate arrays are maintained: IY(N) for any occurrence, IN(N) for numerics $48_{10} \leqslant N \leqslant 57_{10}$, and IX(N) for spaces 32_{10}.

Subprogram 8

This prints the sequential numeric string analysis for half-byte encoding susceptibility. This subprogram uses the IM(N) array generated by SUB-1. It uses the algorithm

$$\left[\left[\frac{\text{String size} + 1}{2} \right] + 2 \right] * \text{Count}$$

to derive the characters saved by half-byte encoding.

Subprogram 9

This isolates character pairs and calculates their frequency of occurrence. It begins with the first couplet in the string and continues, incrementing by two, until the string is exhausted. No attempt is made to shift boundaries of couplets.

A two-dimensional array (28 × 26) is maintained to count the following pair combinations, where the underline symbolizes a blank character:

_A	A_	AA	. . .	ZA
_B	B_	AB	. . .	ZB
_C	C_	AC	. . .	ZC
.	.	.		.

$$\cdot \qquad \cdot \qquad \cdot \qquad \qquad \cdot$$
$$\cdot \qquad \cdot \qquad \cdot \qquad \qquad \cdot$$
$$\_Z \quad Z\_ \qquad \cdot \qquad AZ \quad \ldots \qquad ZZ$$

An additional count is maintained for embedded pairs of blanks or spaces: e.g. bounded by none, blanks thereby not susceptible to other forms of encoding. In order to maintain a symmetric array, which is sorted by SUB-11, the Q-cell is used since this pair is never encountered in the English language.

Initial decimal values are established to represent pairs and DO loops are performed in the following manner:

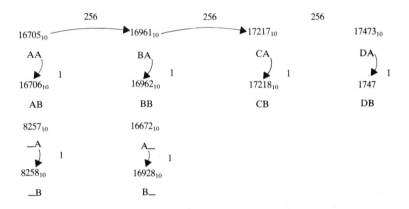

The J index is used in the program to establish initial values. Due to an unexplainable 'bug' in the system used for development, the starting values had to be inflated by 16. The values in cards 4750, 4860, 4990 and 5070 should be changed to the above to operate properly on a different system.

Subprogram 10

This prints the paired-character analysis report after SUB-11 sorts the array. One page is required to display the top 132 frequencies of occurrence. The array is folded into 22 rows of 6 columns each for ease of reference.

A final summary count of combinations is displayed at the foot of the page which may be used to derive a count of those additional combinations beyond the bounds of the table.

Subprogram 11

This performs an internal parallel sort of the paired frequency array IP (N1,N2) with character array C(N) in descending order of frequency. To facilitate the technique used in SUB-6, a linear conversion is performed to give IP(N1, N2) the appearance of a single dimension corresponding to C(N).

Subprogram 12

This computes file entropy and produces the final report:

$$\text{Entropy} = \sum_{i=1}^{M} P_i \log_2 P_i$$

where P_i is the probability of occurrence of characters in the data file: for example, if E occurs 100 times in a 1000 character file

$$P_i(E) = \frac{100}{1000} = 0.1$$

A.3 PROGRAM TRANSFERABILITY

Several instructions are hardware sensitive and, by their nature, are not directly transferable between word-oriented hardware. The FORTRAN compiler must be examined and, if need be, three or four instructions modified.

For example, the program derives the ordinal decimal value of each character inputed and uses it as an array subscript to increment counts of occurrence. The Honeywell compiler requires an integer-right-shift (IRS) function to align the left-justified ASCII character to a proper 36-bit double word boundary.

For example, card 1380 aligns datum in the following manner (datum = A = 65):

	0	8 9	17 18	26 27	35
Before:	65	0	0	0	

IRS(A(I),27)

	0	8 9	17 18	26 27	35
After:	0	0	0	65	

To operate on the DECSYSTEM 10, the following specific instructions (cards) should be changed as indicated:

CONVERSION TO DECSYSTEM 10
Change the specific instructions (cards) as follows:
(1) Change card 1310 to: 2 FORMAT(132R1)
(2) Change card 1380 to: IP2 = A(I)
(3) Change card 4720 to: IV = (A(I)*256)
(4) Change card 4730 to: IV = IV + A(I + 1)
(5) Change card 4750 to: IF (IV − 8224)923, 920, 923
(6) Change card 4860 to: J = 8257
(7) Change card 4990 to: J = 16672
(8) Change card 5070 to: J = 16705
(9) Change card 5960 to: 1200 E = E + P(I)*ALOG(P(I))

Note: The generic functions ALOG and ALOG 10 are poorly discussed in DECSYSTEM 10 publications. The specific function desired is a log to the base two. If ALOG does not provide this properly, substitute as follows in card 5960:

$$\sum_i P_i \frac{\log_{10} P_i}{\log_{10} 2} \quad \text{in lieu of} \quad \sum P_i \log_2 P_i$$

A.4 VARIABLE ASSIGNMENTS

Name	Type	Purpose	Usage	I = Endogenous X = Exogenous
A(132)	DIM	ASCII record	Main	X
B(129)	DIM	Graphic symbols	SUB3,6	I
IA(132)	DIM	Line of ASCII character in octal notation	Main; SUB1,2	I
IN(133)	DIM	Numeric strings	SUB1,4	I
IX(133)	DIM	Blank strings	SUB2,5	I
IY(133)	DIM	All strings	SUB7,8	I
Z( )	DIM			
NI	INT	Linelength to search	Main; SUB1,2,4,5	X
X	Char.	File name	SUB3,4,5	X
JI	INT	Record count	Main; SUB4,5	I

A.4 *(continued)*

Name	Type	Purpose	Usage	I = Endogenous X = Exogenous
I	INT	Index	Main; SUB1,2,3, 4,5,6	I
J	INT	Index		
K	INT	Index	SUB1,2,3, 6	I
M	INT	Flag	SUB3	I
P(128)	Doub. Prec.	Percentage of occurrence	SUB3,4,5	I
IR(128)	Doub. Prec.	Count of occurrence	Main; SUB3,4,5, 6	I
IP1	INT	Octal equivalent of character	Main	I
L	INT	Index	Main	I
IPI	INT	Sort index	SUB6	I
IV	INT	Trailing space suppression flag	Main	X
N	INT	Adjusted linelength	Main; SUB1,2,4, 5	I
IM(133)	DIM	Mixed numeric and specific characters	SUB8,1	I
NC	REAL	Trailing space counter	Main	I
IC & ICI	INT	Half-byte compression character count	SUB8	I
ITN$_x$, ITX, ITY$_x$, ITT$_x$, ITS$_x$	INT	Total cells	SUB5	I
E	INT	Entropy calculation	SUB12	I
BI	INT	Bits after compression	SUB12	I
B4	INT	Characters after compression	SUB12	I
B2	INT	Characters before compression	SUB12	I
B3	INT	Theoretical maximum compression	SUB12	I

.

A.5 BASIC PROGRAM: OPERATIONAL DESCRIPTION

The original DATANALYSIS program was written in 1980 for operation on large-scale computer systems. Although the use of FORTRAN IV permitted the program to be easily transported to various large-scale computers, its transferability excluded many popular minicomputers and microcomputers for a variety of reasons to include the lack of an economical FORTRAN compiler. Based upon the large number of requests received from readers of the first edition of this book, work was begun in 1985 to rewrite the program in Microsoft BASIC to accommodate the ever-expanding audience of MS-DOS and PC-DOS compatible computers.

To shorten the execution time of the BASIC program, which was several magnitudes greater than obtained from the use of the FORTRAN program on a large computer system, required several subroutines to be extensively revised. The two-dimensional pair-combination sort, for example, was totally unacceptable from an execution time perspective and was considerably abbreviated in BASIC to sequence columns only in descending order of occurrence. The interpretive version of the BASIC program, called DAT-ANAL.BAS is listed at the end of this appendix. Unfortunately, even reducing the two-dimensional pair-combination sort still requires approximately 15–25 min to complete the analysis of a file containing approximately 20 000 characters. To substantially reduce the required execution time of the BASIC version of DATANALYSIS will require the reader to obtain a compiled version of the program. Readers obtaining the convenience disk offered with the current edition of this book will find a program file named DATANAL.EXE. This is an executable program file that was produced by the use of the Microsoft Quick BASIC compiler and can operate on any 256K MS-DOS compatible system. Other files included on the referenced disk are: BRUNIO.LIB which is the Quick BASIC run-time module library; BRUNIO.EXE which is the Quick BASIC run-time module; DATANAL.OBJ which is the object version of the DATANALYSIS program; DATANAL.LST which is the listing of the source file produced by the compilation process; and DATANAL.MAP, which is a file that lists all external symbols in the program and their extensions.

The BASIC version of DATANALYSIS was structured to allow operations on systems with or without an attached parallel printer. Any file saved in ASCII can be analysed by this program.

For the sake of run-time efficiency, use the program as is if the file is mostly in lower case. The program could be modified to accommodate both cases; however, this would greatly sacrifice both execution speed and memory, since it would double the size of the program's IP and C$ arrays. For those readers with 80286-based PCs and BASIC compilers that can access over 384K of memory, a program expansion to accomodate both cases might be well worthwhile. As the reader will note from reviewing the program listing at the end of this appendix, an extensive number of comments have been included to facilitate the analysis of the program's logic as well as to enable the program to be modified by the reader. Any improvements, comments or suggestions will be greatly appreciated by the author.

To execute the compiled BASIC version of DATANALYSIS requires you to first load either MS-DOS or PC-DOS and then insert the convenience disk in drive A. At the prompt A>, enter the command DATANAL. The following paragraphs describe the main routine and subroutines included in the BASIC version of DATANALYSIS.

A.6 MAIN ROUTINE

The routine first builds two symbolic arrays filled with those characters associated with the frequency counters. The first array contains the 127 ASCII characters followed by a summary symbol and a temporary work slot used while sorting the array. The second array contains all of the ASCII character pairs normally encountered. The array, although structured in one dimension, can be viewed as a two-dimensional array directly proportional to the paired-integer array IP (28,26). The DATA statement was chosen to minimize external I/O.

The routine then asks three questions prior to performing the actual analysis:

ENTER ASCII FILENAME—Any [DRIVE:]FILENAME EXTENSION which identifies the file to be analyzed, this is displayed on each report for future reference. The file must be in ASCII format.

IS FILE MOSTLY IN LOWER CASE—For pair analysis the array is initialized with lower case 97_{10} to 122_{10} in lieu of 65_{10} to 90_{10}.

DO YOU DO YOU WANT PRINTED OUTPUT—Allows the program to be run on a system without an attached parallel printer.

A record or string is then read. Each character is converted to its ordinal decimal value and the value is used to subscript into an array of tallies. Before the next record is read, three subprograms are called and the alphanumeric string is passed to each subprogram for further analysis. These subprograms are: SUB-1 to resolve purely numeric strings, SUB-7 to resolve repetitious strings, and SUB-9 to resolve pair combinations.

The remaining subprograms are called upon encountering the end-of-file to sort and print the eight reports.

Subprogram 1

This calculates sequential numeric strings which are susceptible to half-byte encoding. The following special characters normally found in financial programs are also included as part of the string:

$$\begin{aligned}
\$ \quad &= 36_{10}. \\
* \quad &= 42_{10} \\
, \quad &= 44_{10} \\
- \quad &= 45_{10} \\
. \quad &= 46_{10} \\
/ \quad &= 47_{10}
\end{aligned}$$

Half-byte numeric packing would permit compression of:

$***1,234.56
12/12/80-2/11/81
026-36-1048
800-555-1212
45, 675, 109, 210.86
1941/1945/1952–1954

Subprogram 2

This prints the execution report summary.

Subprogram 3

This prints the frequency of occurrence table first in ordinal sequence, then, after sorting by SUB-6, in descending frequency of occurrence for ease of analysis. The array is folded into a table consisting of 4 columns and 32 rows to fit on a single page.

Subprogram 4

This prints the repeated character string analysis report. Only strings of *identical* characters are included. Void string lengths are omitted to conserve printing.

Subprogram 5

This prints a further analysis of that displayed by SUB-4 in that it derives the actual savings achieved by employing data-compression encoding techniques. For example, $4 \leq R \leq 256$ when compressed as:

SPECIAL CHARACTER	COUNT	COMPRESSED CHARACTER

Subprogram 6

This performs an internal parallel sort of the frequency array, with its associated ASCII symbol, in descending order of frequency. Simply stated, for every movement of an IR(N) value there is a corresponding of a B$(N) symbol.

Subprogram 7

This calculates the sequential repeating characters displayed by SUB-4 and SUB-5. Three separate arrays are maintained: IY(N) for any occurrence, IN(N) for numerics $48_{10} \leq N \leq 57_{10}$, and IX(N) for spaces 32_{10}.

Subprogram 8

This prints the sequential numeric string analysis for half-byte encoding susceptibility. This subprogram uses the IM(N) array generated by SUB-1.

It uses the algorithm

$$\left[\left[\frac{\text{String size} + 1}{2}\right] + 2\right] * \text{Count}$$

to derive the characters saved by half-byte encoding.

Subprogram 9

This isolates character pairs and calculates their frequency of occurrence. It begins with the first couplet in the string and continues, incrementing by two, until the string is exhausted. An attempt is made to shift boundaries of couplets when a non-alphabetic character is encountered.

A two-dimensional array (28 * 26) is maintained to count the following pair combinations, where the underline symbolizes a blank character:

_A	A_	AA	. . .	ZA
_B	B_	AB	. . .	ZB
_C	C_	AC	. . .	ZC
.	.	.		.
.	.	.		.
.	.	.		.
_Z	Z_	AZ	. . .	ZZ

An additional count is maintained for imbedded pairs of blanks or spaces: e.g. bounded by none, blanks thereby not susceptible to other forms of encoding. In order to maintain a symmetric array, which is sorted by SUB-11, the Q-cell is used since this pair is never encountered in the English language.

Subprogram 10

This prints the paired-character analysis report after SUB-11 sorts each column of the array in descending order of occurrence. One page is required to display the top 132 frequencies of occurrence. The array is folded into 22 rows of 6 columns each for ease of reference.

A final summary count of combinations is displayed at the foot of the page which may be used to derive a count of those additional combinations beyond the bounds of the table.

Subprogram 11

This performs an internal parallel sort of the paired-frequency array IP(N1,N2) with character array C$(N) in descending order of frequency. To facilitate the technique used in SUB-6, a linear conversion is performed to give IP(N1,N2) the appearance of a single dimension corresponding to C$(N).

Subprogram 12

This computes the file entropy and produces the final report:

$$\text{Entropy} = \sum_{i=1}^{M} P_i \log_2 P_i$$

where P_i is the probability of occurrence of characters in the data file: for example, if E occurs 100 times in a 1000 character file

$$P_i(\text{E}) = \frac{100}{1000} = 0.1$$

A.7 VARIABLE ASSIGNMENTS

Name	Type	Purpose	Usage	I = Endogenous X = Exogenous
A(132)	DIM	ASCII record	Main	X
B(129)	DIM	Graphic symbols	SUB3,6	I
IA(132)	DIM	Line of ASCII characters in octal notation	Main; SUB1,2	I
IN(133)	DIM	Numeric strings	SUB1,4	I
IX(133)	DIM	Blank strings	SUB2,5	I
IY(133)	DIM	All strings	SUB7,8	I
Z( )	DIM			

A.7 *(continued)*

Name	Type		Purpose	Usage	I = Endogenous X = Exogenous
NI	INT		Linelength to search	Main; SUB1,2,4,5	I
F$	Char.		File name	SUB3,4,5	X
JI	INT		Record count	Main; SUB4,5	I
I	INT		Index	Main; SUB1,2,3, 4,5,6	I
J	INT		Index		
K	INT		Index	SUB1,2,3,6	I
M	INT		Sort flag	SUB3	I
P(128)	DIM		Percentage of occurrence	SUB3,4,5	I
IR(128)	DIM		Count of occurrence	Main; SUB3,4,5,6	I
IP2	INT		Decimal equivalent of character	Main	I
IM(133)	DIM		Mixed numeric and specific characters	SUB8, 1	I
IC & ICI	INT		Half-byte compression character count	SUB8	I
ITN_x, ITX, ITY_x, ITT_x, ITS_x	INT		Total cells	SUB5	I
E	INT		Entropy calculation	SUB12	I
BI	INT		Bits after compression	SUB12	I
B4	INT		Characters after compression	SUB12	I
B2	INT		Characters before compression	SUB12	I
B3	INT		Theoretical maximum compression	SUB12	I
	D$	CHAR	LPT1: or SCRN: option	Main	X
	V$	CHAR	Upper/lower case flag	Main	X

A.8 FORTRAN DATANALYSIS PROGRAM LISTING

```
C *MAIN**MAIN FREQ ROUTINE**HELD & MARSHALL****DATANALYSIS**1980*        00000100
C *THIS PROGRAM WAS WRITTEN TO ANALYZE FILES FOR SUSCEPTABILITY *       00000110
C *TO VARIOUS COMPRESSION TECHNIQUES. IT IS WRITTEN IN INDUSTRY *       00000120
C *STANDARD FORTRAN IV FOR RUNNING IN TIME-SHARING OR BATCH MODE*       00000130
C *HARDWARE SENSITIVE INSTRUCTIONS HAVE BEEN FLAGGED BY COMMENT *       00000140
C * SEE APPENDIX A OF DOCUMENTATION FOR PROGRAM TRANSFERABILITY *       00000150
C *TO RUN H66/80 TSS: RUN # XXXX "09" (WHERE XXXX=PERMFILE NAME)        00000160
      DIMENSION A(132),B(129),IA(132),IN(133),IM(133),IX(133),IY(132)   00000170
     &,Z(132)                                                           00000180
      DIMENSION C(729),IP(28,26)                                        00000190
      DOUBLE PRECISION IR(128),P(128)                                   00000200
      CHARACTER *1 A                                                    00000210
      CHARACTER *2 B,C                                                  00000220
      CHARACTER *7 X                                                    00000230
      INTEGER OUTPUT/6/,INPUT/5/,FILIN/9/                               00000240
C     STRUCTURE GRAPHIC SYMBOL ARRAY FOR  FREQ OF OCCURRENCE TABLE      00000250
      DATA(B(L),L=1,129)/                                               00000260
     &2HSH,2HEX,2HSX,2HET,2HEQ,2HAK,2HBL,2HBS,2HHT,2HLF,                00000270
     &2HVT,2HFF,2HCR,2HSO,2HSI,2HDE,2HD1,2HD2,2HD3,2HD4,                00000280
     &2HNK,2HSY,2HEB,2HCN,2HEM,2HSB,2HEC,2HFS,2HGS,2HRS,                00000290
     &2HUS,2HSP,2HEP,2H" ,2H# ,2HS ,2HZ ,2HS ,2H' ,2H( ,                00000300
     &2H) ,2H* ,2H, ,2H+ ,2H, ,2H/ ,2HO ,2H1 ,2H2 ,                    00000310
     &2H3 ,2H4 ,2H5 ,2H6 ,2H7 ,2H8 ,2H9 ,2H: ,2H; ,2H< ,                00000320
     &2H= ,2H> ,2HQM,2H@ ,2HA ,2HB ,2HC ,2HD ,2HE ,2HF ,                00000330
     &2HG ,2HH ,2HI ,2HJ ,2HK ,2HL ,2HM ,2HN ,2HO ,2HP ,                00000340
     &2HQ ,2HR ,2HS ,2HT ,2HU ,2HV ,2HW ,2HX ,2HY ,2HZ ,                00000350
     &2H[ ,2H\ ,2H] ,2H↑ ,2H+ ,2H@ ,2HA ,2HB ,2HC ,2HD ,                00000360
     &2HE ,2HF ,2HG ,2HH ,2HI ,2HJ ,2HK ,2HL ,2HM ,2HN ,                00000370
     &2HO ,2HP ,2HQ ,2HR ,2HS ,2HT ,2HU ,2HV ,2HW ,2HX ,                00000380
     &2HY ,2HZ ,2H[ ,2H  ,2H] ,2H  ,2HDL,2H**,2H??/                     00000390
C     STRUCTURE PAIRED SYMBOL ARRAY                                     00000400
      DATA(C(J),J=1,729)/                                               00000410
     &2H+A,2H+B,2H+C,2H+D,2H+E,2H+F,2H+G,2H+H,2H+I,2H+J,                00000420
     &2H+K,2H+L,2H+M,2H+N,2H+O,2H+P,2H+Q,2H+R,2H+S,2H+T,                00000430
     &2H+U,2H+V,2H+W,2H+X,2H+Y,2H+Z,2HA+,2HB+,2HC+,2HD+,                00000440
     &2HE+,2HF+,2HG+,2HH+,2HI+,2HJ+,2HK+,2HL+,2HM+,2HN+,                00000450
     &2HO+,2HP+,2H++,2HR+,2HS+,2HT+,2HU+,2HV+,2HW+,2HX+,                00000460
     &2HY+,2HZ+,2HAA,2HAB,2HAC,2HAD,2HAE,2HAF,2HAG,2HAH,                00000470
     &2HAI,2HAJ,2HAK,2HAL,2HAM,2HAN,2HAO,2HAP,2HAQ,2HAR,                00000480
     &2HAS,2HAT,2HAU,2HAV,2HAW,2HAX,2HAY,2HAZ,2HBA,2HBB,                00000490
     &2HBC,2HBD,2HBE,2HBF,2HBG,2HBH,2HBI,2HBJ,2HBK,2HBL,                00000500
     &2HBM,2HBN,2HBO,2HBP,2H3Q,2HBR,2HBS,2HBT,2HBU,2HBV,                00000510
     &2HBW,2HBX,2HBY,2HBZ,2HCA,2HCB,2HCC,2HCD,2HCE,2HCF,2HCG,           00000520
     &2HCH,2HCI,2HCJ,2HCK,2HCL,2HCM,2HCN,2HCO,2HCP,2HCQ,                00000530
     &2HCR,2HCS,2HCT,2HCU,2HCV,2HCW,2HCX,2HCY,2HCZ,2HDA,                00000540
     &2HDB,2HDC,2HDD,2HDE,2HDF,2HDG,2HDH,2HDI,2HDJ,2HDK,                00000550
     &2HDL,2HDM,2HDN,2HDO,2HDP,2HDQ,2HDR,2HDS,2HDT,2HDU,                00000560
     &2HDV,2HDW,2HDX,2HDY,2HDZ,2HEA,2HEB,2HEC,2HED,2HEE,                00000570
     &2HEF,2HEG,2HEH,2HEI,2HEJ,2HEK,2HEL,2HEM,2HEN,2HEO,                00000580
     &2HEP,2HEQ,2HER,2HES,2HET,2HEU,2HEW,2HEX,2HEY,                     00000590
     &2HEZ,2HFA,2HFB,2HFC,2HFD,2HFE,2HFF,2HFG,2HFH,2HFI,                00000600
     &2HFJ,2HFK,2HFL,2HFM,2HFN,2HFO,2HFP,2HFQ,2HFR,2HFS,                00000610
     &2HFT,2HFU,2HFV,2HFW,2HFX,2HFY,2HFZ,2HGA,2HGB,2HGC                 00000620
     &2HGD,2HGE,2HGF,2HGG,2HGH,2HGI,2HGJ,2HGK,2HGL,2HGM                 00000630
     &2HGN,2HGO,2HGP,2HGQ,2HGR,2HGS,2HGT,2HGU,2HGV,2HGW,                00000640
     &2HGX,2HGY,2HGZ,2HHA,2HHB,2HHC,2HHD,2HHE,2HHF,2HHG,                00000650
     &2HHH,2HHI,2HHJ,2HHK,2HHL,2HHM,2HHN,2HHO,2HHP,2HHQ,                00000660
     &2HHR,2HHS,2HHT,2HHU,2HHV,2HHW,2HHX,2HHY,2HHZ,2HIA,                00000670
     &2HIB,2HIC,2HID,2HIE,2HIF,2HIG,2HIH,2HII,2HIJ,2HIK,                00000680
     &2HIL,2HIM,2HIN,2HIO,2HIP,2HIQ,2HIR,2HIS,2HIT,2HIU,                00000690
     &2HIV,2HIW,2HIX,2HIY,2HIZ,2HJA,2HJB,2HJC,2HJD,2HJE,                00000700
     &2HJF,2HJG,2HJH,2HJI,2HJJ,2HJK,2HJL,2HJM,2HJN,2HJO,                00000710
     &2HJP,2HJQ,2HJR,2HJS,2HJT,2HJU,2HJV,2HJW,2HJX,2HJY,                00000720
     &2HJZ,2HKA,2HKB,2HKC,2HKD,2HKE,2HKF,2HKG,2HKH,2HKI,                00000730
     &2HKJ,2HKK,2HKL,2HKM,2HKN,2HKO,2HKP,2HKQ,2HKR,2HKS,                00000740
     &2HKT,2HKU,2HKV,2HKW,2HKX,2HKY,2HKZ,2HLA,2HLB,2HLC,                00000750
     &2HLD,2HLE,2HLF,2HLG,2HLH,2HLI,2HLJ,2HLK,2HLL,2HLM,                00000760
     &2HLN,2HLO,2HLP,2HLQ,2HLR,2HLS,2HLT,2HLU,2HLV,2HLW,                00000770
```

```
      &2HLX,2HLY,2HLZ,2HMA,2HMB,2HMC,2HMD,2HME,2HMF,2HMG,        00000780
      &2HMH,2HMI,2HMJ,2HMK,2HML,2HMM,2HMN,2HMO,2HMP,2HMQ,        00000790
      &2HMR,2HMS,2HMT,2HMU,2HMV,2HMW,2HMX,2HMY,2HMZ,2HNA,        00000800
      &2HNB,2HNC,2HND,2HNE,2HNF,2HNG,2HNH,2HNI,2HNJ,2HNK,        00000810
      &2HNL,2HNM,2HNN,2HNO,2HNP,2HNQ,2HNR,2HNS,2HNT,2HNU,        00000820
      &2HNV,2HNW,2HNX,2HNY,2HNZ,2HOA,2HOB,2HOC,2HOD,2HOE,        00000830
      &2HOF,2HOG,2HOH,2HOI,2HOJ,2HOK,2HOL,2HOM,2HON,2HOO,        00000840
      &2HOP,2HOQ,2HOR,2HOS,2HOT,2HOU,2HOV,2HOW,2HOX,2HOY,        00000850
      &2HOZ,2HPA,2HPB,2HPC,2HPD,2HPE,2HPF,2HPG,2HPH,2HPI,        00000860
      &2HPJ,2HPK,2HPL,2HPM,2HPN,2HPO,2HPP,2HPQ,2HPR,2HPS,        00000870
      &2HPT,2HPU,2HPV,2HPW,2HPX,2HPY,2HPZ,2HQA,2HQB,2HQC,        00000880
      &2HQD,2HQE,2HQF,2HQG,2HQH,2HQI,2HQJ,2HQK,2HQL,2HQM,        00000890
      &2HQN,2HQO,2HQP,2HQQ,2HQR,2HQS,2HQT,2HQU,2HQV,2HQW,        00000900
      &2HQX,2HQY,2HQZ,2HRA,2HRB,2HRC,2HRD,2HRE,2HRF,2HRG,        00000910
      &2HRH,2HRI,2HRJ,2HRK,2HRL,2HRM,2HRN,2HRO,2HRP,2HRQ,        00000920
      &2HRR,2HRS,2HRT,2HRU,2HRV,2HRW,2HRX,2HRY,2HRZ,2HSA,        00000930
      &2HSB,2HSC,2HSD,2HSE,2HSF,2HSG,2HSH,2HSI,2HSJ,2HSK,        00000940
      &2HSL,2HSM,2HSN,2HSO,2HSP,2HSQ,2HSR,2HSS,2HST,2HSU,        00000950
      &2HSV,2HSW,2HSX,2HSY,2HSZ,2HTA,2HTB,2HTC,2HTD,2HTE,        00000960
      &2HTF,2HTG,2HTH,2HTI,2HTJ,2HTK,2HTL,2HTM,2HTN,2HTO,        00000970
      &2HTP,2HTQ,2HTR,2HTS,2HTT,2HTU,2HTV,2HTW,2HTX,2HTY,        00000980
      &2HTZ,2HUA,2HUB,2HUC,2HUD,2HUE,2HUF,2HUG,2HUH,2HUI,        00000990
      &2HUJ,2HUK,2HUL,2HUM,2HUN,2HUO,2HUP,2HUQ,2HUR,2HUS,        00001000
      &2HUT,2HUU,2HUV,2HUW,2HUX,2HUY,2HUZ,2HVA,2HVB,2HVC,        00001010
      &2HVD,2HVE,2HVF,2HVG,2HVH,2HVI,2HVJ,2HVK,2HVL,2HVM,        00001020
      &2HVN,2HVO,2HVP,2HVQ,2HVR,2HVS,2HVT,2HVU,2HVV,2HVW,        00001030
      &2HVX,2HVY,2HVZ,2HWA,2HWB,2HWC,2HWD,2HWE,2HWF,2HWG,        00001040
      &2HWI,2HWJ,2HWK,2HWL,2HWM,2HWN,2HWO,2HWP,2HWQ,             00001050
      &2HWR,2HWS,2HWT,2HWU,2HWV,2HWW,2HWX,2HWY,2HWZ,2HXA,        00001060
      &2HXB,2HXC,2HXD,2HXE,2HXF,2HXG,2HXH,2HXI,2HXJ,2HXK,        00001070
      &2HXL,2HXM,2HXN,2HXO,2HXP,2HXQ,2HXR,2HXS,2HXT,2HXU,        00001080
      &2HXV,2HXW,2HXX,2HXY,2HXZ,2HYA,2HYB,2HYC,2HYD,2HYE,        00001090
      &2HYF,2HYG,2HYH,2HYI,2HYJ,2HYK,2HYL,2HYM,2HYN,2HYO,        00001100
      &2HYP,2HYQ,2HYR,2HYS,2HYT,2HYU,2HYV,2HYW,2HYX,2HYY,        00001110
      &2HYZ,2HZA,2HZB,2HZC,2HZD,2HZE,2HZF,2HZG,2HZH,2HZI,        00001120
      &2HZJ,2HZK,2HZL,2HZM,2HZN,2HZO,2HZP,2HZQ,2HZR,2HZS,        00001130
      &2HZT,2HZU,2HZV,2HZW,2HZX,2HZY,2HZZ,2H??/                  00001140
C        HOW MANY CHAR. TO SEARCH IN INPUT RECORD               00001150
         WRITE(OUTPUT,23)                                       00001160
   23 FORMAT("ENTER FILE TYPE")                                 00001170
         READ(INPUT,24)X                                        00001180
   24 FORMAT(A7)                                                00001190
C        READ IN FILE TYPE FOR REPORT                           00001200
         WRITE(OUTPUT,21)                                       00001210
   21 FORMAT("ENTER INPUT LINELENGTH")                          00001220
         READ(INPUT,22)N1                                       00001230
   22 FORMAT(I3)                                                00001240
         WRITE(OUTPUT,25)                                       00001250
   25 FORMAT("TO SUPRESS TRAILING SPACES ENTER 1")              00001260
         READ(INPUT,26)IV                                       00001270
   26 FORMAT(I1)                                                00001280
C        READ A RECORD FROM DESIGNATED FILE; CHECK FOR EOF      00001290
    1 READ(FILIN,2,END=4)(A(I),I=1,127)                         00001300
    2 FORMAT(132A1)                                             00001310
         J1=J1+1                                                00001320
         NC=0                                                   00001330
C     INCREMENT COUNTERS IN THE IR ARRAY BY USING ORDINAL EQUIV OF  00001340
C     THE CHARACTER AS THE SUBSCRIPT TO THE ARRAY.              00001350
         DO 3 I=1,N1                                            00001360
C     NOTE-FOLLOWING 2 INST HARDWARE SENSITIVE-SEE APPENDIX A.  00001370
         IP2=IRS(A(I),27)                                       00001380
         IA(I)=IP2                                              00001390
         IR(IP2)=IR(IP2)+1                                      00001400
         IF (IV.EQ.1.AND.IA(I).EQ.32) GOTO 7                    00001410
         NC=0                                                   00001420
         GO TO 3                                                00001430
    7 NC=NC+1                                                   00001440
    3 IR(128)=IR(128)+1                                         00001450
C     SUBTRACT TRAILING SPACE COUNT FROM SUMMARY ARRAY          00001460
         IR(32)=IR(32)-NC                                       00001470
         IR(128)=IR(128)-NC                                     00001480
```

```
C     REDUCE LINE LENGTH BY TRAILING SPACE COUNT IF OPTIONED    00001490
      N=N1-NC                                                    00001500
      CALL SUB1(IA,IM,N)                                         00001510
      CALL SUB7(IA,IX,IY,IN,N)                                   00001520
      CALL SUB9(A,IP,N)                                          00001530
      GOTO 1                                                     00001540
    4 CONTINUE                                                   00001550
      N=N1                                                       00001560
C     PAUSE "POSITION PAPER NOW"                                 00001570
      CALL SUB2(X)                                               00001580
      CALL SUB3(IR,P,B,X)                                        00001590
      CALL SUB6(IR,B)                                            00001600
      CALL SUB3(IR,P,B,X)                                        00001610
      CALL SUB4(IN,IX,IY,IR,P,X,J1,N)                            00001620
      CALL SUB5(IN,IX,IY,IR,P,X,J1,N)                            00001630
      CALL SUB8(IM,IR,P,X,N)                                     00001640
      CALL SUB11(IP,C)                                           00001650
      CALL SUB10(IP,IX,B,C)                                      00001660
      CALL SUB12(IR,P,X)                                         00001670
      STOP                                                       00001680
      END                                                        00001690
C       SUB-1**CALCULATE NUMERIC STRINGS**                       00001700
      SUBROUTINE SUB1(IA,IM,N)                                   00001710
      DIMENSION IA(132),IM(133)                                  00001720
      I=1                                                        00001730
   11 IF(IA(I).GE.48.AND.IA(I).LE.57)GO TO 20                    00001740
      IF(IA(I).GE.44.AND.IA(I).LE.47)GO TO 20                    00001750
      IF(IA(I).EQ.42)GO TO 20                                    00001760
      IF(IA(I).EQ.36)GO TO 20                                    00001770
   15 I=I+1                                                      00001780
      IF(I-N)11,11,40                                            00001790
   20 K=1                                                        00001800
      I=I+1                                                      00001810
      IT=IA(I)                                                   00001820
      M=0                                                        00001830
   30 IF(IA(I).GE.48.AND.IA(I).LE.57)GO TO 25                    00001840
      IF(IA(I).GE.44.AND.IA(I).LE.47)GO TO 25                    00001850
      IF(IA(I).EQ.42)GO TO 25                                    00001860
      IF(IA(I).EQ.36)GO TO 25                                    00001870
   39 IF (M.EQ.0) GO TO 15                                       00001880
      IM(K)=IM(K)+1                                              00001890
      GO TO 15                                                   00001900
   25 I=I+1                                                      00001910
      K=K+1                                                      00001920
C     ELIMINATE FULLY REPITITIOUS STRINGS FROM CONSIDERATION     00001930
      IF(IA(I-1).EQ.IT) GO TO 16                                 00001940
      M=1                                                        00001950
   16 IF (I-N)30,30,39                                           00001960
   40 RETURN                                                     00001970
      END                                                        00001980
C       SUB-2**PRINT EXECUTION REPORT SUMMARY**                  00001990
      SUBROUTINE SUB2(X)                                         00002000
      INTEGER OUTPUT/6/                                          00002010
      CHARACTER *7 X                                             00002020
      WRITE(OUTPUT,201)                                          00002030
  201 FORMAT(1H1,30X,"DATANALYSIS")                              00002040
      WRITE(OUTPUT,204)                                          00002050
      WRITE(OUTPUT,202)                                          00002060
  202 FORMAT(1H0,24X,"EXECUTION  REPORT  SUMMARY")               00002070
      WRITE(OUTPUT,204)                                          00002080
      WRITE(OUTPUT,203)X                                         00002090
  203 FORMAT(1H0,24X,"FILE ANALYZED:",4X,A7)                     00002100
      WRITE(OUTPUT,204)                                          00002110
  204 FORMAT(1H0)                                                00002120
      WRITE(OUTPUT,205)                                          00002130
  205 FORMAT(1H0,15X,"SEGMENT",10X,"DESCRIPTION")                00002140
      WRITE(OUTPUT,206)                                          00002150
  206 FORMAT(1H0,18X,"I",13X,"SYSTEM STANDARD FREQUENCY OF OCCURRENCE 00002160
     &E")                                                        00002170
      WRITE(OUTPUT,207)                                          00002180
  207 FORMAT(1H0,18X,"II",12X,"SORTED FREQUENCY OF OCCURRENCE")   00002190
      WRITE(OUTPUT,208)                                          00002200
  208 FORMAT(1H0,18X,"III",11X,"REPEATED CHARACTER STRING ANALYSIS") 00002210
```

```
            WRITE(OUTPUT,209)                                       00002220
        209 FORMAT(1H0,18X,"IV",12X,"RUN LENGTH ENCODING SUSCEPTIBILITY") 00002230
            WRITE(OUTPUT,210)                                       00002240
        210 FORMAT(1H0,18X,"V",13X,"HALF-BYTE  ENCODING SUSCEPTIBILITY") 00002250
            WRITE(OUTPUT,211)                                       00002260
        211 FORMAT(1H0,18X,"VI",12X,"DIATOMIC COMPRESSION ANALYSIS")  00002270
            WRITE(OUTPUT,212)                                       00002280
        212 FORMAT(1H0,18X,"VII",11X,"ENTROPY ANALYSIS")            00002290
            WRITE(OUTPUT,204)                                       00002300
            RETURN                                                  00002310
            END                                                     00002320
C       SUB-3**PRINT FREQUENCY OF OCCURRANCE TABLE**                00002330
            SUBROUTINE SUB3(IR,P,9,X)                               00002340
            DOUBLE PRECISION IR(128),P(128)                         00002350
            DIMENSION B(129)                                        00002360
            INTEGER OUTPUT/6/                                       00002370
            CHARACTER *2 B                                          00002380
            CHARACTER *7 X                                          00002390
C       NOW CALCULATE PERCENTAGES                                   00002400
            DO 8 K=1,128                                            00002410
          8 P(K)=IR(K)/IR(128)                                      00002420
C       PRINT FULL TABLE - 4 COLUMNS/32 ROWS                        00002430
            IF (M.EQ.1) GO TO 9                                     00002440
            WRITE(OUTPUT,301)                                       00002450
        301 FORMAT(1H1,"SEGMENT I",11X,"SYSTEM STANDARD FREQUENCY OF  00002460
           & OCCURRANCE",6X,"DATANALYSIS")                          00002470
            GO TO 12                                                00002480
          9 WRITE(OUTPUT,302)                                       00002490
        302 FORMAT(1H1,"SEGMENT II",11X,"SORTED FREQUENCY OF OCCUR   00002500
           &RENCE",14X,"DATANALYSIS")                               00002510
         12 WRITE(OUTPUT,303)X                                      00002520
        303 FORMAT(18X,"TABLE OF CHARACTERS FOUND IN ",A7," FILE")   00002530
            WRITE(OUTPUT,305)                                       00002540
        305 FORMAT(1H0,"CHAR   COUNT    %   CHAR   COUNT    %        00002550
           & CHAR   COUNT    %   CHAR   COUNT    %")                00002560
            DO 5 I=1,32                                             00002570
          5 WRITE(OUTPUT,6)B(I),IR(I),P(I),B(I+32),IR(I+32),P(I+32), 00002580
           &B(I+64),IR(I+64),P(I+64),B(I+96),IR(I+96),P(I+96)       00002590
          6 FORMAT(4(A4,0PF8.0,2PF8.2))                             00002600
            M=1                                                     00002610
            WRITE(OUTPUT,304)                                       00002620
        304 FORMAT(1H0,"** DENOTES TOTAL CHARACTERS IN FILE")       00002630
            RETURN                                                  00002640
            END                                                     00002650
C       SUB-4**PRINT REPITITIOUS STRING ANALYSIS **                 00002660
            SUBROUTINE SUB4(IN,IX,IY,IR,P,X,J1,N)                   00002670
            DOUBLE PRECISION IR(128),P(128)                         00002680
            DIMENSION IN(133),IX(133),IY(133)                       00002690
            INTEGER OUTPUT/6/                                       00002700
            CHARACTER *7 X                                          00002710
            WRITE(OUTPUT,401)                                       00002720
        401 FORMAT(1H1,"SEGMENT III",30X,"DATANALYSIS")             00002730
            WRITE(OUTPUT,402)X                                      00002740
        402 FORMAT(1H0,"REPEATED CHARACTER STRING ANALYSIS FOR ",A7," FILE 00002750
           &")                                                      00002760
            WRITE(OUTPUT,403)                                       00002770
        403 FORMAT(1H0,"STRING ****NUMBER OF OCCURRENCES******")    00002780
            WRITE(OUTPUT,404)                                       00002790
        404 FORMAT("LENGTH  NUMERICS SPACES  OTHER  TOTAL")         00002800
            DO 51 I=3,N                                             00002810
            IN(N+1)=IN(N+1)+(IN(I)*I)                               00002820
            IX(N+1)=IX(N+1)+(IX(I)*I)                               00002830
            IY(N+1)=IY(N+1)+(IY(I)*I)                               00002840
            IF(IY(I).EQ.0) GO TO 51                                 00002850
         50 WRITE(OUTPUT,61)I,IN(I),IX(I),(IY(I)-IN(I)-IX(I)),IY(I) 00002860
         61 FORMAT(I4,4I8)                                          00002870
         51 CONTINUE                                                00002880
            WRITE(OUTPUT,41)                                        00002890
         41 FORMAT(1H0,"**ANALYSIS SUMMARY**")                      00002900
            WRITE(OUTPUT,42)J1                                      00002910
         42 FORMAT("RECORDS PROCESSED ",I6)                         00002920
```

```
      WRITE(OUTPUT,43)IY(N+1)                                          00002930
   43 FORMAT("TOTAL REPETITIONS",I6)                                   00002940
      WRITE(OUTPUT,71)IR(128)                                          00002950
   71 FORMAT("TOTAL CHARACTERS IN FILE",0PF8.0)                        00002960
      P(128)=IY(N+1)/IR(128)                                           00002970
      WRITE(OUTPUT,81)P(128)                                           00002980
   81 FORMAT("PERCENT REPETITIOUS",2PF8.2)                             00002990
      RETURN                                                           00003000
      END                                                              00003010
C     SUB-5**PRINT RUN-LENGTH ENCODING ANALYSIS **                     00003020
      SUBROUTINE SJB5(IN,IX,IY,IR,P,X,J1,N)                            00003030
      DOUBLE PRECISION IR(128),P(128)                                  00003040
      DIMENSION IN(133),IX(133),IY(133)                                00003050
      INTEGER OUTPUT/6/                                                 00003060
      CHARACTER *7 X                                                   00003070
      WRITE(OUTPUT,501)                                                00003080
  501 FORMAT(1H1,"SEGMENT IV",45X,"DATANALYSIS")                       00003090
      WRITE(OUTPUT,502)                                                00003100
  502 FORMAT(1H0,12X,"RUN LENGTH ENCODING COMPRESSION SUSCEPTIBILITY   00003110
     &")                                                               00003120
      WRITE(OUTPUT,503)X                                               00003130
  503 FORMAT(12X,"FOR REPEATED CHARACTER STRINGS IN ",A7," FILE")      00003140
      WRITE(OUTPUT,53)                                                 00003150
   53 FORMAT(1H0,"STRING  ****REPEATED CHARACTERS*****   CHAR.         00003160
     & SAVED BY COMPRESSION")                                          00003170
      WRITE(OUTPUT,54)                                                 00003180
   54 FORMAT("LENGTH  NUMERICS SPACES   OTHER   TOTAL    NUMERICS      00003190
     & SPACES OTHER TOTAL")                                            00003200
      WRITE(OUTPUT,55)                                                 00003210
   55 FORMAT(1H0)                                                      00003220
      DO 63 I=3,N                                                      00003230
      ITN1=ITN1+(IN(I)*I)                                              00003240
      ITX1=ITX1+(IX(I)*I)                                              00003250
      ITY1=ITY1+(IY(I)*I)                                              00003260
      ITN2=(I-3)*IN(I)                                                 00003270
      ITX2=(I-3)*IX(I)                                                 00003280
      ITY2=(I-3)*(IY(I)-IX(I)-IN(I))                                   00003290
      ITT2=(I-3)*(IY(I))                                              00003300
      ITN3=ITN3+ITN2                                                   00003310
      ITX3=ITX3+ITX2                                                   00003320
      ITY3=ITY3+ITY2                                                   00003330
      ITT3=ITT3+ITT2                                                   00003340
      IF(IY(I).EQ.0) GO TO 63                                          00003350
      IYT1=(IY(I)*I)-(IN(I)*I)-(IX(I)*I)                               00003360
   52 WRITE(OUTPUT,62)I,(IN(I)*I),(IX(I)*I),IYT1,(IY(I)*I),ITN2,ITX2   00003370
     &,ITY2,                                                           00003380
     &ITT2                                                             00003390
   62 FORMAT(I4,8I8)                                                   00003400
   63 CONTINUE                                                         00003410
      ITS1=IR(128)                                                     00003420
      ITS2=(ITN1/IR(128)*100)                                          00003430
      ITS3=(ITX1/IR(128)*100)                                          00003440
      ITS4=((ITY1-ITX1-ITN1)/IR(128)*100)                             00003450
      ITS5=(ITY1/IR(128)*100)                                          00003460
      ITS6=(ITN3/IR(128)*100)                                          00003470
      ITS7=(ITX3/IR(128)*100)                                          00003480
      ITS8=(ITY3/IR(128)*100)                                          00003490
      ITS9=(ITT3/IR(128)*100)                                          00003500
      I=99999                                                          00003510
      WRITE(OUTPUT,505)                                                00003520
  505 FORMAT(1H0)                                                      00003530
      WRITE(OUTPUT,62)I,ITN1,ITX1,(ITY1-ITN1-ITX1),ITY1,ITN3,ITX3,IT   00003540
     &Y3,ITT3                                                          00003550
      WRITE(OUTPUT,506)ITS1                                            00003560
  506 FORMAT("SUMMARY INFORMATION: TOTAL CHAR. IN DATA FILE:",I6)      00003570
      WRITE(OUTPUT,507)                                                00003580
  507 FORMAT(" PERCENTAGE SEQUENTIAL REPEATED CHAR:")                  00003590
      WRITE(OUTPUT,508)ITS2                                            00003600
  508 FORMAT("  NUMERIC:            ",I6)                              00003610
      WRITE(OUTPUT,509)ITS3                                            00003620
  509 FORMAT("  BLANK(SPACES):      ",I6)                              00003630
      WRITE(OUTPUT,510)ITS4                                            00003640
  510 FORMAT("  NONNUMERIC NONBLANK:",I6)                              00003650
```

```
        WRITE(OUTPUT,511)ITS5                                  00003660
    511 FORMAT(" TOTAL REPEATED:       ",I6)                   00003670
        WRITE(OUTPUT,512)                                      00003680
    512 FORMAT(1H0,"POTENTIAL COMPRESSION REDUCTION (%):")     00003690
        WRITE(OUTPUT,513)ITS6                                  00003700
    513 FORMAT("  NUMERIC:             ",I6)                   00003710
        WRITE(OUTPUT,514)ITS7                                  00003720
    514 FORMAT("  BLANK(SPACES):       ",I6)                   00003730
        WRITE(OUTPUT,515)ITS8                                  00003740
    515 FORMAT("  NONNUMERIC NONBLANK:",I6)                    00003750
        WRITE(OUTPUT,516)ITS9                                  00003760
    516 FORMAT("  TOTAL:               ",I6)                   00003770
        RETURN                                                 00003780
        END                                                    00003790
C      SUB-6**SORT SYMBOL ARRAY IN DESCENDING SEQUENCE**       00003800
        SUBROUTINE SUB6(IR,B)                                  00003810
        DOUBLE PRECISION IR(128)                               00003820
        DIMENSION B(129)                                       00003830
        CHARACTER *2 B                                         00003840
C      SORT THE FREQUENCY AND SYMBOL ARRAYS IN DESCENDING ORDER; 00003850
C      WHERE IR(N) = VALUE AND B(N) = ASSOCIATED SYMBOL.       00003860
        DO 10 I = 1,126                                        00003870
        IP1 = I+1                                              00003880
        DO 10 K=IP1,126                                        00003890
        IF(IR(I).GE.IR(K))GO TO 10                             00003900
        TEMP = IR(I)                                           00003910
        IR(I) = IR(K)                                          00003920
        IR(K) = TEMP                                           00003930
        B(129) = B(I)                                          00003940
        B(I) = B(K)                                            00003950
        B(K) = B(129)                                          00003960
     10 CONTINUE                                               00003970
        RETURN                                                 00003980
        END                                                    00003990
C      SUB-7**CALCULATE SEQUENTIAL REPEATING CHARACTERS***     00004000
        SUBROUTINE SUB7(IA,IX,IY,IN,N)                         00004010
        DIMENSION IA(132),IX(133),IY(133),IN(133)             00004020
C      CALCULATE SEQUENTIAL REPEATING CHARACTERS IN STRING     00004030
        I=1                                                    00004040
        K=1                                                    00004050
     73 IP=IA(I)                                               00004060
        IF(IP.EQ.IA(I+1)) GO TO 75                             00004070
     74 K=1                                                    00004080
        I=I+1                                                  00004090
        IF(I-N) 73,73,79                                       00004100
     75 K=K+1                                                  00004110
        I=I+1                                                  00004120
        IF(I-N) 68,68,69                                       00004130
     68 IF(IP.EQ.IA(I+1)) GO TO 75                             00004140
     69 IY(K)=IY(K)+1                                          00004150
        IF(IP.GE.48.AND.IP.LE.57) GO TO 76                     00004160
        IF(IP.EQ.32) GO TO 77                                  00004170
     78 GOTO 74                                                00004180
     76 IN(K)=IN(K)+1                                          00004190
        GOTO 74                                                00004200
     77 IX(K)=IX(K)+1                                          00004210
        GOTO 74                                                00004220
     79 RETURN                                                 00004230
        END                                                    00004240
C       SUB-8**PRINT SEQUENTIAL NUMERIC STRING ANALYSIS**      00004250
        SUBROUTINE SUB8(IM,IR,P,X,N)                           00004260
        DOUBLE PRECISION IR(128),P(128)                        00004270
        DIMENSION IM(133)                                      00004280
        INTEGER OUTPUT/6/                                      00004290
        CHARACTER *7 X                                         00004300
        WRITE(OUTPUT,801)                                      00004310
    801 FORMAT(1H1,"SEGMENT V",50X,"DATANALYSIS")              00004320
        WRITE(OUTPUT,802)                                      00004330
    802 FORMAT(1H0,12X,"HALF-BYTE ENCODING COMPRESSION SUSCEPTIBILITY" 00004340
       &)                                                      00004350
        WRITE(OUTPUT,803)X                                     00004360
```

```
     803 FORMAT(8X,"FOR SEQUENTIAL (NON-REPEATING) NUMERICS IN ",A7," F   00004370
        &ILE")                                                            00004380
         WRITE(OUTPUT,804)                                                00004390
     804 FORMAT(1H0,"STRING      NUMBER OF     TOTAL     COMPRESSED  CHA   00004400
        &RACTERS")                                                        00004410
         WRITE(OUTPUT,805)                                                00004420
     805 FORMAT("LENGTH     OCCURRANCES  CHARACTERS CHARACTERS     SAVED   00004430
        &")                                                               00004440
         DO 80 I=4,N                                                      00004450
         IM(N+1)=(IM(N+1)+IM(I)*I)                                        00004460
         IF(IM(I).EQ.0) GO TO 80                                          00004470
         IC=((((I+1)/2)+2)*IM(I)                                          00004480
         IC1=IC1+IC                                                       00004490
         WRITE(OUTPUT,82)I,IM(I),(IM(I)*I),IC,((IM(I)*I)-IC)              00004500
      82 FORMAT(I4,4I13)                                                  00004510
      80 CONTINUE                                                         00004520
         WRITE(OUTPUT,806)                                                00004530
     806 FORMAT(1H0,"**ANALYSIS SUMMARY**")                               00004540
         WRITE(OUTPUT,83)IR(128)                                          00004550
      83 FORMAT("TOTAL CHARACTERS IN FILE",0PF8.0)                        00004560
         WRITE(OUTPUT,807)IM(N+1)                                         00004570
     807 FORMAT("TOTAL CHAR. SUSCEPTIBLE TO COMPRESSION",I6)              00004580
         WRITE(OUTPUT,808)(IM(N+1)-IC1)                                   00004590
     808 FORMAT("TOTAL CHARACTERS SAVED  BY COMPRESSION",I6)              00004600
         P(128)=(IM(N+1)-IC1)/IR(128)                                     00004610
         WRITE(OUTPUT,84)P(128)                                           00004620
      84 FORMAT("PERCENT FILE COMPRESSION REDUCTION",2PF8.2)              00004630
         RETURN                                                           00004640
         END                                                             00004650
C       SUB-9**ISOLATE CHARACTER PAIRS IN STRINGS (DIATOMIC)**           00004660
         SUBROUTINE SUB9(A,IP,N)                                         00004670
         DIMENSION A(132),IP(28,26)                                      00004680
         I=1                                                             00004690
C       NOTE-"J" VALUES INFLATED BY 16 DUE TO HONEYWELL BUG.             00004700
C       NOTE-FOLLOWING 2 INST. HARDWARE SENSITIVE-SEE APPENDIX A.        00004710
     901 IV=IRS(A(I),19)                                                 00004720
         IV=IV+(IRS(A(I+1),27))                                          00004730
C       CHECK FOR IMBEDDED BLANK PAIRS;USE Q+ COUNTER                    00004740
         IF(IV-8240)923,920,923                                          00004750
     920 IV1=IRS(A(I+2),27)                                              00004760
         IF(IV1.EQ.32)GO TO 923                                          00004770
         IF(I-1)922,922,921                                              00004780
     921 IV1=IRS(A(I-1),27)                                              00004790
         IF(IV1.EQ.32)GO TO 923                                          00004800
     922 IP(2,17)=IP(2,17)+1                                             00004810
     923 CONTINUE                                                        00004820
         IC=1                                                            00004830
         IR=0                                                            00004840
C       NOW CHECK FOR BLANK/LETTER                                      00004850
         J=8273                                                          00004860
     902 IR=IR+1                                                         00004870
         IF(IV-J)903,905,903                                            00004880
     903 IF(IR-26)904,907,907                                           00004890
     904 J=J+1                                                          00004900
         GO TO 902                                                      00004910
     905 IP(IC,IR)=IP(IC,IR)+1                                          00004920
     906 I=I+2                                                          00004930
         IF(I-N)901,901,918                                             00004940
     907 IC=2                                                           00004950
         IR=0                                                           00004960
C       NOW CHECK FOR LETTER/BLANK                                      00004970
C       USE J=24880 FOR LOWER CASE                                     00004980
         J=16688                                                        00004990
     908 IR=IR+1                                                        00005000
         IF(IV-J)909,905,909                                           00005010
     909 IF(IR-26)910,911,911                                          00005020
     910 J=J+256                                                       00005030
         GO TO 908                                                     00005040
C       NOW CHECK FOR LETTER/LETTER                                    00005050
C       USE J=24945 FOR LOWER CASE                                     00005060
     911 J=16721                                                       00005070
     912 IR=0                                                          00005080
```

```
            IC=IC+1                                                      00005090
      913 IR=IR+1                                                        00005100
            IF(IV-J)914,905,914                                          00005110
      914 IF(IR-26)915,916,916                                           00005120
      915 J=J+1                                                          00005130
            GO TO 913                                                    00005140
      916 IF(IC-28)917,906,906                                           00005150
      917 J=J+231                                                        00005160
            GO TO 912                                                    00005170
      918 RETURN                                                         00005180
            END                                                          00005190
C       SUB-10**PRINT PAIRED CHARACTER ANALYSIS REPORT**                 00005200
            SUBROUTINE SUB10(IP,IX,B,C)                                  00005210
            DIMENSION IP(28,26),IX(133),B(129),C(729)                    00005220
            INTEGER OUTPUT/6/                                            00005230
            CHARACTER *2 B,C                                             00005240
            WRITE(OUTPUT,101)                                            00005250
      101 FORMAT(1H1,"SEGMENT VI",50X,"DATANALYSIS")                     00005260
            WRITE(OUTPUT,102)                                            00005270
      102 FORMAT(1H0,15X,"PAIRED CHARACTER COMPRESSION ANALYSIS")        00005280
            WRITE(OUTPUT,103)                                            00005290
      103 FORMAT(1H0," PAIR/COUNT  PAIR/COUNT  PAIR/COUNT  PAIR/COUNT    00005300
          & PAIR/COUNT PAIR/COUNT ")                                     00005310
            I=1                                                          00005320
            N=0                                                          00005330
            DO 110 J=1,28                                                00005340
            DO 110 K=1,26                                                00005350
            IF(IP(J,K).EQ.0) GO TO 110                                   00005360
C       PRINT ONLY THE TOP 132 PAIR OCCURRENCES                         00005370
            IF(N-22)106,106,110                                          00005380
      106 IX(I)=IP(J,K)                                                  00005390
            IPS=IPS+IX(I)                                                00005400
            M=((J-1)*26)+K                                               00005410
            B(I)=C(M)                                                    00005420
            I=I+1                                                        00005430
            IF(I-6)110,110,109                                           00005440
      109 WRITE(OUTPUT,105)B(1),IX(1),B(2),IX(2),B(3),IX(3),B(4),IX(4),  00005450
          &B(5),IX(5),B(6),IX(6)                                         00005460
      105 FORMAT(6(A6,I6))                                               00005470
            I=1                                                          00005480
            N=N+1                                                        00005490
      110 CONTINUE                                                       00005500
C       FINISH OFF PRINT LINE NOW IF PARTIALLY FILLED                   00005510
            IF(I-1)112,112,114                                           00005520
      114 DO 113 I=I,6                                                   00005530
            B(I)=B(128)                                                  00005540
            IX(I)=0                                                      00005550
      113 CONTINUE                                                       00005560
      111 WRITE(OUTPUT,105)B(1),IX(1),B(2),IX(2),B(3),IX(3),B(4),IX(4),  00005570
          &B(5),IX(5),B(6),IX(6)                                         00005580
      112 WRITE(OUTPUT,115)IPS                                           00005590
      115 FORMAT(1H0,"TOTAL COMBINATIONS FOUND:",I6)                     00005600
            RETURN                                                       00005610
            END                                                          00005620
C        SUB-11**SORT  PAIRED CHARACTER ARRAY ***                       00005630
            SUBROUTINE SUB11(IP,C)                                       00005640
            DIMENSION IP(28,26),C(729)                                   00005650
            CHARACTER *2 C                                               00005660
C       SORT THE TWO-DIMENSION PAIRS ARRAY & ASSOCIATED SYMBOLS         00005670
C       WHERE IP(N1,N2) = VALUE AND C(N) = RELATED PAIR SYMBOL.         00005680
            DO 1101 J=1,28                                               00005690
            DO 1101 K=1,26                                               00005700
            KK=K                                                         00005710
            DO 1101 J1=J,28                                              00005720
            DO 1101 K1=KK,26                                             00005730
            KK=1                                                         00005740
            IF(IP(J,K).GE.IP(J1,K1)) GO TO 1101                         00005750
            TEMP=IP(J,K)                                                 00005760
            IP(J,K)=IP(J1,K1)                                            00005770
            IP(J1,K1)=TEMP                                               00005780
```

```
C       PERFORM LINEAR CONVERSION OF TWO DIMENSIONS INTO ONE.      00005790
        M1=((J-1)*26)+K                                            00005800
        M2=((J1-1)*26)+K1                                          00005810
        C(729)=C(M1)                                               00005820
        C(M1)=C(M2)                                                00005830
        C(M2)=C(729)                                               00005840
 1101 CONTINUE                                                     00005850
      RETURN                                                       00005860
      END                                                          00005870
C       SUB-12**COMPUTE ENTROPY & PRINT ANALYSIS REPORT**          00005880
      SUBROUTINE SUB12(IR,P,X)                                     00005890
      DOUBLE PRECISION IR(128),P(128),ZERO                         00005900
      INTEGER OUTPUT/6/                                            00005910
      CHARACTER *7 X                                               00005920
      ZERO=0.D0                                                    00005930
      DO 1201 I=1,127                                              00005940
      IF(P(I)-ZERO)1201,1201,1200                                  00005950
 1200 E=E+P(I)*DLOG2(P(I))                                         00005960
 1201 CONTINUE                                                     00005970
      E=-1*E                                                       00005980
      B1=E*IR(128)                                                 00005990
      B2=IR(128)*8                                                 00006000
      B3=(B2-B1)/B2*100                                            00006010
      B4=B1/8                                                      00006020
      WRITE(OUTPUT,1202)                                           00006030
 1202 FORMAT(1H1,"SEGMENT VII",50X,"DATANALYSIS")                  00006040
      WRITE(OUTPUT,1203)X                                          00006050
 1203 FORMAT(1H0,15X,"ENTROPY ANALYSIS FOR ",A7," FILE")           00006060
      WRITE(OUTPUT,1204)E                                          00006070
 1204 FORMAT(1H0,10X,"ENTROPY: ",0PF8.2," BITS/CHARACTER")         00006080
      WRITE(OUTPUT,1205)                                           00006090
 1205 FORMAT(1H0,10X,"FILE CONTAINS:")                             00006100
      WRITE(OUTPUT,1206)IR(128)                                    00006110
 1206 FORMAT(1H0,15X,0PF8.0," CHARACTERS")                         00006120
      WRITE(OUTPUT,1207)B2                                         00006130
 1207 FORMAT(1H0,15X,0PF8.0," BITS")                               00006140
      WRITE(OUTPUT,1211)B3                                         00006150
 1211 FORMAT(1H0,10X,"THEORETICAL STATISTICAL COMPRESSION: ",0PF8.2,00006160
     8"%")                                                         00006170
      WRITE(OUTPUT,1209)                                           00006180
 1209 FORMAT(1H0,10X,"FILE WOULD REQUIRE:")                        00006190
      WRITE(OUTPUT,1210)B4                                         00006200
 1210 FORMAT(1H0,15X,0PF8.0," CHARACTERS")                         00006210
      WRITE(OUTPUT,1212)B1                                         00006220
 1212 FORMAT(1H0,15X,0PF8.0," BITS")                               00006230
      RETURN                                                       00006240
      END                                                          00006250
```

A.9 BASIC LANGUAGE DATANALYSIS PROGRAM LISTING

```
10 '****************************************************************
20 '* COPYWRITE GILBERT HELD & THOMAS MARSHALL - DATANALYSIS       *
30 '* THIS PROGRAM WAS WRITTEN TO ANALYSE/FILES FOR SUSCEPTIBILITY *
40 '* TO VARIOUS COMPRESSION TECHNIQUES.  REFER TO DOCUMENTATION.  *
50 '****************************************************************
60 '----- INITIALIZATION -----------
70 DIM A(132),B$(129),IA(132),IN(133),IM(133),IX(133),IY(132)
80 DIM Z(132),C$(729),IP(26,28),IR(128),P(128)
90 WIDTH 80:CLS            'CLEAR SCREEN & SET WIDTH TO 80
100 ON ERROR GOTO 4050     'ERROR HANDLER
110  '- - SETUP PROCESSING OF INPUT FILE  - -
120  LOCATE ,,1
130  PRINT "ENTER ASCII FILENAME IN THE FORMAT [DRIVE:]FILESPEC";
140  INPUT F$: OPEN F$ FOR INPUT AS #2
150 PRINT "IS FILE MOSTLY LOWER CASE(Y/N)";
160 INPUT V$
170 IF V$ = "Y" OR V$ = "y" THEN Z= 97 ELSE Z= 65
```

```
180   PRINT "DO YOU WANT PRINTED OUTPUT (Y/N)";
190   INPUT D$
200   IF D$= "y" OR D$= "Y" THEN D$="LPT1:" ELSE D$="SCRN:"
210   OPEN D$ FOR OUTPUT AS #1
220   ' STRUCTURE GRAPHIC SYMBOL ARRAY
230   PRINT "DATANALYSIS - INITIALIZATION..."
240 DATA SH,SX,EX,ET,EQ,AK,BL,BS,HT,LF,VT,FF,CR,SO,SI,DL,D1,D2,D3,D4
250 DATA NK,SY,EB,CN,EM,SB,EC,FS,GS,RS,US,SP
260 FOR I=1 TO 32:READ A$:B$(I)=A$:NEXT I
270 FOR I= 33 TO 127
280 B$(I) = CHR$(I):NEXT I:B$(127)="DL":B$(128)="**"
290 '***********************************************************
300 '*   STRUCTURE THE PAIRED SYMBOL ARRAY FIRST              *
310 '***********************************************************
320 ' 1ST SPACE/LETTER COMBINATIONS
330 K=1
340 I=32
350 FOR J= 2 TO 2+25
360 C$(K)= CHR$(I)+ CHR$(J)
370 K=K+1
380 NEXT J
390 ' NOW LETTERS/SPACE  COMBINATIONS
400 J=32
410 FOR I=2 TO 2+25
420 C$(K)= CHR$(I)+CHR$(J)
430 K=K+1
440 NEXT I
450 ' NOW LETTER/LETTER COMBINATIONS
460 FOR I=2 TO 2+25
470 FOR J=2 TO 2+25
480 C$(K)= CHR$(I)+CHR$(J)
490 K=K+1
500 NEXT J
510 NEXT I
520 PRINT "PATIENCE - INPUT PROCESSING";
530 IF EOF(2) THEN 760
540 LINE INPUT #2, X$     'READ FULL LINE WITH PUNCTUATION
550 PRINT ".";            'TELL THEM WE'RE STILL ALIVE
560 K= LEN(X$)            'SAVE LENGTH OF INPUT STRING
570 FOR I= 1 TO K         'AND SET UP END OF STRING
580 A$= MID$(X$,I,1)      'PULL OUT A CHARACTER TO ANALYSE
590 '*************************************************************
600 '*INCREMENT COUNTERS BY THE ORDINAL EQUIV OF CHAR AS SUBSCRIPT*
610 '*************************************************************
620 IP2=ASC(A$)           'DERIVE DECIMAL REPRESENTATION
630 IR(IP2)= IR(IP2)+1    'ADD TO DISPLACEMENT COUNTER
640 IR(128)= IR(128)+1    'ADD TO THE TOTAL CHAR READ
650 IA(I)= IP2            'STRING THE RECORD OUT IN ONE DIMENSION
660 N1= N1+1              'ADD TO THE CHARACTER COUNT
670 NEXT I                'GET NEXT INPUT CHARACTER
680 GOSUB 880             'SUB 1 - CALCULATE NUMERICS
690 GOSUB 1180            'SUB 7 - CALCULATE REPEATS
700 GOSUB 1940            'SUB 9 - ISOLATE PAIRS
710 J1=J1+1               'ADD TO RECORD COUNT
720 N=N1                  'SAVE LAST RECORD LENGTH
730 N1=0                  'ZERO LENGTH FOR NEW RECORD
740 GOTO 530              'AND GO GET MORE INPUT
750 BEEP  '******** END OF MAINLINE PROGRAM ********************
760 GOSUB 4060            'SUB 2-PRINT THE EXECUTION REPORT
770 GOSUB 1420            'SUB 3-PRINT FREQ./OCCURRENCE ANALYSIS
780 GOSUB 3880            'SUB 6-SORT FREQ. ARRAY
790 GOSUB 1420            'SUB 3-REPRINT FREQ./OCCURRENCE ANALYSIS
800 GOSUB 1690            'SUB 4-PRINT STRING ANALYSIS
810 GOSUB 2770            'SUB 5-PRINT RUNLENGTH ANALYSIS
820 GOSUB 3300            'SUB 8-PRINT NUM. STRING ANALYSIS
830 GOSUB 2540            'SUB 11-SORT PAIR ARRAY
840 GOSUB 2250            'SUB 10-PRINT PAIR ARRAY
850 GOSUB 3620            'SUB 12-COMPUTE & PRINT ENTROPY
860 END                   'T-T-T-THATS ALL FOLKS
870 '***************************************************
880 '*      SUBROUTINE 1 - CALCULATE NUMERIC STRINGS   *
890 '***************************************************
900 I=1
910 IF IA(I)>= 48 AND IA(I)<= 57 THEN 980
920 IF IA(I)>= 44 AND IA(I)<= 47 THEN 980
930 IF IA(I) = 42 THEN 980
940 IF IA(I) = 36 THEN 980
```

```
950 I=I+1                          'NOT A NUMERIC OR SYMBOL
960 IF I> N1 THEN 1160            'RECORD STRING PROCESS COMPLETE
970 GOTO 910
980 K=1
990 I=I+1
1000 IT=IA(I)
1010 M=0
1020 IF IA(I)>= 48 AND IA(I)<= 57 THEN 1090   'NUMERIC?
1030 IF IA(I)>= 44 AND IA(I)<= 47 THEN 1090   'SYMBOL?
1040 IF IA(I) = 42 THEN 1090                  'ASTERISK?
1050 IF IA(I) = 36 THEN 1090                  'DOLLAR?
1060 IF M=0 THEN 950
1070 IM(K)= IM(K)+1               'ADD TO STRING SIZE COUNT
1080 GOTO 950
1090 I=I+1
1100 K=K+1
1110 ' ELIMINATE FULLY REPITITIOUS STRINGS FROM CONSIDERATION
1120 IF IA(I-1)= IT THEN 1140
1130 M=1
1140 IF I> N1 THEN 1060
1150 GOTO 1020
1160 RETURN
1170 '*****************************************************
1180 '*        SUBROUTINE 7 - CALCULATE SEQ. REPEATING CHAR. *
1190 '*****************************************************
1200 I=1
1210 K=1
1220 IC= IA(I)                    'PULL CHAR. FROM STRING
1230 IF IC= IA(I+1) THEN 1280     'SAME AS NEXT IN STRING?
1240 K=1
1250 I= I+1
1260 IF I> N1 THEN 1400           'END OF RECORD
1270 GOTO 1220
1280 K=K+1                        'BUMP REPITITION COUNT
1290 I= I+1
1300 IF I> N1 THEN 1320           'END OF STRING?
1310 IF IC = IA(I+1) THEN 1280    'LOOP ON REPITIONS
1320 IY(K) = IY(K)+1              'ADD TO "ANY" COUNT
1330 IF IC>= 48 AND IC<= 57 THEN 1360   ' ITS NUMERIC
1340 IF IC = 32 THEN 1380         ' ITS A SPACE
1350 GOTO 1240
1360 IN(K) = IN(K)+1              'ADD TO REPEAT COUNT
1370 GOTO 1240
1380 IX(K)= IX(K)+1               'ADD TO SPACE COUNT
1390 GOTO 1240
1400 M=0:RETURN                   'RESET TOGGLE & RETURN
1410 '*****************************************************
1420 '*        SUBROUTINE 3 - PRINT FREQ OF OCCURRENCE TABLE      *
1430 '*****************************************************
1435 IF D$= "SCRN:" THEN WIDTH #1,255    'ELIM. DOUBLE SPACE
1440 ' 1ST CALCULATE PERCENTAGES
1450 FOR K= 1 TO 128
1460 P(K)= IR(K)/IR(128)          'IR(128) IS TOTAL CHAR STORE
1470 NEXT K
1480 ' NOW PRINT FULL TABLE - 4 COLUMNS/32 ROWS
1490 GOSUB 3580                   'SET TOP OF PAGE
1500 IF M=1 THEN 1530             'THIS TIME IT IS SORTED
1510 PRINT #1, SPC(5)"SEGMENT I";SPC(11)"STANDARD FREQ. OF OCCURRENCE"
1520 GOTO 1540
1530 PRINT #1,SPC(5)"SEGMENT II";SPC(11)"SORTED  FREQ. OF OCCURRENCE"
1540 PRINT #1,SPC(18)"TABLE OF CHARACTERS FOUND IN ";F$;" FILE"
1550 PRINT #1,
1560 PRINT #1,"CHAR    COUNT     %   CHAR   COUNT     %   CHAR   COUNT     %";
1570 PRINT #1,"   CHAR   COUNT     %"
1580 PRINT #1,
1590 P1$= " \\ ######   .##    "
1600 FOR I = 1 TO 32
1610 PRINT #1,USING P1$;B$(I);IR(I);P(I);
1620 PRINT #1,USING P1$;B$(I+32);IR(I+32);P(I+32);
1630 PRINT #1,USING P1$;B$(I+64);IR(I+64);P(I+64);
1640 PRINT #1,USING P1$;B$(I+96);IR(I+96);P(I+96)
1650 NEXT I
1660 M=1
1670 RETURN
1680 '*****************************************************
1690 '*        SUBROUTINE 4 - PRINT REPITITIOUS STRING ANALYSIS  *
1700 '*****************************************************
1710 GOSUB 3580              'SET TOP OF PAGE
1720 PRINT #1,"SEGMENT III";SPC(11)"REPEATED CHARACTER STRING ANALYSIS"
```

```
1730 PRINT #1,
1740 PRINT #1,"STRING *****NUMBER OF|OCCURRENCES***"
1750 PRINT #1,"LENGTH  NUMERICS SPACES  OTHER   TOTAL"
1760 PRINT #1,
1770 P2$="####    ####    ####    ####    #####"
1780 FOR I=3 TO N      .  'IGNORE STRINGS LESS THAN THREE
1790 IN(N+1)=IN(N+1)+(IN(I)*I)      'ADD TO NUMERIC TOTAL
1800 IX(N+1)=IX(N+1)+(IX(I)*I)      'ADD TO SPACE TOTAL
1810 IY(N+1)=IY(N+1)+(IY(I)*I)      'ADD TO SUM TOTAL
1820 IF IY(I)=0 THEN 1840           'SKIP IF ZERO COUNT
1830 PRINT #1,USING P2$;I;IN(I);IX(I);(IY(I)-IN(I)-IX(I));IY(I)
1840 NEXT I
1850 PRINT #1,
1860 PRINT #1,"**ANALYSIS SUMMARY**"
1870 PRINT #1," RECORDS PROCESSED ";J1
1880 PRINT #1," TOTAL REPITITIONS ";IY(N+1)
1890 PRINT #1," CHARACTERS IN FILE ";IR(128)
1900 P(128)=IY(N+1)/IR(128)*100
1910 PRINT #1," PERCENT REPITITIOUS ";INT(P(128))
1920 RETURN
1930 '*************************************************************
1940 '*       SUBROUTINE 9 - ISOLATE PAIRS IN STRINGS (DIATOMIC) *
1950 '*************************************************************
1960 I=1
1970 ' CHECK FOR IMBEDED BLANK PAIRS; USE Q_ COUNTER FOR TALLY
1980 IR=17:IC=2
1990 IF IA(I) <> 32 THEN 2020
2000 IF IA(I+1) <> 32 THEN 2020
2010 GOTO 2190                      'ITS A HIT
2020 ' NOW CHECK FOR BLANK/LETTER
2030 IR=IA(I+1)-(Z-1):IC=1          'SET TO ROW N, COL 1
2040 IF IA(I) <> 32 THEN 2070
2050 IF IA(I+1) < Z OR IA(I+1) > Z+25 THEN 2070   'IS IT WITHIN RANGE?
2060 GOTO 2190                      'ITS A HIT
2070 'NOW CHECK FOR LETTER/BLANK
2080 IR=IA(I)-(Z-1):IC=2            'SET TO ROW N,COL 2
2090 IF IA(I) < Z OR IA(I) > Z+25 THEN 2120      'IS IT WITHIN RANGE?
2100 IF IA(I+1) <> 32 THEN 2120
2110 GOTO 2190                      'ITS A HIT
2120 ' NOW CHECK FOR LETTER/LETTER
2130 IC= IA(I)-(Z-3)               'SET COLUMN TO 1ST PAIR CHAR
2140 IR= IA(I+1)-(Z-1)             'SET ROW TO 2ND PAIR CHAR
2150 IF IA(I) < Z OR IA(I) > Z+25 THEN 2180    '1ST WITHIN RANGE?
2160 IF IA(I+1) < Z OR IA(I+1) > Z+25 THEN 2180 '2ND WITHIN RANGE?
2170 GOTO 2190                      'ITS A HIT
2180 I=I+1:GOTO 2210                'NO HITS, STEP JUST ONE
2190 IP(IR,IC)=IP(IR,IC)+1          'INCREMENT PAIR COUNT IN ARRAY
2200 I=I+2                          'STEP TWO FOR NEXT PAIR TEST
2210 IF I>=N1 THEN 2230
2220 GOTO 1970                      'CONTINUE TO END OF RECORD
2230 RETURN
2240 '*********************************************************
2250 '*        SUBROUTINE 10 - PRINT PAIRED CHAR. ANALYSIS    *
2260 '*********************************************************
2270 GOSUB 3580                     'SET TOP OF PAGE
2280 PRINT #1,"SEGMENT VI";SPC(11)"PAIRED CHARACTER DIATOMIC ANALYSIS"
2290 PRINT #1,
2300 PRINT #1,"PAIR/COUNT  PAIR/COUNT  PAIR/COUNT  PAIR/COUNT  PAIR/COUNT  PAIR/
COUNT"
2310 PRINT #1,
2320 I=1
2330 N=0
2340 P3$="\\ #####    \\ #####    \\ #####    \\ #####    \\ #####    \\ #####"
2350 FOR J=1 TO 26
2360 FOR K=1 TO 28
2370 IF IP(J,K)< 2 THEN 2510        'SKIP 0 AND 1 COUNTS
2380 ' PRINT ONLY THE TOP 132 PAIRS COUNT
2390 IF N < 23 THEN 2410
2400 J=26:K=28:GOTO 2510            'IM DONE
2410 IX(I)= IP(J,K)
2420 IPS=IPS+IX(I)
2430 M=((K-1)*26)+ J
2440 B$(I)=C$(M)
2450 IF B$(I)= "Q " OR B$(I)="q " THEN B$(I)= "  " 'IMBEDDED BLANK PAIR
2460 I=I+1
2470 IF I <=6 THEN 2510             'SETUP SIX PAIRS TO THE LINE
2480 PRINT #1,USING P3$;B$(1);IX(1);B$(2);IX(2);B$(3);IX(3);B$(4);IX(4);B$(5);IX
(5);B$(6);IX(6)
```

```
2490 I=1
2500 N=N+1
2510 NEXT K
2520 NEXT J
2530 RETURN
2540 '*************************************************************
2550 '*           SUBROUTINE 11 - SORT PAIRED CHAR. ARRAY          *
2560 '*************************************************************
2570 ' SORT THE TWO DIMENSION PAIRS ARRAY (IP) & ASSOC. SYMBOLS (C)
2580 PRINT:PRINT "(NOW SORTING PAIR ARRAY)";
2590 FOR K=1 TO 28              ' SET COLUMN LOOP
2600  FOR J=1 TO 25             ' SET ROW LOOP
2610   FOR JJ=J+1 TO 26         ' SET WITHIN-COLUMN LOOP
2620    IF IP(J,K) >= IP(JJ,K) THEN 2710
2630    TMP=IP(J,K)             'TEMP SAVE THE GREATER COUNT
2640    IP(J,K)=IP(JJ,K)        'SWAP HIGHER COUNT
2650    IP(JJ,K)=TMP            'WITH LOWER COUNT
2660    M1=((K-1)*26)+J         'CALC LOWER SYMBOL ADDR
2670    M2=((K-1)*26)+JJ        'CALC HIGHER SYMBOL ADDR
2680    C$(729)=C$(M1)          'TEMP SAVE THE SYMBOL
2690    C$(M1)=C$(M2)           'SWAP 1
2700    C$(M2)=C$(729)          'SWAP 2
2710   NEXT JJ                  'COMPLETE 3RD LOOP
2720  NEXT J                    'COMPLETE 2ND LOOP
2730   PRINT ".";               'LET EM KNOW WE'RE ALIVE
2740  NEXT K                    'COMPLETE 1ST LOOP
2750 RETURN
2760 '*************************************************************
2770 '*  SUBROUTINE 5 - RUN LENGTH ENCODING ANALYSIS              *
2780 '*************************************************************
2790 GOSUB 3580           'SET TOP OF PAGE
2800 PRINT #1,"SEGMENT IV - RUN LENGTH ENCODING ANALYSIS"
2810 PRINT #1,
2820 PRINT #1,"STRING ****** REPEATED CHARACTERS *****   CHAR. SAVED"
2830 PRINT #1,"LENGTH  NUMERICS  SPACES   OTHER    TOTAL    NUMERICS";
2840 PRINT #1," SPACES  OTHER  TOTAL"
2850 PRINT #1,
2860 P4$=" ####      ####    ####   ####  #####       ####    ####  ####  ####"
2870 FOR I=3 TO N
2880 ITN1=ITN1+(IN(I)*I)            'TALLY NUMERICS
2890 ITX1=ITX1+(IX(I)*I)            'TALLY SPACES
2900 ITY1=ITY1+(IY(I)*I)            'TALLY OTHER
2910 ITN2=(I-3)*IN(I)
2920 ITX2=(I-3)*IX(I)
2930 ITY2=(I-3)*(IY(I)-IX(I)-IN(I))
2940 ITT2=(I-3)*(IY(I))
2950 ITN3=ITN3+ITN2
2960 ITX3=ITX3+ITX2
2970 ITY3=ITY3+ITY2
2980 ITT3=ITT3+ITT2
2990 IF (IY(I)=0) THEN 3020    'SKIP 0 COUNTS
3000 IYT1=(IY(I)*I)-(IN(I)*I)-(IX(I)*I)
3010 PRINT#1,USING P4$;I;(IN(I)*I);(IX(I)*I);IYT1;(IY(I)*I);ITN2;ITX2;ITY2;ITT2
3020 NEXT I
3030 ITS1=IR(128)                  'PICKUP TOTAL CHAR INPUT
3040 ITS2=(ITN1/IR(128)*100)       'COMPUTE NUMERIC %
3050 ITS3=(ITX1/IR(128)*100)       'COMPUTE SPACE %
3060 ITS4=((ITY1-ITX1-ITN1)/IR(128)*100)   'COMPUTE OTHER %
3070 ITS5=(ITY1/IR(128)*100)
3080 ITS6=(ITN3/IR(128)*100)
3090 ITS7=(ITX3/IR(128)*100)
3100 ITS8=(ITY3/IR(128)*100)
3110 ITS9=(ITT3/IR(128)*100)
3120 PRINT #1,
3130 PRINT #1,USING P4$;I;ITN1;ITX1;(ITY1-ITN1-ITX1);ITY1;ITN3;ITX3;ITY3;ITT3
3140 PRINT #1,
3150 PRINT #1,"SUMMARY INFORMATION: TOTAL CHAR READ";ITS1
3160 PRINT #1,
3170 PRINT #1,"PERCENTAGE SEQUENTIAL REPEATED CHAR:"
3180 PRINT #1,"   NUMERIC:";INT(ITS2)
3190 PRINT #1,"   BLANKS(SPACES):";INT(ITS3)
3200 PRINT #1,"   NONNUMERIC/NONBLANK:";INT(ITS4)
3210 PRINT #1,"   TOTAL REPEATED:";INT(ITS5)
3220 PRINT #1,
3230 PRINT #1," POTENTIAL COMPRESSION REDUCTION(%):"
3240 PRINT #1,"    NUMERIC:";INT(ITS6)
3250 PRINT #1,"    BLANK(SPACES):";INT(ITS7)
3260 PRINT #1,"    NONNUMERIC/NONBLANK:";INT(ITS8)
3270 PRINT #1," TOTAL:";INT(ITS9);"%"
3280 RETURN
```

```
3290 '************************************************************
3300 '*       SUBROUTINE 8 - NUMERIC STRING ANALYSIS           *
3310 '************************************************************
3320 GOSUB 3580            'SET TOP OF PAGE
3330 PRINT #1,"SEGMENT V - HALF BYTE ENCODING ANALYSIS":PRINT
3340 PRINT #1,"FOR SEQUENTIAL (NON-REPEATING) NUMERIC DATA"
3350 PRINT #1,
3360 PRINT #1,"STRING       NUMBER OF      TOTAL        COMPRESSED   CHAR"
3370 PRINT #1,"LENGTH       OCCURANCES     CHAR.        CHAR.     SAVED"
3380 PRINT #1,
3390 P5$= "  ###        ####       ####       ####       ####     ###"
3400 FOR I=4 TO N
3410 IM(N+1)=IM(N+1)+(IM(I)*I)
3420 IF (IM(I)=0) THEN 3460         'SKIP 0 COUNTS
3425 IF I> 15 THEN IC= .5 ELSE IC= 0 'EXTRA HALF-BYTE OVER 15
3430 IC= IM(I)*CINT(IC+1.5+(I/2)+.4) 'COMPUTE COMPRESSION
3440 IC1=IC1+IC
3450 PRINT #1,USING P5$;I;IM(I);(IM(I)*I);IC;((IM(I)*I)-IC)
3460 NEXT I
3470 PRINT #1,
3480 PRINT #1,"*ANALYSIS SUMMARY*"
3490 PRINT #1,"TOTAL CHAR. IN FILE=";IR(128)
3500 PRINT #1,"TOTAL CHAR. SUSCEPTIBLE| TO COMPRESSION:";IM(N+1)
3510 PRINT #1,"TOTAL CHAR. SAVED BY COMPRESSION:";INT(IM(N+1)-IC1)
3520 P(128)=(IM(N+1)-IC1)/IR(128)*100    'COMPUTE PERCENTAGE
3530 PRINT #1,"PERCENT FILE COMPRESSION REDUCTION:";INT(P(128))
3540 RETURN
3550 '************************************************************
3560 '* SETS TOP OF FORM OR SCREEN DELAY BASED ON OPTION        *
3570 '************************************************************
3580 IF D$= "LPT1:" THEN 3600
3590 PRINT:PRINT "STRIKE ENTER WHEN READY";:INPUT G$
3600 PRINT #1, CHR$(12)              'SET TOP OF FORM
3610 RETURN
3620 '************************************************************
3630 '* SUBROUTINE 12 - COMPUTE & PRINT ENTROPY                *
3640 '************************************************************
3650 GOSUB 3580            'SET TOP OF PAGE
3660 FOR I= 1 TO 127
3670 IF P(I) = 0 THEN 3690
3680 E= E+P(I)* LOG(P(I))           'SEE DOCUMENTATION
3690 NEXT I
3700 E= -1*E
3710 B1= E*IR(128)
3720 B2= IR(128)*8
3730 B3= (B2-B1)/B2*100
3740 B4= B1/8
3760 PRINT #1, "SEGMENT VII - ENTROPY ANALYSIS"
3770 PRINT #1,
3780 PRINT #1, "ENTROPY:  ";E;" BITS/CHARACTER"
3790 PRINT #1, "FILE CONTAINS:"
3800 PRINT #1, INT(IR(128));" CHARACTERS"
3810 PRINT #1, INT(B2);" BITS"
3820 PRINT #1, "THEORETICAL STATISTICAL COMPRESSION: ";B3
3830 PRINT #1, "FILE WOULD REQUIRE:"
3840 PRINT #1, INT(B4);"  CHARACTERS"
3850 PRINT #1, INT(B1);" BITS"
3860 GOSUB 3580            'SET TOP OF PAGE
3870 RETURN
3880 '************************************************************
3890 '* SUBROUTINE 6 - SORT FREQ OCCURRENCE ARRAY DESCENDING *
3900 '************************************************************
3910 PRINT:PRINT "(NOW SORTING FREQUENCY TABLE)";
3920 FOR I= 1 TO 125
3930 FOR K= I+1 TO 126
3940 IF (IR(I)) >= IR(K) THEN 4010      'GET GREATER COUNT
3950 TEMP= IR(I)                        'AND SWAP...
3960 IR(I)= IR(K)
3970 IR(K)= TEMP
3980 B$(129)= B$(I)
3990 B$(I)= B$(K)
4000 B$(K)= B$(129)
4010 NEXT K
4020 PRINT ".";                         'LET EM KNOW WE'RE ALIVE
4030 NEXT I
4040 RETURN
4050 PRINT "**ERROR";ERR;" ENCOUNTERED ON LINE";ERL;"***":BEEP:STOP
```

```
4060 '***************************************************
4070 '*   SUBROUTINE 2 - PRINT EXECUTION REPORT SUMMARY *
4080 '***************************************************
4090 FOR I= 1 TO 10:PRINT #1,:NEXT I     'SKIP 10 LINES
4100 PRINT #1,:PRINT #1,SPC(30)"DATANALYSIS"
4110 PRINT #1,:PRINT #1,SPC(24)"EXECUTION  REPORT  SUMMARY"
4120 PRINT #1,:PRINT #1,SPC(24)"FILE ANALYSED: ";F$
4130 PRINT #1,:PRINT #1,SPC(15)"SEGMENT";SPC(10)"DESCRIPTION"
4140 PRINT #1,:PRINT #1,SPC(18)"I";SPC(13)"SYSTEM STANDARD FREQUENCY OF OCCURRENCE
CE"
4150 PRINT #1,:PRINT #1,SPC(18)"II";SPC(12)"SORTED FREQUENCY OF OCCURRENCE"
4160 PRINT #1,:PRINT #1,SPC(18)"III";SPC(11)"REPEATED CHARACTER STRING ANALYSIS"

4170 PRINT #1,:PRINT #1,SPC(18)"IV";SPC(12)"RUN LENGTH ENCODING SUSCEPTIBILITY"
4180 PRINT #1,:PRINT #1,SPC(18)"V";SPC(13)"HALF-BYTE ENCODING SSUSCEPTIBILITY"
4190 PRINT #1,:PRINT #1,SPC(18)"VI";SPC(12)"DIATOMIC COMPRESSION ANALYSIS"
4200 PRINT #1,:PRINT #1,SPC(18)"VII";SPC(11)"ENTROPY ANALYSIS"
4210 RETURN
4220 PRINT "**ERROR";ERR;" ENCOUNTERED ON LINE";ERL;"***":BEEP:STOP
```

APPENDIX B

SHRINK PROGRAM DESCRIPTIONS AND LISTINGS

For illustrative purposes, we have combined run-length, diatomic and half-byte encoding compression routines into two programs which we collectively call SHRINK. The first program, whose listing is contained in Figure B.1, is called MERGEC.BAS. As the reader may surmise from the name of this BASIC program, it represents the merging of the three previously mentioned compression techniques. The second BASIC program presented in this appendix was developed to decompress the data compressed by MERGEC.DAT. This program is called MERGED.BAS and its listing is contained in Figure B.2.

Like all BASIC programs presented in this book, the reader should note that the understanding of the coding techniques, and not program efficiency, was of primary concern. Thus, almost every line of each BASIC program contains a comment defining the function of the line. Since interpretive BASIC checks each comment during program execution, this excessive documentation considerably slows the execution of each program. Owing to this, it is highly recommended that the reader who wishes to use these programs excludes all comments from inclusion in the program. In addition, the compilation of each program by the use of a BASIC compiler will greatly increase the operating efficiency of each program.

B.1 MERGEC.BAS AND MERGED.BAS

The MERGEC.BAS program listed in Figure B.1 has some interesting changes from the previous programs that were used to

```
10 '*************************************************************
20 '* MERGEC.BAS PROGRAM COMBINES ALL COMPRESSION TECHNIQUES   *
30 '* INTO ONE PROGRAM.  THE COMPANION PROGRAM, MERGED.BAS IS  *
40 '* USED TO DECOMPRESS THIS PROGRAMS OUTPUT (COMPRESS.DAT)   *
50 '* INTO ITS ORIGINAL FORM.  IT ALLOWS UP TO 254 CHARACTER   *
60 '* INPUT STRINGS AND MIXED UPPER/LOWER CASE.  IF NO LOWER    *
70 '* CASE PAIRS ARE ENCOUNTERED IN THE 1ST 100 CHARACTERS THE *
80 '* PROGRAM ADJUSTS ITS LOOKUPS TO UPPER CASE ONLY IN ORDER  *
90 '* TO SHORTEN RUN TIME.  AUTHOR: THOMAS R. MARSHALL  1986    *
100 '*************************************************************
110 DIM O$(256), C(256)
120 WIDTH 80:CLS
130 '**********MAIN ROUTINE*********************
140 '* THIS ROUTINE READS RECORDS FROM AN ASCII *
150 '* FILE INTO A STRING CALLED X$ WHICH IS    *
160 '* THEN PASSED TO SUBROUTINES FOR COMPRESSION
170 '*******************************************
180 PRINT "ENTER ASCII FILENAME. EG, [DRIVE:]FILESPEC";
190 INPUT F$: OPEN F$ FOR INPUT AS #2
200 OPEN "COMPRESS.DAT" FOR OUTPUT AS #3
210 PRINT "PATIENCE - INPUT PROCESSING"
220 GOSUB 1150          'SETUP PAIR TABLE
230 IF EOF(2) THEN GOTO 1940
240 LINE INPUT #2, X$
250 N= LEN(X$)
260 GOSUB 340           'RUN LENGTH ENCODE
270 GOSUB 680:N=I-1     'SWAP I/O BUFFERS
280 GOSUB 820           'DIATOMIC ENCODE
290 GOSUB 700:N=I-1     'SWAP I/O BUFFERS
300 GOSUB 1250          'HALF BYTE ENCODE
310 GOSUB 740           'TALLY ONLY
320 GOSUB 770           'PRINT BUFFER
330 GOTO 230
340 '*****RUN LENGTH ENCODING SUBROUTINE********
350 '* THIS ROUTINE PROCESSES RECORDS FROM X$  *
360 '* AND COMPRESSES OUT REPETITIVE CHARACTERS*
370 '* USING O$ AS THE OUTPUT BUFFER.          *
380 '*******************************************
390 K=1:J=1                    'RESET INDICES
400 FOR I= 1 TO N              'STEP THRU RECORD
410 A$= MID$(X$,I,1)           'EXTRACT A CHAR
420 IF A$= MID$(X$,I+1,1) THEN 490 'SAME AS NEXT?
430 IF K>3 THEN 530            'COMPRESS
440 IF K>1 THEN 610            'DON'T COMPRESS
450 O$(J)=A$                   'STUFF IN OUTPUT BUFFER
460 J=J+1                      'BUMP BUFFER INDEX
470 NEXT I                     'GO BACK FOR MORE
480 RETURN                     'END OF STRING
490 B$=A$                      'SAVE REPEATED CHAR
500 K=K+1                      'BUMP COUNT
510 GOTO 470                   'KEEP LOOKING
520 '*************************************************
530 'INSERT COMPRESSION NOTATION IN OUTPUT BUFFER
540 '*************************************************
550 O$(J)=CHR$(128)            'SET FLAG FOR RUN-LENGTH
560 O$(J+1)=B$                 'INSERT REPEATED CHAR
570 O$(J+2)=CHR$(K)            'INSERT COUNT
580 IF K=13 THEN O$(J+2)=CHR$(125) 'TRANSLATE CR
590 J=J+3:K=1                  'RESET INDEX
600 GOTO 470
610 O$(J)=B$                   'STUFF 1ST REPEAT CHAR
620 O$(J+1)=B$                 'STUFF 2ND REPEAT CHAR
630 J=J+2:K=1                  'RESET INDEX
640 GOTO 470                   'DONE
650 '*****TALLY THE COMPRESSION COUNT & WRITE BUFFER******
660 '* DISPLAY BEFORE & AFTER RESULTS OF COMPRESSION     *
670 '* AND SHOW THE NET RESULTS OBTAINED BY EACH METHOD  *
680 '*****************************************************
690 N1=N1+N                    'TALLY INPUT CHAR COUNT
```

Figure B.1

```
700 IF N=0 THEN X$=SPACE$(1)        'ALLOW FOR NEW PARA ONLY
710 FOR I= 1 TO J-1
720 MID$(X$,I,1)= O$(I)             'SWAP I/O FOR NEXT ROUTINE
730 NEXT I
740 T=N-J+1                         'NET DIFFERENCE IN BUFFERS
750 T1=T1+T                         'SAVE COUNT FOR SUMMARY
760 RETURN
770 FOR I=1 TO J-1
780 PRINT #3, O$(I);                'WRITE OUT BUFFER
790 NEXT I
800 PRINT #3, ""                    'FORCE END OF WRITE
810 RETURN
820 '*****DIATOMIC COMPRESSION SUBROUTINE*******  *
830 '* THIS ROUTINE PROCESSES RECORDS FROM X$    *
840 '* AND COMPRESSES OUT COMMON PAIRS           *
850 '* USING O$ AS THE OUTPUT BUFFER.            *
860 '***********************************************
870 I=1                             'RESET INDICES
880 FOR J= 1 TO N-1                 'STEP THRU RECORD
890 A$= MID$(X$,J,2)                'EXTRACT A PAIR
900 IF N1>100 AND LCC=0 THEN LC=25 'NO LOWER CASE
910 FOR K = 1 TO LC                 'SETUP PAIR TABLE LOOP
920 IF A$=P$(K) THEN GOSUB 1030     'IS INPUT PAIR IN TABLE?
930 NEXT K                          'NO - TRY NEXT
940 IF M = 1 THEN 960               'IF MATCH FLAG SET?
950 O$(I) = MID$(A$,1,1)            'NO-STUFF 1ST CHAR IN BUFFER
960 I=I+1                           'BUMP INPUT STRING INDEX
970 M=0                             'RESET MATCH FLAG
980 NEXT J                          'GO BACK FOR MORE
990 IF J=N+1 THEN J=I:GOTO 1020     'ONE TOO MANY
1000 O$(I)= MID$(X$,J,1)            'GET LAST CHAR
1010 J=I+1                          'RESET INDEX
1020 RETURN                         'DONE
1030 M=1                            'SET PAIR MATCH FLAG
1040 '****************************************************
1050 'INSERT COMPRESSION NOTATION IN OUTPUT BUFFER
1060 V = K + 199                    'INDEX OUT TO SUBSTITUTE CHAR
1070 O$(I)=CHR$(V)                  'INSERT PAIR SUBSTITUTION
1080 J=J+1                          'FORCE INPUT SHIFT 2 OVER PAIR
1090 IF K>25 THEN LCC=1             'FOUND LOWER CASE PAIR
1100 K = LC                         'FORCE END OF PAIR SEARCH
1110 RETURN                         'GO BACK FOR MORE
1120 '****************************************************
1130 '*  CONSTRUCT PAIR COMBINATION TABLE            *
1140 '****************************************************
1150 DIM P$(50)                     'JEWELL CHAR. COMBINATION PAIRS
1160 DATA "E "," T",TH," A","S ",RE,IN,HE,ER," I"," O","N ",ES,
1170 DATA " B",ON,"T ",TI,AN,"D ",AT,TE," C"," S",OR,"R "
1180 DATA "e "," t",th," a","s ",re,in,he,er," i"," o","n ",es,
1190 DATA " b",on,"t ",ti,an,"d ",at,te," c"," s",or,"r "
1200 FOR I = 1 TO 50                'SETUP PAIR TABLE
1210 READ Z$                        'GET COMMON PAIR
1220 P$(I) = Z$: NEXT I             'AND STUFF INTO PAIR TABLE
1230 LC=50:LCC=0                    'SETUP LOOP COUNT & LC FLAG
1240 RETURN                         'DONE - TABLE COMPLETE
1250 '*****HALF-BYTE ENCODING SUBROUTINE*********
1260 '* THIS ROUTINE PROCESSES RECORDS FROM X$   *
1270 '* AND ENCODES  MIXED  STRINGS OF DATA INTO*
1280 '* HALF-BYTE OR 4 BIT REPRESENTATION USING *
1290 '* DOUBLE BUFFERING WITH O$ AS OUTPUT BUFF.*
1300 '*********************************************
1310 K=1:J=1                        'RESET INDICES
1320 FOR I=1 TO N STEP 2            'STEP THRU RECORD
1330 IF I=N-1 THEN  1530            'EVEN STRING SIZE
1340 C(I)=0:C(I+1)=0                'RESET ENCODE FLAGS
1350 A$= MID$(X$,I,1)               'GET 1ST BYTE
1360 B$= MID$(X$,I+1,1)             'GET 2ND BYTE
1370 IF A$= "$" THEN C(I)= 1        'SET 1ST ENCODE FLAG
1380 IF A$= "," THEN C(I)= 2
```

Figure B.1 (*continued*)

```
1390 IF A$= "." THEN C(I)= 3
1400 IF A$= "*" THEN C(I)= 4
1410 IF A$< "0" OR A$> "9" THEN 1430   'SKIP OTHERS
1420 C(I)= 5
1430 IF B$= "$" THEN C(I+1)= 1    'SET 2ND ENCODE FLAG
1440 IF B$= "," THEN C(I+1)= 2
1450 IF B$= "." THEN C(I+1)= 3
1460 IF B$= "*" THEN C(I+1)= 4
1470 IF B$< "0" OR B$> "9" THEN 1490   'SKIP OTHERS
1480 C(I+1)= 5
1490 IF C(I)= 0 OR C(I+1)= 0 THEN 1530  'NOT CANDIDATE
1500 K=K+2                        'BOTH NUMERIC-BUMP COUNT
1510 NEXT I                       'GO BACK FOR MORE
1520 RETURN                       'END OF STRING
1530 IF K > 4 THEN GOSUB 1620     'ENOUGH TO ENCODE
1540 IF K > 1 THEN GOSUB 1880     'DON'T ENCODE
1550 O$(J) = MID$(X$,I,1)         'OUTPUT 1ST CHAR.
1560 O$(J+1) = MID$(X$,I+1,1)     'OUTPUT 2ND CHAR.
1570 J=J+2:K=1                    'BUMP OUTPUT-RESET COUNT
1580 IF I=N THEN J=J-1            'ONE TOO MANY
1590 IF J=N+2 THEN J=N+1          'EVEN STRING, SUB 1
1600 GOTO 1510                    'AND GO FOR MORE
1610 '***** SUBROUTINE TO PERFORM HALF-BYTE ENCODING *****
1620 O$(J)=CHR$(129)              'FLAG FOR BYTE PACKING
1630 MASK1= &HF0                  '11110000
1640 MASK2= &HF                   '00001111
1650 O$(J+1)=CHR$(K-1)            'INSERT LENGTH OF STRING
1660 J=J+2                        'BUMP OUTPUT INDEX
1670 FOR L=(I-K)+1 TO I-2 STEP 2 'SETUP ENCODE LOOP
1680 ON C(L) GOTO 1690,1700,1710,1720,1730 'USE FLAG TO ENCODE
1690 X=&HA0:GOTO 1750             '10100000
1700 X=&HB0:GOTO 1750             '10110000
1710 X=&HC0:GOTO 1750             '11000000
1720 X=&HD0:GOTO 1750             '11010000
1730 X=VAL(MID$(X$,L,1))          'GET NUM VALUE OF BYTE 1
1740 X=X*16                       'SHIFT 4 BITS LEFT
1750 X=X AND MASK1                'MASK LOWER HALF-BYTE
1760 ON C(L+1) GOTO 1770,1780,1790,1800,1810 'USE ENCODE FLAG
1770 Y=&HA:GOTO 1820              '00001010
1780 Y=&HB:GOTO 1820              '00001011
1790 Y=&HC:GOTO 1820              '00001100
1800 Y=&HD:GOTO 1820              '00001101
1810 Y=VAL(MID$(X$,L+1,1))        'GET NUM VALUE OF BYTE 2
1820 Y=Y AND MASK2                'MASK UPPER HALF-BYTE
1830 Z= X OR Y                    'OR THE TWO TOGETHER
1840 O$(J)= CHR$(Z)               'OUTPUT BYTE TO BUFFER
1850 J=J+1                        'BUMP OUTPUT INDEX
1860 NEXT L                       'GO BACK FOR MORE
1870 K=1:RETURN                   'RESET COUNT AND RETURN
1880 '***** SUBROUTINE FOR STRING NOT WORTH ENCODING *****
1890 FOR L=(I-K)+1 TO I-2         'PICKUP SHORT STRING
1900 O$(J)=MID$(X$,L,1)           'STUFF IN OUTPUT BUFFER
1910 J=J+1                        'BUMP OUTPUT INDEX
1920 NEXT L                       'GO BACK FOR MORE
1930 K=1:RETURN                   'RESET COUNT AND RETURN
1940 CLOSE: OPEN F$ FOR INPUT AS #2
1950 PRINT "FILE ";F$;" BEFORE COMPRESSION:"
1960 LINE INPUT #2,X$
1970 IF EOF(2) THEN 2000
1980 PRINT X$
1990 GOTO 1960
2000 PRINT X$:OPEN "COMPRESS.DAT" FOR INPUT AS #3
2010 PRINT "FILE ";F$;" AFTER COMPRESSION:"
2020 LINE INPUT #3,O$
2030 IF EOF(3) THEN 2060
2040 PRINT O$
2050 GOTO 2020
2060 PRINT O$:PRINT T1;" TOTAL CHARACTERS ELIMINATED FROM ";
2070 PRINT N1;"OR ";INT((T1/N1)*100);"%":CLOSE:END
```

Figure B.1 *(continued)*

```
10 '*******************************************************
20 '* MERGED.BAS PROGRAM WAS WRITTEN TO DECOMPRESS       *
30 '* FILES ENCODED BY ITS COMPANION PROG MERGEC.BAS.    *
40 '* THE INPUT FILE IS NORMALLY COMPRESS.DAT BUT CAN    *
50 '* BE CHANGED TO ACCOMMODATE ANY ENCODED FILE.        *
60 '* THE DECOMPRESSED OUTPUT FILE IS DECOMP.DAT AND     *
70 '* SHOULD BE SAVED UNDER ANOTHER NAME AFTER EACH      *
80 '* RUN OF MERGED.BAS. AUTHOR: THOMAS R. MARSHALL      *
90 '*******************************************************
100 DIM O$(256)
110 WIDTH 80:CLS
120 '**********MAIN ROUTINE***********************
130 '* THIS ROUTINE READS RECORDS FROM AN ASCII *
140 '* FILE INTO A STRING CALLED X$ WHICH IS    *
150 '* THEN PASSED TO DECOMPRESSION SUBROUTINE  *
160 '*********************************************
170 PRINT "ENTER ASCII FILENAME. EG, COMPRESS.DAT";
180 INPUT F$: OPEN F$ FOR INPUT AS #2
190 OPEN "DECOMP.DAT" FOR OUTPUT AS #3
200 GOSUB 1030             'CONSTRUCT PAIR TABLE
210 PRINT "PATIENCE - INPUT PROCESSING"
220 IF EOF(2) THEN GOTO 1530
230 LINE INPUT #2, X$
240 N= LEN(X$)
250 GOSUB 330              'RUN LENGTH DECODE
260 GOSUB 620:N=I-1        'SWAP I/O BUFFERS
270 GOSUB 760              'DIATOMIC DECODE
280 GOSUB 640:N=I-1        'SWAP I/O BUFFERS
290 GOSUB 1120            'HALF BYTE DECODE
300 GOSUB 680             'PICKUP LAST COUNT
310 GOSUB 710             'PRINT BUFFERS
320 GOTO 220
330 '*****RUN LENGTH DECODING SUBROUTINE********
340 '* THIS ROUTINE PROCESSES RECORDS FROM X$  *
350 '* AND DECOMPRESSES RUN-ENCODED CHARACTERS *
360 '* USING O$ AS THE OUTPUT BUFFER.          *
370 '*******************************************
380 K=1:J=1                  'RESET INDICES
390 FOR I= 1 TO N            'STEP THRU RECORD
400 A$= MID$(X$,I,1)         'EXTRACT A CHAR
410 IF A$= CHR$(128) THEN 470    'COMPRESSION FLAG?
420 O$(J)=A$                 'STUFF IN OUTPUT BUFFER
430 J=J+1                    'BUMP BUFFER INDEX
440 NEXT I                   'GO BACK FOR MORE
450 RETURN                   'END OF STRING
460 '*******************************************************
470 'DECODE COMPRESSION NOTATION TO OUTPUT BUFFER
480 '*******************************************************
490 K$= MID$(X$,I+2,1)       'GET REPEAT COUNT
500 A$= MID$(X$,I+1,1)       'GET REPEAT CHAR
510 K= ASC(K$)               'SET UP INDEX
520 IF K=125 THEN K=13       'TRANSLATE CR
530 FOR L= J TO J+K-1        'SET OUTPUT LOOP
540 O$(L)= A$                'STUFF REPEAT CHAR
550 NEXT L                   'KEEP GOING
560 J= L                     'BUMP OUTPUT INDEX
570 I= I+3                   'BUMP INPUT INDEX
580 GOTO 400                 'DONE
590 '*****TALLY THE DECOMPRESSION COUNT & WRITE BUFFER****
600 '* DISPLAY BEFORE & AFTER RESULTS OF DECOMPRESSION   *
610 '* AND SHOW THE NET RESULTS OBTAINED BY EACH METHOD  *
620 '*****************************************************
630 N1=N1+N                  'TALLY INPUT CHAR COUNT
640 X$=SPACE$(J-1)           'EXPAND INPUT BUFFER
650 FOR I= 1 TO J-1
660 MID$(X$,I,1)= O$(I)      'SWAP I/O FOR NEXT ROUTINE
670 NEXT I
680 T=J-1-N                  'NET DIFFERENCE IN BUFFERS
690 T1=T1+T                  'SAVE COUNT FOR SUMMARY
700 RETURN
710 FOR I=1 TO J-1
720 PRINT #3, O$(I);         'WRITE OUT BUFFER
```

Figure B.2

```
730 NEXT I
740 PRINT #3, ""                     'END WRITE
750 RETURN
760 '*****DIATOMIC    DECODING SUBROUTINE********
770 '* THIS ROUTINE PROCESSES RECORDS FROM X$   *
780 '* AND DECOMPRESSES PAIR-ENCODED CHARACTERS*
790 '* USING O$ AS THE OUTPUT BUFFER.          *
800 '********************************************
810 K=1:J=1:V=0                      'RESET INDICES
820 FOR I= 1 TO N                    'STEP THRU RECORD
830 A$= MID$(X$,I,1)                 'EXTRACT A CHAR
840 IF A$> CHR$(199) THEN 900        'COMPRESSED PAIR?
850 O$(J)=A$                         'STUFF IN OUTPUT BUFFER
860 J=J+1                            'BUMP BUFFER INDEX
870 NEXT I                           'GO BACK FOR MORE
880 RETURN                           'END OF STRING
890 '**************************************************
900 'DECODE COMPRESSION NOTATION TO OUTPUT BUFFER
910 '**************************************************
920 K= ASC(A$)                       'GET ORDINAL EQUIV.
930 K= K-199                         'SUBTRACT FOR INDEX
940 T$= P$(K)                        'STUFF PAIR IN BUFFER
950 O$(J)=MID$(T$,1,1)
960 O$(J+1)=MID$(T$,2,1)
970 J= J+2                           'BUMP OUTPUT INDEX
980 V= V+1                           'SUM VARIABLE COUNT
990 GOTO 870                         'DONE
1000 '*********************************************
1010 "*  CONSTRUCT PAIR COMBINATION TABLE       *
1020 '*********************************************
1030 DIM P$(50)                      'JEWELL CHAR. COMBINATION PAIRS
1040 DATA "E "," T",TH," A","S ",RE,IN,HE,ER," I"," O","N ",ES,
1050 DATA " B",ON,"T ",TI,AN,"D ",AT,TE," C"," S",OR,"R "
1060 DATA "e "," t",th," a","s ",re,in,he,er," i"," o","n ",es,
1070 DATA " b",on,"t ",ti,an,"d ",at,te," c"," s",or,"r "
1080 FOR I = 1 TO 50                 'SET UP PAIR TABLE
1090 READ Z$                         'GET COMMON PAIR
1100 P$(I) = Z$: NEXT I              'AND STUFF INTO PAIR TABLE
1110 RETURN                          'DONE - TABLE COMPLETE
1120 '*****HALF BYTE   DECODING SUBROUTINE********
1130 '* THIS ROUTINE PROCESSES RECORDS FROM X$   *
1140 '* AND DECOMPRESSES BYTE-ENCODED CHARACTERS*
1150 '* USING O$ AS THE OUTPUT BUFFER.          *
1160 '********************************************
1170 J=1                             'RESET INDEX
1180 FOR I= 1 TO N                   'STEP THRU RECORD
1190 A$= MID$(X$,I,1)                'EXTRACT A CHAR
1200 IF A$= CHR$(129) THEN 1280      'COMPRESSION FLAG?
1210 O$(J)=A$                        'STUFF IN OUTPUT BUFFER
1220 J=J+1                           'BUMP BUFFER INDEX
1230 NEXT I                          'GO BACK FOR MORE
1240 RETURN                          'END OF STRING
1250 '******************************************************
1260 'DECODE COMPRESSION NOTATION TO OUTPUT BUFFER        *
1270 '******************************************************
1280 MASK1= &HF0                     '11110000
1290 MASK2= &HF                      '00001111
1300 K= ASC(MID$(X$,I+1,1))          'GET STRING LENGTH
1310 M= I+2+(K/2)-1                  'SET END OF STRING
1320 FOR L=I+2 TO M                  'SETUP LOOP TO DECODE
1330 Z= ASC(MID$(X$,L,1))            'GET BYTE
1340 X= (Z AND MASK1)/16            'MASK LOWER HALF-BYTE
1350 IF X< 10 THEN 1410              'ITS NUMERIC
1360 IF X= 10 THEN O$(J)= "$"        'SPECIAL
1370 IF X= 11 THEN O$(J)= ","        'SPECIAL
1380 IF X= 12 THEN O$(J)= "."        'SPECIAL
1390 IF X= 13 THEN O$(J)= "*"        'SPECIAL
1400 GOTO 1420                       'SKIP IF SPECIAL
1410 O$(J)= CHR$(X+48)               'OUTPUT 1ST NUMERIC
1420 Y= Z AND MASK2                  'MASK UPPER HALF-BYTE
1430 IF Y< 10 THEN 1490              'ITS NUMERIC
1440 IF Y= 10 THEN O$(J+1)= "$"      'SPECIAL
```

Figure B.2 (*continued*)

```
1450 IF Y= 11 THEN O$(J+1)= ","    'SPECIAL
1460 IF Y= 12 THEN O$(J+1)= "."    'SPECIAL
1470 IF Y= 13 THEN O$(J+1)= "*"    'SPECIAL
1480 GOTO 1500                     'SKIP IF SPECIAL
1490 O$(J+1)= CHR$(Y+48)           'OUTPUT 2ND NUMERIC
1500 J= J+2                        'BUMP OUTPUT BY TWO
1510 NEXT L:I= M                   'CONTINUE, BUMP INPUT INDEX
1520 GOTO 1230                     'GO BACK FOR MORE
1530 CLOSE: OPEN F$ FOR INPUT AS #2
1540 PRINT K$
1550 PRINT "FILE ";F$;" BEFORE DECOMPRESSION:"
1560 LINE INPUT #2,X$
1570 IF EOF(2) THEN 1600
1580 PRINT X$
1590 GOTO 1560
1600 PRINT X$:OPEN "DECOMP.DAT" FOR INPUT AS #3
1610 PRINT "FILE ";F$;" AFTER DECOMPRESSION:"
1620 LINE INPUT #3,O$
1630 IF EOF(3) THEN 1660
1640 PRINT O$
1650 GOTO 1620
1660 PRINT O$:PRINT T1;" TOTAL CHARACTERS INSERTED"
1670 CLOSE:END
```

Figure B.2 (*continued*)

indicate a specific compression technique. First, the Jewell table has been expanded to include lower case characters as indicated in lines 1160 to 1190. To reduce the processing time of the program, the first 100 characters in a file to be compressed are examined in the diatomic compression subroutine. If a lower case pair is encountered, Jewell character combination pairs to include lower case pairs are matched against the data file. Otherwise, it is assumed that the file consists of upper case text and data is only matched against upper case pairs during processing.

Because of the expanded Jewell character-pair table, the base of the characters used to replace pairs of characters has been changed from ASCII 224 to ASCII 199. Thus, ASCII codes from 199 to 249 are now used to represent paired-character substitution. Another change from previous examples was the change in the run-length flag, from ASCII 125 to ASCII 128. This was done to ensure all compression-indicating characters were above ASCII 127.

It should be noted that files with graphic characters above ASCII 127 can cause unexpected results to occur. This is due to the possibility of those characters being misinterpreted as a flag character, which will provide a false indication of a particular type of compression when the decompression program operates upon previously compressed data. This problem can be alleviated by modifying the MERGEC.BAS program to insert a second compression-indicating character after one occurs naturally in the input data. Then, the MERGED.BAS program can be modified to check the character following every compression-indicating character. If the second character is the same as the first, the program would then strip one character and ignore the second as it represents naturally occurring data and does not signify that compression occurred. For readers desiring to expand the scope of these programs, the previously described modifications may represent an interesting challenge as well as result in a program that can compress tokenized BASIC programs.

B.2 PROGRAM OPERATIONS

Unless altered by the reader, MERGEC.BAS will create a file named COMPRESS.DAT which represents a compressed form of the input file specified when the program is executed.

Figure B.3 represents a typical electronic mail message one might transmit. This message contains 776 characters. Since many electronic mail services charge for both connect time and the number of characters transmitted, any reduction in data may result in a commensurate reduction in transmission cost.

Figure B.4 illustrates the resulting compressed file after MERGEC.BAS operated upon the sample data file listed in Figure B.3. The reader should note that some of the compression flag characters are equivalent to very interesting printer control characters, which

```
J.J. ASTOR
ASTORIA, OREGON

MY GOOD SIR;

I AM RESPONDING TO YOUR CORRESPONDENCE LAST REGARDING THE DISPOSITION
OF PROCEEDS FROM SALE OF SAID PROPERTY.   THE GROSS PROCEEDS REALIZED
WERE $832,746,381.99.

FROM THIS, WE HAVE TAKEN THE LIBERTY OF DEDUCTING MINOR EXPENSES IN THE
FOLLOWING MANNER:

A.· TRANSFER FEES        $136,941
B. REALITY FEES         $8,327,436
C. LEGAL FEES           $9,938,862
D. ADVERTISING           $422,977
E. TAXES                $1,646,311
F. SUNDRY               $7,139,774
G. MISCELLANEOUS      $462,114,283

THE NET PROCEEDS RESIDE IN A NON-INTEREST BEARING ACCOUNT UNTIL
INSTRUCTIONS TO THE CONTRARY ARE RECEIVED.   TO OUR VALUED CLIENT WE
REMAIN-

                            VERY TRULY YOURS,

                            DEWEY, CHEATHAM & HOWE
```

Figure B.3

is the reason for the listing of the compressed file only vaguely resembling the original data file. As indicated, 245 characters representing 31 per cent of the original data were eliminated, due to the mixture of the three compression routines used in the program.

Several important items concerning the compressed file warrant further discussion, especially if one desires to transmit such data over an electronic mail service. First, when you compress the data, be sure to remove any destination information from the file. This is because the electronic mail system cannot understand your routing requests if they are compressed. Secondly, prior to transmitting compressed data, the reader should ascertain if the electronic mail service supports the extended ASCII character set, which is sometimes called 8-bit ASCII. If the electronic mail service does not support extended ASCII you will not be able to transmit

```
FILE astor AFTER COMPRESSION:
J.J.╥STα
ASTα╥A,╥═G╫

MY GOO█SIR;

I╥M ═SP╫D╬G╓O YOUR █α═SP╫DENC╙AS╪═GARD╬G╓┴ DISPOSI┘╫
OF PROCEED╟FROM█AL╙OF█AI█PROP╨TY. ╓┴ GROS╟PROCEED╟═ALIZED
W╨╙$ ┼ ┼ ╠ ╬ ▬

FROM╓HIS, W╙HAV╙TAKE╙╨╙IB╨TY╥F DEDUC┘NG M╬α EXPENS╘╤╙E
FOLLOW╬G M╓N╨:

A.╓R╓SF╨ FE╘$k1
B. ═AL ITY FE╘
                ¿|'┤6
C. LEGAL FE╘        $
                    2
D.╥DV╨┘S╬G
          $B+7
E.╓AX╘ $
F.█UNDRY }$4
G. MISCELL╓EOUS






ñb▒▓

╨╙NE╪PROCEED╟═SID╙╨╥ N╫-╬█═S╪BEAR╬G╥CCOUN╪UN┘L
╟STRUC┘╫╟TO╓┴ █╫TRARY╥═ ═CEIVED. ╓O╥UR VALUE█CLIEN╪WE
═MA╬

 'V╨Y╓RULY YOURS,

 'DEWEY, █╙█HAM & HOWE
 245  TOTAL CHARACTERS ELIMINATED FROM  776 OR  31 %
Ok
```

Figure B.4

compressed data since compression-indicating characters are all above ASCII 127. Lastly, let us pose a question to the reader. From examining Figure B.4, could you determine what the original message stated?

While compression is no substitute for the utilization of encryption devices, it may make it much more difficult for an unauthorized reader to decipher a message.

Prior to leaving the reader to SHRINK IT themselves, let us review the complete compression and decompression of a small file. This is illustrated in Figure B.5. At the top of Figure B.5 our four-line file to which we assigned the name tst is listed. Next, upon loading and executing the program MERGEC.BAS we are prompted

```
Lets take a look at the benefits of compression when we
have different types of data to include large numbers
such as $123,456,789.98 and repeating strings in a file,
such as --------------.

ENTER ASCII FILENAME. EG, [DRIVE:]FILESPEC? tst
PATIENCE - INPUT PROCESSING
FILE tst BEFORE COMPRESSION:
Lets take a look at the benefits of compression when we
have different types of data to include large numbers
such as $123,456,789.98 and repeating strings in a file,
such as --------------.
FILE tst AFTER COMPRESSION:
Letµtakⅼa lookσ≥∑ⅼbenefitµof°ompⅼssi± wθθwe
havⅼdiffⱱenⱱtyp€ⅿf d‡aⱷoδncludⅼlargⅼnumbⱱs
suchσµí #┤∨┐         ┌8σnⅉ ⱷpe‡ⱷg-tⱼⱷgµⱷσ file,

suchσµ-_

  53  TOTAL CHARACTERS ELIMINATED FROM  187 OR  28 %
Ok
```

Running MERGEC.BAS

```
ENTER ASCII FILENAME. EG, COMPRESS.DAT? compress.dat
PATIENCE - INPUT PROCESSING


FILE compress.dat BEFORE DECOMPRESSION:
Letµtakⅼa lookσ≥∑ⅼbenefitµof°ompⅼssi± wθθwe
havⅼdiffⱱenⱱtyp€ⅿf d‡aⱷoδncludⅼlargⅼnumbⱱs
suchσµí #┤∨┐         ┌8σnⅉ ⱷpe‡ⱷg-tⱼⱷgµⱷσ file,

suchσµ-_

FILE compress.dat AFTER DECOMPRESSION:
Lets take a look at the benefits of compression when we
have different types of data to include large numbers
such as $123,456,78920T8 and repeating strings in a file,
such as --------------.
  54  TOTAL CHARACTERS INSERTED
Ok
```

Running MERGED.BAS

Figure B.5

to enter the ASCII file we wish to compress. As indicated, the program lists the original file as well as its compressed form.

The second half of Figure B.5 illustrates the execution of MERGED.BAS, which will convert a compressed file back into its original form. Since MERGEC.BAS automatically used the filename compress.dat to store compressed data, we used that file as input to MERGED.BAS. As indicated, the file is faithfully reconstructed into its original form; however, from careful examination, 53 characters were eliminated and 54 were inserted according to the printout. In case the reader is puzzled, it should be noted that in the case of half-byte encoding, the saving of an odd number of bytes was rounded down while the insertion of actual characters is counted, resulting upon occasion in a one character discrepancy in comparing character removals and character insertions. This, however, has no effect upon the decoding of previously compressed data.

REFERENCES

Aronson, J. (1977) Data compression—a comparison of methods. *National Bureau of Standards*, PB-269 296, June.

Dishon, Y. (1977). Data compaction in computer systems. *Computer Design*, April, 85–90.

Jewell, G. C. (1976). Text compaction for information retrieval systems. *IEEE SMC Newsletter*, **5**, No. 1.

Lempel, A. and Zvi, J. (1977). A universal algorithm for sequential data compression. *IEEE Transactions on Information Theory*, **IT-23**, No. 5.

McCullough, T. (1977). Data compression in high-speed digital facsimile. *Telecommunications*, July, 40–43.

Moilanen, U. (1978). Information preserving codes compress binary pictorial data. *Computer Design*, November, 134–136.

Peterson, J. L., Bitner, J. R., and Howard, J. H. (1978). The selection of optimal tab settings. *Communications of the ACM*, **21**, No. 12, 1004–1007.

Rubin, F. (1976). Experiments in text file compression. *Communications of the ACM*, **19**, No. 11, 617–623.

Ruth, S., and Kreutzer, P. (1972). Data compression for large business files. *Datamation*, **18**, No. 9, 62–66.

Snyderman, M., and Hunt, B. (1970). The myriad virtues of text compaction. *Datamation*, **1**, December, 36–40.

Ziv, J., and Lempel, A. (1977). A universal algorithm for sequential data compression. *IEEE Transactions on Information Theory*, **IT-23**, No. 3.

FURTHER READING

Andrews, C. A., Davies, J. M., and Schwarz, E. (1967). Adaptive data compression. *Proceedings of the IEEE*, **55**, No. 3.

Ash, R. (1965). *Information Theory*, Interscience, New York.

Barton, I. J., Creasey, S. E., Lynch, M. F., and Snell, M. J. (1974). An information-theoretic approach to text searching in direct access systems. *Communications of the ACM*, **17**, No. 6, 345–350.

Bemer, R. W. (1960). Do it by the numbers—digital shorthand. *Communications of the ACM*, **3**, N810, 530–536.

Bentley, J. L., Skator, D. D., Tarjan, R. E., and Wei, V. K. (1986). A locally adaptive data compression scheme. *Communications of the ACM*, **29**, No. 4, 320–330.

Blasbalg, H., and Van Blerkom, R. (1972). Message compression. *IRE Transactions on Space Electronics and Telemetry*, September, 228–238.

Bookstein, A., and Fouty, G. (1976). A mathematical model for estimating the effectiveness of bigram coding. *Information Proceedings and Management*, **12**, 111–116.

Bray, J. M., Nelson, V. P., deMaine, P. A. D., and Irwin, J. D. (1985). Data-compression techniques ease storage problems. *Computer Design*, October, 102–105.

Clare, A. G., Cook, G. M., and Lynch, M. F. (1972). The identification of variable-length, equifrequency character strings in a natural language data base. *Computer Journal*, **15**.

Corbin, H. (1981). An introduction to data compression. *BYTE*, April, 218–250.

Cortesi, D. (1982). An effective text-compression algorithm. *BYTE*, January, 397–403.

Costlow, T. (1989). Compression doubles QIC capacity. *Electronic Engineering Times*, January, 4.

Costlow, T. (1989). What's new in data compression. *Electronic Engineering Times*, January, 53–57.

Cullum, R. D. (1972). A method for the removal of redundancy in printed text. *NTIS*, AD751 407, September.

Davidson, L. D. (1966). Theory of adaptive data compression. In A. V. Balakrishinan (Ed.), *Advances in Communications Systems*, Academic Press, New York, 173–192.

Davisson, L. D. (1967). An approximate theory of prediction for data compression. *IEEE Transactions on Information Theory*, **IT-13**, No. 2, 274–278.

Davisson, L. D. (1968). Data compression using straight line interpolation. *IEEE Transactions on Information Theory*, **IT-14**, No. 3, 300–304.

Davisson, L. D. (1968). The theoretical analysis of data compression systems. *Proceedings of the IEEE*, **56**, No. 2, 176–186.

Davisson, L. D., and Gray, R. M. (1976). *Data Compression*, Dowden, Hutchinson and Ross, Dowden.

De Main, P. A. D., Kloss, K., and Marron, B. A. (1967). The SOLID System III. alphanumeric compression. Washington: US Government Printing Office, NBS Technical Note 413, August.

Doherty, R. (1989). System puts real-time squeeze on color videos. *Electronic Engineering Times*, February.

Ehrman, L. (1967). Analysis of some redundancy removal bandwidth compression techniques. *Proceedings of the IEEE*, **55**, No. 3, 278–287.

Ellias, P. (1955). Predictive coding. *IRE Transactions*, **IT-1**, 16–44.

Fano, R. M. (1949). The transmission of information. Research Laboratory for Electronics, Massachusetts Institute of Technology, Technical Report, No. 65.

Forney, G. D., and Tao, W. Y. (1976). Data compression increases throughout. *Data Communications*, May/June.

Gilbert, E. N., and Moore, E. F. (1959). Variable-length binary encodings. *Bell System Technical Journal*, April, 933–967.

Gottlieb, B., Hagereth, S. E., Denot, P. G. H., and Rabinowitz, H. S. (1975). A classification of compression methods and their usefulness for a large data processing center. *Proceedings of the National Computer Conference*, 453–458.

Hann, B. (1974). A new technique for compression and storage of data. *Communications of the ACM*, **17**, No. 8.

Harker, J. (1982). Byte oriented data compression techniques. *Computer Design*, October, 95–100.

Heaps, H. S. (1972). Storage analysis of a compression coding for document data bases. *Information*, **10**, No. 1.

Held, G. (1979). Eliminating those blanks and zeros in data transmission. *Data Communications*, **8**, No. 9, 75–77.

Honien, Liu. (1968). A file management system for a large corporate information system data bank. *Fall Joint Computer Conference*, Vol. 33, Part I, 145–156.

Hu, T. C., and Tucker, A. C. (1971). Optimal computer search trees and variable-length alphabetical codes. *SIAM Journal of Applied Mathematics*, **21**, No. 4, 514–532.

Huffman, D. A. (1952). A method for the construction of minimum redundancy codes. *Proceedings of the IRE*, **40**, 1098–1101.

Karp, R. M. (1961). Minimum-redundancy coding for the discrete noiseless channel. *IEEE Transactions on Information Theory*, **IT-7**, 27–38.

Kortman, C. M. (1965). Data compression and adaptive telemetry. *IEEE Western Electronic Show and Convention (WESCON)*, Vol. 9, Paper 14.4.

Kurmiss, J. M. (1974). An experiment in adaptive encoding. IBM Technical Report Troo. 2524, Poughkeepsie, NY.

Lesk, M. E. (1970). Compressed text storage. *Computing Science Technical Report*, No. 3, Bell Telephone Laboratories.

Ling, H., and Palermo, F. P. (1975). Block-oriented information compression. *IBM Journal of Research and Development*, March.

Lynch, F. L., Petrie, H. J., and Snell, M. J. (1973). Analysis of the microstructure of titles in the INSPEC data-base. *Information Storage and*

Retrieval, **9**, 331–337.

Lynch, M. F. (1973). Compression of bibliographic files using an adaption of run-length coding. *Information Storage and Retrieval*, **9**, 207–214.

Marron, B. A., and De Maine, P. A. D. (1967). Automatic data compression. *Communications of the ACM*, **10**, No. 3, 711–715.

Mayne, A., and James, E. B. (1975). Information compression by factorising common strings. *Computer Journal*, **18**, No. 2, 157–160.

McCarthy, J. P. (1973). Automatic file compression. *Proceedings of the International Computer Symposium*, North-Holland, Amsterdam, 511–516.

Moilanen, U. (1978). Information preserving codes compress binary pictorial data. *Computer Design*, November, 134–136.

Mulford, J. B., and Ridall, R. K. (1971). Data compression techniques for economic processing of large commercial files. *ACM Symposium on Information Storage and Retrieval*, 207–215.

Mommens, J. H., and Ravir, J. (1974). Coding for data compaction. *IBM Research Report*, RC 5150, T. J. Watson Research Center, Yorktown Heights, NY.

Nordling, K. (1982). A data compression modem. *Telecommunications*, September, 67–70.

Oliver, B. M. (1952). Efficient coding. *Bell System Technical Journal*, **21**, No. 4, 724–750.

Ott, G. (1967). Compact encoding of stationary Markov sources. *IEEE Transactions on Information Theory*, **IT-13**, 82–86.

Peterson, J. L. (1979). Text compression. *BYTE*, December, 106–118.

Pountain, D. (1987). Run-length encoding. *BYTE*, June, 317–320.

Powell, D. (1989). The hidden benefits of data compression. *Networking Management*, October, 46–54.

Ruth, S. R., and Villers, J. M. (1972). *Data Compression and Data Compaction*, Government Clearing House, Study Number AD 723525.

Schieber, W. D., and Thomas, G. (1971). An algorithm for the compaction of alphanumeric data. *Journal of Library Automation*, **4**, 198–206.

Schuegraf, E. F., and Heaps, H. S. (1973). Selection of equifrequent word fragments for information retrieval. *Information Storage and Retrieval*, **9**, 697–711.

Schuegraf, E. F., and Heaps, H. S. (1974). A comparison of algorithms for data base compression by the use of fragments as language elements. *Information Storage and Retrieval*, **10**, 309–319.

Schwartz, E. S., and Kalleck, B. (1964). Generating a canonical prefix encoding. *Communications of the ACM*, **7**, 166–169.

Seither, M. (1989). Data compression doubles capacity of ¼-inch tape drives. *System Integration*, May.

Shannon, C. E. (1948). A mathematical theory of communications. *Bell System Technical Journal*, **27**, 379–423 and 623–656.

Thiel, L. H., and Heaps, H. S. (1972). Program design for retrospective searches on large data bases. *Information Storage and Retrieval*, **8**, 1–20.

Tropper, R. (1982). Binary-coded text: a text-compression method. *BYTE*, April, 398–412.

Wagner, Robert A. (1973). Common phrases and minimum-space text storage. *Communications of the ACM*, **16**, No. 3, 148–152.

Wells, M. (1972). File compression using variable length encodings. *Computer Journal*, April, 308–313.

INDEX

Index compiled by Geoffrey C. Jones